The Uses
of the Canon

THE USES OF THE CANON

Elizabethan Literature and Contemporary Theory

HOWARD FELPERIN

CLARENDON PRESS · OXFORD

Oxford University Press, Walton Street, Oxford OX2 6DP

Oxford New York Toronto
Delhi Bombay Calcutta Madras Karachi
Petaling Jaya Singapore Hong Kong Tokyo
Nairobi Dar es Salaam Cape Town
Melbourne Auckland

and associated companies in
Berlin Ibadan

Oxford is a trade mark of Oxford University Press

Published in the United States
by Oxford University Press, New York

First published 1990
First published in paperback (with corrections) 1992

British Library Cataloguing in Publication Data
Felperin, Howard
The uses of the canon: Elizabethan literature and
contemporary theory.
1. English literature, 1558–1702. Criticism
I. Title
820.9003
ISBN 0–19–812244–6
ISBN 0–19–812265–9 (pbk.)

Library of Congress Cataloging in Publication Data
Felperin, Howard.
The uses of the canon: Elizabethan literature and contemporary
theory / Howard Felperin.
p. cm.
1. English literature—Early modern, 1500–1700—History and
criticism—theory, etc.   2. Shakespeare, William, 1564–1616—
Criticism and interpretation.   3. Canon (Literature)   I. Title.
PR421.F45   1990
820.9'003—dc20   90–7006
ISBN 0–19–812244–6
ISBN 0–19–812265–9 (pbk.)

Printed and bound in
Great Britain by Bookcraft Ltd.,
Midsomer Norton, Bath

Preface

This volume brings together essays of mine, written for a variety of occasions, on Shakespeare and his contemporaries. Several have not previously been published, and others have appeared only in Australia. Dating from the mid-1970s, they coincide with the explosive emergence of literary–critical theory known at the time as the 'crisis in English'. Its shock waves are registered even in the earliest of them and even from the distance of the antipodes. More recent essays attempt to discriminate and measure its subsequent repercussions on the reading of Renaissance texts. Gathering them together here may concentrate their impact back upon continuing theoretical practice in the field in such a way as to alter its course and enlarge its horizons. It might also sharpen their challenge to a more reactionary or nostalgic criticism still stuck at a pre-theoretical stage.

The characteristic procedure of these essays is to bring to bear—and sometimes to book—the claims of contemporary theory in the aggressive demystification of Elizabethan literature now under way. This involves a certain attention to the theoretical regimes that dominate academic criticism today, as well as the more direct engagement with canonical texts that has endowed them with their defining aura of commentary. The critical theory most often brought to bear in the pages that follow—let the reader be warned straightaway—is a kind of deconstruction. The theory most often brought to book is one or another version of the 'new historicism', also known in America as 'cultural poetics' and in Britain as 'cultural materialism'. Such a burst of terminology—the continuing fallout of the theoretical explosion of the 1970s—requires some preliminary clarification.

Though an American coinage sometimes refused by its British practitioners, the 'new historicism' still strikes me as a useful umbrella-term to cover the collective endeavour on both sides of the Atlantic to re-situate 'literature' generally and 'early modern literature' especially within their historical and cultural contexts—and within ours. This project came to seem a necessary reagent to the dehistoricized textualism of the structuralism and deconstruction that preceded it. The 'new historicism'—particularly in its American manifestation—thus represents a late and weakened version of that unmasking of the historical interestedness of the text—of 'high culture' itself—whose strong form has traditionally been Marxism. Why a weak form* of materialist critique should have been thrown up in the 1970s and 1980s, and why its attempt to politicize literary studies should give us pause, will emerge in due course.

While the ensuing essays certainly question a number of the assumptions and aims of the 'new historicism', and do so in the sceptical spirit of deconstruction, in no way do they attempt to stage anything like a 'showdown', as of mighty opposites, between the two. As variations of a contemporary 'hermeneutics of suspicion', these theoretical practices have too many opponents in common among the numerous 'hermeneutics of faith' in place within and in power outside academia for any such simple opposition between them to make sense, either politically or philosophically. After all, it was from the deconstructive textualism theoretically dominant in the 1970s that the new contextualisms emergent in the 1980s derived some of their most potent 'strategies of intervention'. The novel methods by which deconstruction challenged ingrained doctrines of presence and privilege in the text seemed for a time eminently compatible with an older critique of ideology and power in society, and readily co-optable to it.

Yet the reluctance or inability of deconstruction to move beyond the aporia it discovered in literary and philosophical texts into the potential agency of their social and political recontextualization provoked the 'new historicism' at once to accuse it of conservatism or complacency and to claim to have supplanted it in theoretical import and urgency. In one sense such claims have been justified: does anyone outside philosophy departments any longer perform the sort of pure textualist analysis with which deconstruction began in the work of Derrida and de Man? But such claims can also be inverted: in its politicization of their textual tactics, the 'new historicism' may be seen as a kind of 'applied deconstruction'. In any case, not only have rumours of the death of deconstruction been greatly exaggerated; it remains alive and well in the very activities that were supposed to have succeeded it.

But there is a deeper, more pressing and troubling sense in which the careers of deconstruction and the 'new historicism' are so intertwined as to make the idea of open conflict between them seem quixotic. Because each is finally a 'conventionalism' rather than a 'realism'—however reluctant the latter might be to accept this epistemological status—there would be no way to decide the outcome of such a conflict. For the most funda- mental and far-reaching of the post-structuralist strategies deployed by the 'new historicism' was its 'textualizing' of history and culture in the first place, its re-framing of them as discursive constructs. While this move was necessary to open an appeal from the pseudo-objective 'facts' of an older historical empiricism to 'texts' and 'discourses' now explicitly political and therefore newly *reconstructible*, it also opened its own 'constructions' from within to rejection as *mere* construc- tions.

The weakness of this new 'conventionalism', then, is a new vulnerability to the charge of relativism, in so far as its claim to objective validity or verifiability has been abandoned. Having insisted on the textuality of history and culture, what *extra- textual* grounds are left on which to mount the claim that one's own interpretations are correct or privileged, or to meet the charge from a resurgent 'right' that they are not? The decon- structive aporia beyond which the new historicism was sup- posed to have moved us thus returns in the form of a relativism that goes to the heart of its own project. Having left behind an older 'empiricist' or 'realist' historical narrative constituted by 'facts' and connected by 'cause and effect' for a 'conventionalist' historical hermeneutics consisting only of 'texts' and 'dis- courses', there is nothing solid to fall back on when its 'know- ledge' is relativized as only a matter of opinion or interpretation.

This vulnerability is particularly acute today, when historical and humanistic studies are increasingly regarded as the opposi- tional ideology of a political group or the outworn faith of an antiquarian cult, and in either case marginalized as a luxury society can no longer afford. While the pseudo-objectivity of older empirical models in the social and human 'sciences' could not be maintained for ever, they had the advantage while they lasted of offering some methodological resistance to being dismissed as merely subjective or ideological. The problem of relativism thus looms large at a moment when the value of the humanities within an increasingly utilitarian and implicitly reactionary culture is in serious question. It is a problem to which these essays, especially the later ones, will repeatedly return. Unfortunately, neither the 'new historicists' nor I can claim to have found a solution to it.

This came home to me recently after I had accused one 'new historicist' (in an article reprinted here) of relapsing into historical realism only to be accused in a letter to the editor of doing the same thing myself, along with several other post-structuralist Shakespeareans. Interpretive 'realism', the illusion that one's own interpretation has somehow cut textuality at the joints and arrived at the referential heart of the matter, is only an anxious overcompensation for the interpretive relativism to which we 'conventionalists', all of us, are predisposed. Or perhaps it too is a discursive function, the by-product of a logocentrism as deeply ingrained in our institutional practices as original sin was once held to be in our souls, and about as hard to avoid. Apart from politicians, admen, journalists, and others whose livelihood depends on linguistic bad faith of this kind, the worst academic offenders in my experience tend to be older historical empiricists and vulgar Marxists and feminists who alike produce 'definitive'—yet wholly different!—accounts of 'what really happened'.

But this relapse into 'realism' is particularly embarrassing for post-structuralist interpreters of all schools, whose commitment to what Catherine Belsey terms 'discursive knowledge' and Louis Montrose 'the textuality of history' has effectively deprived them of the right of appeal to an outmoded or unsustainable objectivity, or, in Montrose's elegant phrasing, 'the historicity of texts', to substantiate their historical readings and clinch their political points. Short of bracketing everything one writes between inverted commas, there is no avoiding the relapse into a residual interpretive realism from which we have all taken leave—at least in theory. And even if one were to bracket everything thus, one would then be exposed to the opposite and no less vitiating charge of interpretive relativism. Until some deliverance from this dilemma is found, I am afraid the best we can do is acknowledge that we are caught in it, even if that means reconciling ourselves to revisiting—heaven forfend!—the dreaded state of aporia now and again; or, worse yet, learning to live in it permanently.

My own way of acknowledging the incapacity of my readings to tell the truth about the texts they take up has been to foreground their 'writerly' play. Of course I realize this strategy may also be self-defeating. Not only has it exposed me to the charge of dithering between 'conventionalism' and 'realism' like the new historicists whose work I deconstruct, but it has invited misunderstanding of my politics by those who equate 'play' with political cynicism or complacency, particularly when the play is directed towards them. Must all satire be written by Tories? So I have tried in later essays to triangulate my own political position in relation to the texts I interpret and the critics on whom I comment. While 'deconstruction' may have no politics, deconstructionists do, and the reader may be surprised to discover that mine come out not very far from those of the 'new historicists' themselves, in so far as their political positions can be determined. The 'left' is too important to us all to be left to the 'left'.

For our disagreement seems to me at base a matter not of political but of hermeneutic principle. While I subscribe to the text engraved on Marx's tomb, that 'philosophers have only interpreted the world in various ways; the point, however, is to change it'—a 'realist' project with little time for 'relativism' if ever there was one—the relation between interpretation and action, theory and praxis, seems to me one of reciprocity rather than priority. Like the new historicists, I believe that our professional justification for interpreting the texts of the world is to change it for the better; but how can that be done if the interpretations which we perform, and on which we must proceed in order to change it, are only half-baked? Each activity is dependent upon the other, but neither is *guaranteed* by the other.

Unlike some, if not all, 'new historicists', I fail to see a necessary or inescapable relation between politics and criticism. My reading of Elizabethan literature has not compelled upon me, so far as I can tell, one politics or another. Nor has my reading of criticism on it led me to regard political interpretation as the only valid or valuable kind. While reading historical texts doubtless contributes to our political formation, it is certainly not the only activity that does so. Conversely, while contemporary politics doubtless play a part in that reading, they cannot be said to determine or dominate it. Nor can politics alone, however 'correct' or 'sound', validate interpretation, except in the view of the converted. The final essay in this collection illustrates dramatically just how 'non-aligned' the politics of a canonical text repeatedly subjected to political interpretation have been. This is in no way to suggest that *The Tempest*, or the canon for which it stands as the paradigm-case in the essays that follow, is 'above politics'; quite the contrary, it seems to exist at their still centre.

Finally, my differences with the 'new historicists' follow from our disjunct points of entry into the process of reading. What a deconstructionist like myself repeatedly discovers and increasingly values is the resistance the great text throws up against my efforts to impose my preconceptions upon it, to make it say what I want to hear. I confess I have come to enjoy being led by the text, by its train of signifiers, in directions I could not have predicted and might not initially have wished to go— even if the outcome of being led, indeed 'read', in this way is that I end up in the state of aporia without a visa. A more politically assertive or activist criticism begins at the other end of reading, with the signified it desires rather than the signifier it encounters. It knows in advance the meaning it seeks from the text, which it either approves for delivering or, more often nowadays in the case of canonical texts, rebukes for failing to deliver.

This difference carries over into contrasting attitudes to the institutional context within which the practice of serious, i.e. slow, reading is increasingly confined. For most 'new historicists' are also, relatively speaking, 'young historicists'. Their generation came of age during a decade of bitter political conflict, within which universities served as a major theatre of operations. Those who were students at the time still seem to regard the universities in which they now teach as the core, ideally the united core, of a progressive community of the future, or at the very least as a site of resolute resistance to a wider culture more or less hostile and benighted. Their attitude is 'if you're not with us, you're agin' us'. It must be said that in recent years the wider culture has not done much to prove them mistaken.

While recognizing the necessity of struggle at all times—and never more than at present—I fail to see why it is either necessary or desirable for academics, or the humanists among them, to think alike politically. It is not a shared political position but a shared institutional framework that defines the academic 'community', a structure of practices within which political differences take a philosophical, that is, open, explicit, and analytical form. What an academic community properly has in common—what makes it a 'community' in so far as it is one—is a commitment to the expression of differences in those forms, which are inescapably political only in so far as they are usually under threat from the left or the right, and at the present moment from both.

The specifically academic ideal of 'foregrounding conflict', in Gerald Graff's happy phrase, is thus far from 'disinterested'. But neither is it to be identified with any particular political interest or confused with the cultural ideology of 'corporate pluralism' dominant in universities today. For the latter is aimed precisely at *avoiding conflict* by appeasing special interest groups, whereas the former seeks not to preserve a static, determinate, and self-interested 'difference' but to promote dialogue across it. It presupposes the necessity of such a dialogue if we are to change our minds and positions, and the necessity of changing these if the world is to change *for the better* and *for us all*. I can only wonder how many new contextualists, be they historicists or feminists, would agree.

One contribution the present book offers to this process is to raise, but by no means answer, the question of what form a 'newer historicism' might take? For if literary studies are to maintain their centrality as a discipline within an increasingly professionalized academia and culture, they will have to decide what their specific subject-matter is and what specialist knowledge of it they can provide. When the dust of current theoretical controversy begins to clear and the boundaries of the subject are again visible, they will have to coincide—so my argument runs—with the canon and its pedagogical extension in the curriculum. For any criticism bent on abolishing or dissolving the canon in the name of an 'egalitarian' politics or an 'interdisciplinary' theory is effectively committing suicide by relinquishing at once the subject matter and the social rationale specific to it. It will also discover, in the moment of recognition before death, that its attempt to dismantle the canon has only reinforced it.

For the canon is finally the only reason for the existence of literary studies, and all they have left to fall back on in hard times. This is *not* to suggest that it is or should be a fixed body of texts inscribed as it were in stone, or that an historical and political criticism of it is out of bounds. On the contrary, I am suggesting that the canon depends on a continuing cultural negotiation that is deeply political, a process that its successive re-inscriptions cannot help but record. For what constitutes the canonical text is the range of social interests it has been capable of serving—demonstrably diverse and conflicting not only over time but at any given moment. My differences on this point with the new contextualisms, however, turn on the irreducibility of the canonical text to the momentary interests that constitute and re-inscribe it. To read it as if it were captive to the interests of its context and moment is always reductive, even if the elucidation of those interests could be exhaustive. This is only to re-assert the obvious and undeniable *transhistoricity*—as distinct from transcendence or ahistoricity—of the canon, and to regard it as more than the by-product of an amazingly efficient and enduring conspiracy on the part of the powers that be.

Over the past three centuries, Shakespeare's plays have cast a penumbra of commentary richer in amplitude and variety than any other texts, including the Bible, and have become the paradigm-case of modern and secular canonicity: so much so that I doubt whether it is even possible any longer to gain access to them except by way of its mediation. Yet once this is recognized, the inescapable mediation of Shakespeare's plays becomes the subject matter of a newer historicism focused not on some original and 'definitive' context of production but on their multiple and shifting contexts of reproduction and re-inscription at the hands of later interpreters. For the history of re-inscription of Shakespeare's work is at one and the same time the history of 'Shakespeare' and the history of modern culture. Moreover, such a history of the cultural and critical re-inscription of the canon is also the only historical project specific to literary studies rather than parasitical upon other disciplines. So the canon, which is all we finally have to define ourselves, might turn out to be quite a lot after all.

On this recognition, the re-contextualization of Renaissance texts now under way—however demystifying or democratic in intent—turns in effect into the contemporary form of their continuing canonization. Within the largely unwritten history of that cultural process, the currently divergent movements of deconstruction and the new historicism will join together again to provide not only the subject-matter of its later chapters but the discursive resources of its writing. While no more than preliminary to such an enlarged project, the essays collected here may help to perform the hygienic and enabling task of clarifying what such a post-structuralist historicism can and cannot accomplish. For both aspects of the contemporary re-inscription of Donne, Marlowe, and, especially, Shakepeare are foregrounded in the following case studies, in which a self-consciously political critique of the canon is shown to collabor-ate unwittingly in its perpetuation and consolidation. In so doing, they also foreshadow the limitations, not necessarily unwelcome, on any newer historicism we might envision.

H.F.
Sydney, Australia
October 1989

Acknowledgements

Several of the following essays originally appeared in various collections and journals, in some cases under different titles: 'Romance and Romanticism' in *Shakespeare's Romances Reconsidered*, eds. Carol Kay and Henry Jacobs (Lincoln: University of Nebraska Press, 1978); ' "Tongue-tied, Our Queen?" ' in *Shakespeare and the Question of Theory*, eds. Patricia Parker and Geoffrey Hartman (New York and London: Methuen, 1985); 'The Dark Lady Identified' in *Studies in Shakespeare*, eds. G. A. Wilkes and A. P. Riemer (Sydney: Sydney University Press, 1985); 'Contextualizing the Canon' in *Southern Review*, 18/3 (1985); 'Marlowe our Contemporary' in *Textual Practice*, 1/3 (1987). I am grateful to their editors and publishers for permission to reprint them here in revised form.

More informal and abstract debts are always harder to acknowledge adequately, and I beg pardon for inevitable omissions. Francis Barker and Peter Hulme enriched my visits to Essex in 1985, 1988, and 1989 with many conversations, in which their loyal and hospitable opposition strengthened my thinking at crucial stages. Terence Hawkes, whose biographical iconoclasm towards 'Men of English Letters' has influenced not only the 'new' but the 'newer' historicism projected here, has also been a constant critical friend. I owe him more than a pint. The fresh, understated scholarship of Margreta de Grazia on early editions of Shakespeare provides a timely alternative and quiet corrective to overpublicized new-historicist routines. I thank her for sharing it with me before it becomes better known. In the course of our continuing disagreement over the 'realist' position, my colleague John Tulloch has given me an education in its history and theory. Michael Bristol, Russ McDonald, and Ed Pechter offered unsolicited encouragement at various points. Oxford's anonymous readers confirmed precisely my own intuition of the book's weaknesses and are responsible for many subsequent reinforcements.

At a more practical but indispensable level, Kim Scott Walwyn demonstrated yet again her loyalty to her authors and characteristic publishing flair. My research assistants, Martin Buzacott and Rebecca Barnett, repeatedly came to my rescue with their native resourcefulness. My thanks to the Australian Research Council for the grant that enabled me to employ them. The secretarial staff of the School of English at Macquarie persevered nobly in processing a complex typescript. In this connection, I am inexpressibly grateful to my former secretary, the long-suffering and light-hearted Jennifer Newton, for her amazing virtuosity on my behalf.

Contents

1

Historicizing Bardolatry: Or, Where Could Coleridge have been Coming From?

Take pains the genuine meaning to explore;
There sweat, there strain; tug the laborious oar:
Search every comment that your care can find;
Some here, some there, may hit the poet's mind:
When things appear unnatural and hard,
Consult your author, with himself compar'd.

(Roscommon, prefixed to Malone's Edition of
Shakespeare, 1790)

'IDEALISM' AND 'HISTORICISM'

'The dominant critical discourses which hold these [Shake-spearean] texts in place remain committed to idealist con-structions.' Thus writes the editor of a recent collection of essays no less committed to the deconstruction of those dis-courses and the contestation of their dominance in the name of a 'new historicism'.[1] In his entirely plausible account, Coleridge is the crucial figure through whose romantic poetics the late eighteenth-century idolatry of Shakespeare at once achieves its

---

[1] See the introduction to John Drakakis, ed., *Alternative Shakespeares* (London: Methuen, 1985). I use the term 'new historicism' broadly, to refer not only to that movement in America, focused on Shakespeare and Renaissance literature, which also calls itself 'cultural poetics', but also to its counterpart in Britain which goes by the name of 'cultural materialism'. This linkage seems to me justified by their common commitment to a post-structuralist view of history as 'text' rather than 'fact'. Drakakis himself projects a much looser coalition of 'post-structuralism, deconstruction, psycho-analytic criticism, continental semiotics, structural marxism, feminism, the analysis of discursive practices, and cultural materialism'. What links these otherwise divergent critical practices, in his view, is their 'collective commitment to the principle of contestation of meaning' and resistance to 'assimilation into any of the dominant traditions of Shakespeare criticism' (p. 24).

apotheosis and exerts a continuing influence on modern criticism. And Coleridge's Shakespeare is indeed remarkable, not only for its idolatry but for its idealism:

I believe that Shakespeare was not a whit more intelligible in his own day than he is now to an educated man, except for a few local allusions of no consequence. As I said, he is of no age—nor I may add, of any religion, or party or profession. The body and substance of his works came out of the unfathomable depths of his own oceanic mind.[2]

At a stroke, Coleridge's oft-repeated credo divests Shakespeare and his works of virtually any historical and cultural specificity they might once have had and raises both to an almost transcendental level of abstraction. Shakespeare emerges as the original 'god-like' author—omniscient, omnipresent, and inscrutable—the 'chameleon' figure familiar from so much nineteenth- and twentieth-century criticism, 'whose work resists in its very essence any dogged questions that would tie it to time and place'.[3] In the construction of an 'oceanic' consciousness, the one thing for which there is neither time nor place is history, at least not in any materialist sense.

The diminution of Shakespeare's historicity to a 'few local allusions of no consequence' must strike any historical critic, old or new, as a mystification. All the more so, in so far as Coleridge does not seem to be speaking figuratively, in that eulogistic mode in which a poet is not upon oath, even if he is echoing Ben Jonson's 'He was not of an age but for all time'. In fact, in assigning Shakespeare to 'no age' and 'the body and substance of his works' to the spontaneous generation of his oceanic mind, Coleridge seems to echo another Elizabethan text as well, but one more often cited in support of the opposite position. Do Shakespeare's plays not show 'the very age and body of the time his form and pressure', as Hamlet says all

---

[2] Samuel Taylor Coleridge, *Table Talk* [1834], in Terence Hawkes, ed., *Coleridge's Writings on Shakespeare* (Harmondsworth: Penguin, 1969), 122. Quoted by Drakakis, *Alternative Shakespeares*, p. 5. This is not a view, extreme as it is, held casually or expressed only once. Variations on it recur throughout his reflections on Shakespeare, as when he describes Shakespeare as 'the least of all poets coloured in any particulars by the spirit or customs of his age', or says that 'there is nothing common to Shakespeare and to other writers of his day—not even the language they employed'. See his *Shakespearean Criticism*, ed. T. M. Raysor, 2 vols. (London: Dutton, 1936), i.244, ii.125.

[3] Drakakis, *Alternative Shakespeares*, p. 5.

playing should?[4] Are not the historicity of the plays and the case for a historical criticism of them thus grounded in the authority of Shakespeare himself, or at the very least, in the discourse of his own age and stage? What could have moved the likes of Coleridge to such extravagant idealization against the grain of the very Shakespearean text he seems to echo?

This last is not a rhetorical question; it is one of a number of real questions that arise in the wake of the re-historicizing of Shakespeare now under way. Why should he have been so idealized, indeed transcendentalized, as he was in the romantic period? And why should the idealist discourses through which his work was dehistoricized have remained dominant for so long since? Such questions as these are no less historical for being concerned with the occlusion of history. Yet they are infrequently raised by the new historicism and, when they are, its own favoured mode of ideological critique enables only indirect or negative answers to them. For the unmasking of the material and political interestedness of the text can elucidate only its ideological function, the legitimization or promotion of other interests it invariably, if obliquely, serves. Such a critique has only limited purchase on, or interest in, any positive purpose the text might once have served or—perish the thought—might still serve.[5] Unless such questions as these are explicitly addressed, the better part of two centuries of

---

[4] That Shakespeare's plays register the social and political pressures of their own age, even if they do not represent them directly, is of course the argument of the new historicism. For a re-statement of it in terms of Hamlet's advice to the players, see Annabel Patterson, ' "The Very Age and Body of the Time His Form and Pressure" ', in G. Douglas Atkins and David M. Bergeron, eds., *Shakespeare and Deconstruction* (New York: Peter Lang, 1988), 47–68. The most searching new-historicist reflection on Hamlet's reflections on theatrical reflection—though still very much focused on the play's cultural context of production as the 'time' in question—is Stephen Greenblatt's opening chapter, 'The Circulation of Social Energy in Renaissance England', in *Shakespearean Negotiations* (Oxford: Clarendon Press, 1988), 7–20. While this famous passage repeatedly influences his own phrasing, Coleridge seems to resist its historicist implication by changing its emphasis as he echoes it: 'Times and manners lend their form and pressure', he writes, '*to genius*' (my italics). See Robert W. Babcock, *The Genesis of Shakespeare Idolatry 1766–1799* (Chapel Hill: University of North Carolina Press, 1931), 223–4.

[5] A trenchant overview of the limitations of Marxist ideological critique—surely the strong form of new-historicist criticism—and the outline of a broadened historical hermeneutic are set out by Fredric Jameson in the last chapter of *The Political Unconscious: Narrative as a Socially Symbolic Act* (London and New York: Methuen, 1981).

Shakespeare criticism will remain not only a mystification but a mystery.

In the attempt to account for this prolonged and bewildering interlude, let us take for our point of departure the text to which Coleridge seems to concede so little. Though often quoted in the conviction that it voices Shakespeare's own aims and principles as a dramatist and clinches the case for an historical approach to his plays, Hamlet's assertion of the historical embeddedness of theatre is by no means unequivocal. The notions of mimesis, nature, and history on which it rests are no more secure or self-evident in Hamlet's speech than they are in the diverse discourses of drama—classical, medieval, Renaissance—on which he somewhat indiscriminately draws. The 'end' of playing, Hamlet tells us,

> both at first and now, was and is, to
> hold as 'twere the mirror up to nature, to
> show virtue her own feature, scorn her
> own image, and the very age and body of the
> time his form and pressure.

(III.ii.18–22)

For all his insistence on the vividness and accuracy of its mirroring, Hamlet's 'nature' finally consists of eternal moral essences, his theatre is historically unchanging, and his own speech an anachronistic pastiche of disparate discourses. So there is a sense in which Hamlet's own tendency to eternalize and universalize theatrical practice actually invites Coleridge's idealist inversion of his apparent meaning.

If the theatre that mirrors nature and the nature that it mirrors seem to have lost something of their cultural specificity in the circularity of Hamlet's speculations, so too has 'the very age and body of the time'. 'The "age" of the "time" ', comments Dr Johnson, 'can hardly pass.'[6] But his suggested emendation of 'age' to 'face' or 'page', while fixing Hamlet's metaphor, fails to focus his meaning. To which 'time' is Hamlet referring, both here and earlier, when he styles the players 'the abstracts and

---

[6] Cited by H. H. Furness, ed., *Hamlet*, New Variorum edition (Philadelphia: Lippincott, 1879), i. 227–8.

brief chronicles of the time' (II.ii.501–2)? The definite article, as we shall soon see, is quite deceptive. The temporal orientation of theatre remains out of focus in Hamlet's reflections, just as the historical frame of reference for Shakespeare's plays—and for any contextualization of them we might undertake—is out of joint. An historical criticism of Shakespeare that takes its cue from Hamlet will soon be at a loss as to where to direct its research.

The problem of historical reference in Hamlet's famous speech—and in Shakespeare's plays—is by no means an invention of modern criticism, or more particularly, of that school of it known as 'deconstruction'. In the course of the latter eighteenth century—the period that in most accounts frames the rise of Shakespeare idolatry—no fewer than three distinct 'times' were suggested as the time Hamlet had 'in mind'. George Steevens, Johnson's friend and reviser, tried to pin down Hamlet's meaning by conforming it to certain neoclassical doctrines of decorum and verisimilitude. 'To represent the manners of the time', Steevens paraphrases, 'suitable to the period that is treated of, according as it may be ancient or modern.'[7] The time the play mirrors would thus coincide with the 'time' it chronicles, i.e. the historical setting of its ostended action, the moment and context of dramatic representation. In the case of *Hamlet* itself, the time whose form and pressure it would have to show by this logic is medieval Denmark.

To expect with Steevens such a correspondence between history and theatre is surely to expect of Shakespeare's plays either much more or much less than they actually deliver, whether or not one is a historical critic. Virtually any attempt to interpret or produce *Hamlet* as an image of events performed in medieval Denmark would be doomed to reveal precisely the sort of referential inconsistency Ben Jonson liked to point out in Shakespeare's work and expose the play to criticism of a Rymeresque kind and severity. 'If any critics would urge it as an objection,' wrote John Monck Mason of anachronistic scriptural echoes in the ending of *King Lear*, 'that the persons of the Drama are Pagans, and of course unacquainted with the scriptures, they give Shakespeare credit for more accuracy than

[7] Ibid., p. 228.

I fear he possessed.'[8] Hamlet's advice to the players actually substantiates Mason's case and undermines Steevens' by its own carefree juxtaposition of medieval ideas of *theatrum mundi* with neo-classical notions of scenic verisimilitude, the availability of which to a medieval Dane is questionable to say the least.

On the question of the 'time' to which drama properly belongs, neo-classical doctrine never quite managed to resolve the inconsistencies apparent in Hamlet's early version of it. An underlying 'general nature', permanently and universally human, is somehow supposed to show through the local and historical particulars of its verisimilar representation.[9] Thus, while a scrupulous 'period' fidelity might be advanced in theory, eighteenth-century practice—editorial, critical, and especially theatrical—was inclined to 'improve' Shakespeare, i.e. to conform his texts to current cultural and critical norms and update them accordingly. (The cult or fetish of historical and documentary authenticity is actually, as we shall soon see, a later *romantic* development.) With a fully 'methodized' neo-classicism in place, why not adapt Shakespeare's own textual and theatrical practices to it, thereby releasing the light of his genius from the Elizabethan archaisms that partly obscure it? The result, at every level of his Augustan cultural processing, is a radical *contemporization* of Shakespeare, a contemporization that is seen at the same time as a liberation of the eternal form of his work from Elizabethan awkwardness and barbarism. 'He is a classic,' wrote the actress turned moral commentator Mrs Elizabeth Griffith in 1775, 'and contemporary with all ages.'[10]

On such a view, the 'time' that drama represents becomes the moment and context of its cultural re-inscription. In the eighteenth century this means its *literal* as well as figurative re-inscription, as Shakespeare's plays are effectively rewritten in a succession of editions and productions. After all, had not Shakespeare himself gestured more than once towards the

---

[8] John Monck Mason, *Comments on the Several Editions of Shakespeare's Plays* [1785], in Brian Vickers, ed., *Shakespeare: The Critical Heritage*, vi (London: Methuen, 1981), 406.

[9] These tensions, as they appear in Johnson's 'Preface', are acutely analysed by Christopher Norris, 'Post-structuralist Shakespeare: Text and Ideology' in Drakakis, ed., *Alternative Shakespeares*, pp. 47–66.

[10] See Vickers, ed., *Shakespeare: The Critical Heritage*, vi. 137.

future production, and hence the permanent contemporaneity, of his work:

> How many ages hence
> Shall this our lofty scene be acted over
> In states unborn and accents yet unknown?
>
> (*Julius Caesar*, III.i.128–30)

Here Cassius and Brutus, there Cleopatra, elsewhere Prospero, assert a temporal frame of reference for Shakespearean theatre distinct and remote from their own historical moments: i.e., all those unlimited contexts of reproduction and re-inscription that befit and constitute a classic. Why, after all, should 'the very age and body of the time' shown in the archaic mirror of *Hamlet* be restricted to medieval Denmark? Why may it not, once decorously polished and re-framed, reflect eighteenth-century London as well? Or late twentieth-century Berkeley? 'Instead of the very age,' ingeniously urges Monck Mason against Johnson and Steevens, 'I read *every* age and body of the time.'[11] Clearly, we are well on the way to the romantic transcendentalization of Shakespeare with which we began.

THE NEW HISTORICISM OF EDMOND MALONE

Before arriving there, however, we must take account of, indeed come to grips with, the third—and, doubtless, for this our own new-historicist moment, the most obvious—reading of the 'time'. Surely 'the age and body of the time' to which Hamlet refers—one is tempted to add *primarily* refers—is Shakespeare's own time, late Elizabethan England, the provenance, after all, of the play's original inscription and initial production. Compared to this historical moment, those of its dramatic representation and cultural re-inscription nominated by Steevens and Monck Mason respectively must seem pseudo-historical, mere logical extrapolations of neo-classical formalism. 'Speculative criticism on these plays', writes Edmond Malone in the course of correcting one of Monck Mason's intuitive glosses, 'will ever be liable to error unless we add to it an intimate acquaintance with the language and writings of the

---

[11] Mason, *Comments on the Several Editions of Shakespeare's Plays, extended to those of Malone and Steevens* (Dublin, 1807), 445.

predecessors and contemporaries of Shakespeare.'[12] While re-affirming that he was for all time, Malone reminds us that Shakespeare was also of an age—his own.

Against the neo-classical impulses to contemporize and universalize Shakespeare, Malone is the foremost exponent of a new historicism. For at the time it was indeed 'new'. Within the succession of eighteenth-century editors and commentators, Malone has the strongest claim to be called the founder of modern Shakespeare scholarship as an *historical* discipline.[13] (Capell, whose agenda he went on to execute, and not Johnson, is his only real rival.) Referring to Pope's edition, Malone writes that 'by his numerous fanciful alterations the poet was so completely modernized that I am not confident, had he re-visited the glimpses of the moon, he would have understood his own works.'[14] The otherness of an historical text regarded earlier in the century as the product of barbarous outlandish-ness and treated with cavalier irreverence was seen by Malone as an occasion for research and reconstruction of the most painstaking kind, as the Elizabethan age receded ever deeper into the dark backward and abysm of time. In his gloss on Hamlet's speech, the question of the 'time' is re-historicized, against the grain of neo-classical contemporism, to reflect a cultural specificity now fading into indistinction: the end of playing, Malone paraphrases, is 'to *delineate exactly the nuance of the age*, and the *particular humor* of the day'.[15]

Yet it is important for our purposes to recognize that Malone's researches into the authenticity and chronology of Shakespeare's plays, the ambience of his life, the conditions of his stage, and the diverse textual and documentary evidence on which the reconstruction of all of these depend, are instinct with an emergent native romanticism associated with such contemporary figures as James Macpherson, Bishop Percy (with whom Malone conducted a twenty-year correpondence), Thomas Chatterton, and William Henry Ireland (both of whose archaizing fabrications he exposed). At the same time,

[12] Edmond Malone, *Prolegomena* to his 1790 edition, in Vickers, ed., *Shakespeare: The Critical Heritage*, vi. 542–3.

[13] See the illuminating study of Shakespeare in the eighteenth century by Margreta de Grazia, *Shakespeare Verbatim* (Oxford: Clarendon Press, 1991).

[14] See Vickers, ed., *Shakespeare: The Critical Heritage*, vi. 528.

[15] See Furness, ed., *Hamlet*, p. 228.

Shakespeare's plays were being purged of recent 'improvements' and staged once again in their Elizabethan language and form.[16] In this ensemble of late eighteenth-century developments we can discern a pre-romantic nostalgia for remote cultural origins and authentic native traditions common to poets and antiquarians, theatrical managers and historical scholars alike. This new historical consciousness—and in Malone's case, conscientiousness—in the editorial recovery and theatrical revival of Shakespeare's plays is instinct with the cultural dialectic that culminated in the romantic transcendentalization of the plays with which we began. At the same moment Coleridge was idealizing *The Tempest* in his lectures, Malone was identifying the Bermuda pamphlets as its 'historical' source.

The alternative Shakespeares emerging at this time, one newly historicized and the other increasingly idealized, in a certain sense generate one another. My point is not simply that such apparently contradictory developments are already latent in a neo-classical poetics split in its commitments between a 'nature' conceived as historically specific and as transhistorically universal. Nor is it merely a matter of idolatry creating historical interest and vice versa, which is certainly the case. The tireless labours of Malone himself, while aimed at recovering the Elizabethan historicity of Shakespeare and his work, were motivated by his near idolatrous conviction of the timeless universality of both; and those labours certainly contributed in turn to the romantic idealization of Shakespeare into an object of world-cultural idolatry. But even more

[16] Kemble in particular took great pains in his productions at this time to approach something like an Elizabethan textual and theatrical authenticity. See Babcock, *The Genesis of Shakespeare Idolatry*, pp. 87–9; and Louis Marder, *His Exits and His Entrances: The Story of Shakespeare's Reputation* (London: John Murray, 1963), 65. Malone himself remarks on the re-awakening of interest in the historicization of Shakespeare epitomized by his own work in his 'Attempt to Ascertain the Order in which the Plays attributed to Shakespeare Were Written' [1786]: 'An ardent desire to understand and explain his works, has, to the honour of the present age, so much increased within these last thirty years, that more has been done towards their elucidation, during that period, than, perhaps, in a century before . . . Almost every circumstance that tradition or history has preserved, relative to him or his works, has been investigated, and laid before the publick; and the avidity with which all communications of this kind have been received, sufficiently proves, that the time expended in the pursuit has not been wholly misemployed.' (*Prolegomena to the Dramatick Writings of Will. Shakespeare* (London, 1786), pp. v–vi).

crucially, Malone's career illustrates a certain material logic at work in the cultural transmission—and transformation—of Shakespeare in the eighteenth century, a material logic that might explain how these alternative, if not antithetical, Shakespeares could have emerged at almost the same moment.

The mechanism to which I refer is the succession of editions through which Shakespeare's text, with its growing penumbra of commentary, was handed down in the course of the century. The dozen or so distinct editions that appeared between Rowe's of 1709 and Steevens and Reid's First Variorum of 1803 all claimed to make Shakespeare available as never before to an ever expanding audience. At least that was their legitimation. Yet this very same succession of editions, justified on scholarly, educational, and nationalistic grounds and supported by advances in public literacy and printing technology alike, may actually have had the opposite effect and worked progressively to obscure Shakespeare's text and its 'meanings' from the nation it was meant to reach.

Or so claimed John Monck Mason in 1807. After praising the edition of Malone and Steevens, he comments:

The subsequent edition of Mr Isaac Reed [sic], may possibly possess a higher degree of merit, but that I have never seen; being deterred from consulting it, by its formidable dimensions—to analyse a work of twenty-one volumes octavo, was too arduous a task for a man to engage in, who has closed his eightieth year; I likewise apprehended that to swell his edition to that enormous bulk, he must have added at least six cartloads more, to the rubbish with which Shakespeare was before overwhelmed.

I well know that Mr Malone has entered his protest against language of this kind; and pronounced it most *barbarous jargon*, to assert that Shakespeare has been buried under his commentators;—but notwithstanding my deference for his opinion, I shall not retract the expression I have used—for though Johnson tells us, in his admirable preface, that notes are a *necessary* evil; he nowhere says that unnecessary notes are a necessary evil,—and I shall venture to assert, that a great part of those, both of Malone and Steevens, are totally unnecessary.

An edition of Shakespeare, retaining in the text the most approved readings, and omitting every note, except such as tend to explain those passages which really require explanation, is a publication devoutly to be wished—if executed with judgement, it could not fail of general encouragement, and might properly bear the title, *a legible edition of Shakespeare.*[17]

Mason is worth quoting at such length because he at once reveals the problem and re-enacts it through his own testy, owlish, and allusive prose. Shakespeare's text and its meanings had become inaccessible to precisely the extent that the notes, commentaries, and prefatory materials of an entire century had endeavoured to make them available. The full extent of that proliferating accumulation of material is spectacularly illustrated in the great Third Variorum edition, begun by Malone and completed by Boswell the Younger in 1821. Its first three volumes comprised no less than 1,800 pages of 'prolegomena' concerned with Shakespeare's biography, theatre, learning, language, versification, chronology, and text; while the scholarship of the previous century was condensed in the next eighteen. Only then, in the manner of variorum editions before and since, do the editors manage to shoehorn in the text of the plays.

The problem, as Mason citing Johnson notes, begins in the necessary evil of annotation. The paradox of annotation is that to make Shakespeare more 'intelligible'—Coleridge's word with which we began—is to make him less *legible*; to render his meaning accessible is to debar access to his work behind apparatuses; to produce it for the present, to embed it deeper in its own history. In the Third Variorum edition of Malone and Boswell, these paradoxes take the physical and literal form of three daunting volumes of historicizing prolegomena, preliminary discourses to be negotiated before the reader even meets the discourse of the plays in volume four, if indeed he or she ever meets it. The cumbersome apparatus deemed necessary for reading the plays necessitates in turn the deferral of their reading, which is then further deterred by the thousands of notes by diverse hands that form that text's highly visible—and distracting—system of support. When Edward Capell published his ten volumes of excellent text in 1766, and only subsequently his three volumes of commentary in separate instalments, he incurred the ridicule of his fellow editors for some time to come.[18] Yet in thus subverting conventional

---

[17] Mason, *Comments on the Several Editions . . .* , pp. v–vi.

[18] In recent years, Capell has risen dramatically in esteem, both as editor and as commentator. See Alice Walker, 'Edward Capell and his Edition of "Shakespeare"', in

practice, he also recognized a problem to which the vested interests of professional editors required that a blind eye be turned.

'IDEALISM' REVISITED

Against such a background of editorial controversy and such a backlog of accumulated commentary, the romantic transcendentalization of Shakespeare becomes more understandable. If a century of encrusted annotations could provoke old Monck Mason to call for a 'legible' Shakespeare, could it not also move the younger Coleridge to produce one, if not exactly the 'legible Shakespeare' Mason had in mind? Whereas Malone saw himself subjecting current opinion to the test of historical scholarship in order to arrive at a positive knowledge of Shakespeare in his time—one approach to the problem—Coleridge envisioned a universal poetic genius rising above his historical circumstances and modern scholarly controversies all at once—another approach to the problem:

Shakespeare is of no age. It is idle to endeavour to support his phrases by quotations from Ben Jonson, Beaumont and Fletcher, etc. His language is entirely his own, and the younger dramatists imitated him. The construction of Shakespeare's sentences, whether in verse or prose, is the necessary and homogeneous vehicle of his peculiar manner of thinking. His is not the style of an age.[19]

At a stroke, Shakespeare is delivered from the discursive limitations of his contemporaries and from the textual encumbrances of his commentators. What Coleridge has effectively done is to 'publish' Shakespeare afresh, to render his work visible and legible to an expanded audience of 'educated' readers.[20] That this romantic rescue operation depends upon the simultaneous development of a wider cultural support system

Peter Alexander, ed., *Studies in Shakespeare: British Academy Lectures* (London: Oxford University Press, 1964), 132–48; and Vickers, ed., *Shakespeare: The Critical Heritage*, vol. vi, p. xi.

[19] Coleridge, *Table Talk*, in Hawkes, ed., *Coleridge's Writings on Shakespeare*, p. 121.

[20] The audiences of Coleridge's public lectures on Shakespeare at the Royal Institution and elsewhere were distinctly middle-class, in contrast to the broader social cross-section in attendance at Hazlitt's. See Jonathan Bate, *Shakespearean Constitutions: Politics, Theatre, Criticism 1730–1830* (Oxford: Clarendon Press, 1989).

known as 'bourgeois individualism' is not in dispute.[21] It requires—and reinforces—the construction of a psychology and a sociology centred upon the private self, for which Shakespearean characterization, in its foreshadowing of new depths of inwardness, serves as a model. These new reserves of common interiority, at once unique and universal, with their massive potential for audience identification and readerly self-referencing, are essential to Coleridge's Shakespearean criticism. Thus, Shakespeare's characters consist in 'genera intensely individualized' and are 'an involution of the universal in the individual'.[22] Lady Macbeth is a 'class individualized', and Hamlet, of whom Coleridge thought he had a 'smack' himself, 'must have some common connection with the laws of our nature' and 'the constitution of our own minds'.[23]

The 'idealism' for which Coleridge, and romantic criticism generally, is nowadays indicted was basic to a democratization

[21] The rise of the bourgeoisie during the latter eighteenth century to a position of political dominance in the nineteenth, and the restructuring of literary and cultural ideology it entailed, are a recurrent theme of new-historicist and cultural-materialist criticism. See Terry Eagleton, *Criticism and Ideology* (London: Verso, 1977), and *The Function of Criticism* (Oxford: Blackwell, 1983); and especially Jameson, *The Political Unconscious*, where the private bourgeois subject and its aesthetic projection, the romantic author, are seen as ingredients of an overall ideology of containment. On a rigorously Marxist view, both polemical attack on the bourgeois subject and anxious or nostalgic defence of him are equally beside the point. For an example of the latter, see Richard Levin, 'Bashing the Bourgeois Subject', *Textual Practice*, 3/1 (Spring 1989), 76–86.

[22] Coleridge, *Shakespeare Criticism*, ed. Raysor, ii. 33; and *Biographia Literaria*, ed. J. Shawcross, 2 vols. (Oxford: Clarendon Press, 1907), ii. 159.

[23] Coleridge, *Shakespeare Criticism*, i. 137; ii. 223. The view that Shakespeare's work epitomizes the capacity of literature to reveal the inner laws of our subjectivity is by no means unique to Coleridge or German Idealism. William Richardson, Professor of Humanity at Glasgow and inventor of the romantic Hamlet, had already perceived in 1774 that the great poet 'displays passion, traceth its progress and delineates its character'. Shakespeare in particular is an 'unlimited genius', who 'changes himself into every character, and enters easily into every condition of human nature'. His plays will enable us 'to make poetry subservient to philosophy, and to employ it in tracing the principles of human conduct'. See his *Philosophical Analysis and Illustration of Some of Shakespeare's Remarkable Characters* [1774]. Hazlitt's comments on Shakespearean characterization also overlap at many points with Coleridge's: 'Hamlet is a name; his speeches and sayings but the idle coinage of the poet's brain. What then, are they not real? They are as real as our own thoughts. Their reality is in the reader's mind. It is *we* who are Hamlet. This play has a prophetic truth, which is above history' (*Characters of Shakespeare's Plays* (London, 1817), 154). Both comments are cited and usefully situated by Earl Wasserman, 'Shakespeare and the English Romantic Movement', in Herbert M. Schueller, ed., *The Persistence of Shakespeare Idolatry* (Detroit: Wayne State University Press, 1964), 79–103.

of the arts nothing less than revolutionary in its time, albeit in the retrospectively problematic sense of a bourgeois revolution. Thanks to the 'idealist' principles imported by Coleridge from Germany, Shakespeare's meaning was no longer confined either to his own time and culture or to the exclusive proprietorship of gentleman-scholars. Coleridge's idealism thus shifts the site of Shakespearean signification from the cultural and institutional structures unearthed by 'historicism' to the intersubjective transactions of contemporary reader or theatregoer, dramatic character, and universal author.

While some new historicists and cultural materialists may reject such a move as ideologically unsound, it is not only *hermeneutically* sound but hermeneutically necessary—to employ a concept also coming into its own in Germany at this very time. At a certain level, the historical text must always offer itself, and be received, as timeless and universal textuality even as it remains at another level remote and specific historicity—*if it is to be interpreted at all*. Otherwise the historical text would remain mute and impenetrable to any but its own culture and moment. Not only could its 'larger' meanings not be interpreted, but not even its local minutiae could be annotated, since elucidation of the parts of a text requires a previous or anticipatory understanding of the whole no less than interpretation of the whole requires a prior understanding of the parts. The hermeneutic circle encompasses all our textual dealings, whether or not we realize it.

This is of course the extreme or limiting case of the absolutely historical—and totally unintelligible—text, a case no historical criticism could afford to argue without calling into question its own capacity to interpret. It is worth exploring, however, if only to help explain Coleridge's rejection of the historicity of Shakespeare's plays. In its time, this was a 'liberating' move, philosophically and sociologically, and one whose implications —particularly its pedagogical implications for the transmission of the text—need to be carefully reconsidered before we reject it in turn. In foregrounding a common, universal, and trans-historical dimension of Shakespeare's text, Coleridge effectively returned that text to the public domain, enabled it to speak to an historical moment beyond its own and to a broader cross-section of society than previously: specifically to the nineteenth

century on its own bourgeois, individualist, and proto-psycho-
logical terms.

Coleridge was not the only one to attempt this new project,
nor his approach the only way of performing it, though it did
prove to be the most influential way. Despite his own titular
and indeed substantive emphasis on 'character', Hazlitt's approach was at the time as political—and 'left' political—as it
was psychological, and his standing at the present moment
may be higher in consequence, at least among historical
scholars.[24] But even political interpretation such as Hazlitt's
depends upon a way of thinking history, textuality, interpretation, and the relations among them, that allows for the
possibility of analogy and communality between past and
present based on linguistic and cultural continuity, a way of
thinking that allows, in fine, for a certain transhistoricity (as
distinct from ahistoricity or transcendence) of the text.

As an interpreter of texts, Hamlet himself knows all this only
too well. It is very much from the 'idealist' position of Coleridge
that he re-writes *The Murder of Gonzago* to bring out its trans-
historical import—or one of them. And he does so in terms of a
universal psychology: 'I have heard that guilty creatures sitting
at a play . . .' From the viewpoint of Coleridge, we stand in the
same interpretive relation to *Hamlet* as does the Danish court in
relation to *The Murder of Gonzago*: not necessarily in respect of our
complicity in crime but in respect of our capacity for identification. This is the case even before Hamlet re-writes *The Murder*,
since its capacity to be re-written, to be brought to bear upon
the present, depends upon a relation already potentially trans-
historical. This is the case despite our being Danes and Gonzago a
Viennese. Like Coleridge, we must have a 'smack' of Hamlet
ourselves, just as the elder Hamlet, Gertrude, and Claudius
have a smack of Gonzago, Baptista, and Lucianus respectively,
however 'inward' the smack must be. From Coleridge's standpoint, every Shakespearean play becomes a 'Mousetrap', and
we the audience are the mice. In releasing us from the historical
meaning of the text, idealist interpretation only returns us
to our own historical meaning, which has to be at least as
important, to put it mildly.

[24] See particularly Jonathan Bate, 'Shakespeare and the Literary Police', *London
Review of Books*, 29 (September 1988), 26; and his *Shakespearean Constitutions*.

2

Romance and Romanticism

> Where do I look for the romantic spirit? Among the early
> moderns, to Shakespeare, Cervantes, to Italian poetry,
> within that bygone age of knighthood, courtly love, and
> folktale, from which the idea—indeed, the word itself—
> derives.
>
> (Friedrich von Schlegel, 'Letter on the Novel')

FROM 'MYTH' TO 'IRONY'

The recent quickening of interest in Shakespearean, Spenser-
ian, and medieval romance may be seen as part of a broader
movement within modern criticism, an attempt to re-discover
the roots of our literary consciousness in the deeper structures
of fantasy, play, and dreaming that we are all, so to speak, born
into. While this recovery of older romance traditions has proceeded in a serene and scholarly fashion, a more speculative
and polemical side of the same larger project has emerged in the
field of Romanticism, no longer conceived as an isolated period
or movement within literary history but as a continuing artistic
crisis. Despite the contrasting moods that characterize these
fields, the one calm and objective and the other worried and
introspective, their concerns are as intimately related as their
common etymology suggests. Indeed, their contrasting moods
may even suggest a certain dialectical relation between them.
Is it not precisely the untroubled sublimity of the native
tradition of high romance inscribed in the works of Shakespeare,
Spenser, and Milton—a gorgeous and spontaneous abundance
as of unfallen nature itself—that conditions a crisis of anxiety
for the post-Renaissance poets who endeavour to revive that
tradition and bring forth their own second nature? Or so some
theorists of Romanticism would have us believe.[1]

---

[1] See particularly Walter Jackson Bate, *The Burden of the Past and the English Poet*
(Cambridge, Mass.: Harvard University Press, 1970) and Harold Bloom, *The Anxiety of*

That is of course a simplification of the relations between the older mode of romance and the modern movement of Romanticism. But there is a sense in which scholarship in each of these fields is busy reinforcing the prevailing conceptions and misconceptions of the other, because both share certain assumptions governing the way literary history has been periodized. Students of Romanticism have tended to regard the romance literature of the Middle Ages and Renaissance as a well-travelled world, the large historical and structural contours of which are familiar and safe. They imply that our maps of those earlier periods, somewhat like actual Renaissance maps of the known world, are in more or less reliable agreement, while the adventure of charting dark regions is in the area of romantic and post-romantic studies, where every man is his own map-maker and no two maps conform.

At the same time, scholars of that older romance literature have implicitly accepted and reinforced the terms of this myth of romantic modernism. Until quite recently, we have largely ignored all that is dark and unsettling in our subject as if it properly belonged to a later age and retreated into a nostalgic historical humanism with its bland and idealized orthodoxies of 'the great chain of being' and 'the Elizabethan world picture'. In so doing, we have complacently avoided the unsettling modernity that might be said to characterize all great works of literature, however culturally exotic or temporally remote. For this myth of modernism and the pastoralization of the past that complements and reinforces it are themselves romantic constructs under which we all more or less unwittingly labour. Not until we attempt to work ourselves out from under them can we hope to understand either romance or Romanticism better than we do, any more than one can understand one's own society without somehow leaving it.

Influence (New York: Oxford University Press, 1973). It will become apparent in the course of this essay that the view of literary and cultural history expressed in these works is a logical extension of a much more entrenched and uncontroversial conception of modernism, the essential doctrines of which are represented in Richard Ellman and Charles Feidelson, Jr. eds., *The Modern Tradition* (New York: Oxford University Press, 1965). It is an irony of Lionel Trilling's *Sincerity and Authenticity* (Cambridge, Mass.: Harvard University Press, 1972), for example, that the 'cultural mutation' it purports to chronicle and illustrate is already implicit in Shakespeare, with whom Trilling begins.

The work of Northrop Frye, evenly divided as it is between those earlier and later literatures and equally influential in both fields, will serve to illustrate the literary–historical myth I have begun to describe. 'Romanticism', he writes, 'is a "sentimental" form of romance, and the fairy tale, for the most part, a "sentimental" form of folk tale.'[2] Frye's terms are directly adopted from Schiller's famous essay, 'Über naïve und sentimentalische Dichtung', though 'naïve' for Frye means simply 'primitive' or 'popular' and is not historically identified, as it is in Schiller, with 'classical'; while 'sentimental', as in Schiller, means 'later', or 'sophisticated'. In adopting Schiller's terms, however, Frye has also adopted, though less obviously, Schiller's historical scheme. In the theory of modes that opens the *Anatomy*, Frye's division of Western literature into a descending scale from 'myth' through 'romance', 'high mimetic', and 'low mimetic' to 'irony' is correlated to the historical periods in which each mode successively dominates: classical, medieval, Renaissance, eighteenth century, nineteenth century, and modern.

Like Schiller's starker contrast of the 'naïve' or classical poet in touch with the natural world and the 'sentimental' or romantic poet alienated from it by modern civilization, Frye's logical and chronological scheme projects literary history as a disintegration of the presence and univocality of myth into the discontinuities and multivocalities of irony. The history of literature then moves, following hard upon an Enlightenment conception of cultural history that derives as much from Rousseau as from Schiller and Friedrich von Schlegel, from the impersonal universality of myth to the individuality or eccentricity of modern fiction. Frye systematically avoids valorizing this 'progress of poetry' in any of the ways in which it has been successively valorized by various schools of ancients and moderns, classics and romantics, over the past three centuries. Yet he none the less repeats the historical scheme that underlies and generates these schools and their quarrels in the first place. It may turn out that the weakness of Frye's rehabilitation of romance was not his avoidance of history, as is commonly charged, but his inability to do without a certain version of it.

---

[2] Northrop Frye, *Anatomy of Criticism* (Princeton: Princeton University Press, 1957), 35.

Romance for Frye is thus a 'displacement' in a human and secular direction—and Romanticism a further displacement—from the original unity of a putative mythic source:

The redemption myth in the older [Christian] mythology emphasised the free act of God in offering man grace, grace being thought of as essentially the transformation of the human moral will. Such grace proceeded from a divine love or *agape*. Romantic redemption myths . . . throw the emphasis on an *eros*, or love rooted in the human sexual instinct. Such an *eros* develops a distinctively human idealism, and for such idealism the redeeming agent is also human-centered.[3]

The characteristic self-consciousness of modern, that is, romantic, art, which Friedrich von Schlegel pointed out at the beginning of the nineteenth century, is for Frye, as for Schiller and Schlegel before him, the measure of its historical and cultural distance from a naïve mythic source.

For Frye, however, that source is not primarily the mythology of classical antiquity but the Judeo-Christian Scriptures, which he repeatedly reads as the fundamental romance narrative. Since Christian Scripture still retains a 'canonical' status during the Middle Ages and the Renaissance, for the romancer of those earlier periods a reunion with his source and concomitant authorization of his vision is still within reach. Dante, Milton, and Spenser all project the basic movement of scriptural romance from paradise lost to paradise regained, and their work becomes the prototype or, more accurately, the metatype for earlier romance. From Frye's perspective, it could be fairly inferred, there are no secular romances in the Middle Ages and Renaissance since any displacement from Christian myth that might have already occurred is not enough to distort the mythic shape of the work as a whole. Romance for Frye is the *mythos* of an extended summer, long since over but bound to return.

THE DEMYSTIFICATION OF ROMANCE: *THE TEMPEST*

Nothing is more remarkable in Frye's writings on earlier romance than the absence of any suggestion that its representation of pristine mythic form may itself be ironic or problematic for the romancer himself. Even Shakespeare, though generally

[3] Frye, *A Study of English Romanticism* (New York: Columbia University Press, 1968), 20.

considered a secular poet, closes his final romance—which for Frye represents the 'mythos of summer' at its height, a text 'not simply to be read or seen or even studied, but possessed'[4]— with a masque echoing the covenant of seedtime and harvest, an apocalyptic vision of dissolution and re-creation, and a prayer echoing the Christian imperative: 'As you from crimes would pardoned be, | Let your indulgence set me free.'[5] After all, while Shakespeare may be a secular poet, he is also a 'folk poet', a popular dramatist profoundly at one with a culture in which Christian forms and institutions are still dominant. '*The Tempest*', Frye acknowledges, 'is not an allegory, or a religious drama,'[6] since Prospero's renunciation of his magic and vision of apocalypse do not necessarily imply a divine will and an eternal world. But the 'art' which so pervades *The Tempest* is at least the human counterpart of divine grace, a medium of upward transformation to that more idealized human nature and community which constitutes the order of romance.

The assumption is that the erring inhabitants of the historical and daylight world of Milan have been sufficiently reformed as a result of Prospero's art that they will bring back with them something of the heightened nature of the golden or moonlit world of the island. What emerges from *The Tempest* is at least a silver world, an archetypal romance order of an old world inhabited by old men undergoing renovation. It is only fair to Frye, as well as important to my argument, to point out that this reading of *The Tempest* and of earlier romance is not unique to him; it is more or less explicit in the work of Knight, Barber, Tillyard, Traversi, and most of the studies of Shakespearean romance and pastoral that appeared, at an increasing rate, into the early 1970s. Frye's is only the most lucid, systematic, and influential statement of what had become, thanks in part to him, a commonplace of Shakespearean criticism.

There are, however, some unsettling features of the play, particularly of its final act, that simply do not conform to this

[4] Introduction to *The Tempest*, ed. Frye, The Pelican Shakespeare (New York: Penguin, 1970), 24.

[5] *The Tempest*, Epilogue, 19–20. Quotations in my text are from *The Tempest*, ed. Frank Kermode, New Arden Shakespeare (London: Methuen, 1954).

[6] Frye, Introduction to *The Tempest*, p. 17. See also his *A Natural Perspective: The Development of Shakespearean Comedy and Romance* (New York: Columbia University Press, 1965), 141–59.

orthodox view of it. As Frye himself observes, Prospero 'appears to have been a remarkably incompetent Duke of Milan, and not to be promising much improvement after he returns. His talents are evidently dramatic rather than political.'[7] Few commentators have delved into this matter until recently, preferring instead to pursue innocent analogies between Prospero's art and that of his creator or to position that art within a Renaissance debate over the claims of nature and nurture. But Prospero's relation even to his art—not to mention his ethical and political relations—is deeply ambivalent and goes to the heart of the play's romance status. The passion for magic he displays on the island is wholly continuous with that passion for magic and the liberal arts which caused him to lose his dukedom in the first place.

This is not simply because of his over-indulgence in the 'liberal arts' but because those studies carry the potential to draw their practitioner away from ethical and political concerns altogether or move him to seek and impose 'aesthetic' solutions to them. These dangers, while perhaps not serious (until recently) for a graduate student in English, are for a duke, and Prospero's career illustrates both in an extreme form. From the beginning of the play there is a quality of excess, of over-compensation on Prospero's part in exercising on the island the power he had formerly refrained from exercising in the historical world of Milan. He fluctuates, as a duke, between the extremes of benign neglect and a not so benevolent despotism.

The testiness of Prospero's characterization is too insistent to be explained away, as Frye and others try to do, as the nervous tension that accompanies the magician's role or the traditional crankiness of the *senex iratus* of new comedy. In Prospero's opening harangue to Miranda, in which he irritably recounts the history of the Milanese *coup d'état*, his own self-insulation in art is conveniently whitewashed and the blame for his banishment projected outward on to Antonio and Alonso. Prospero's division of the world into simple and self-flattering contrasts of black and white, a technique of romance-making at its most

---

[7] Frye, Introduction to *The Tempest*, p. 20. Since the present essay was written in the mid-1970s, it has been precisely the political dimension of Prospero's career that has preoccupied criticism of the play. See Chapter 9 of this collection for an account of the significant shift marked by the 'new historicism'.

naïve, is repeated in his representation of Caliban, whose faltering aspirations toward humanity he now denies categorically even though he once credited them categorically. His show of superior and unnecessary force in humiliating Ferdinand seems designed as much to display his own power as to correct Ferdinand's faults. Like his other austerity measures, it seems to arise out of an uneasy conscience, out of his own complicity in having created the social disintegration he is now bent on overcorrecting.

If Prospero's art is something less than the purely ethical instrument it was once made out to be, and Prospero himself less than an exemplar of disciplined political virtue, so too the romance order of the final act is something less than it has been represented, and not only by Frye. Several of the cast, under the spell of Prospero's magic, comment on the correspondence of their experience to the romance model Prospero would like that experience to illustrate. Ferdinand concludes from the betrothal masque that 'So rare a wonder'd father and a wife | Makes this place paradise'. Miranda, in perhaps the most famous line of the play, styles the society that emerges from it a 'brave new world'. And Gonzalo, who has already demonstrated his own limited talents at romance-making, chorically sums up what he takes to be the meaning of events: 'Prospero [found] his dukedom | In a poor isle; and all of us ourselves | When no man was his own.' Were *The Tempest* the archetypal romance it is supposed to be, the play would end right here on this uplifting note, which should accord with the ostended dramatic action.

But Gonzalo's summing-up is clearly wishful thinking. It glosses over Prospero's rejoinder to his daughter's exclamation of naïve wonder and joy: ' 'Tis new to thee.' Perhaps more significantly, our desire to assimilate the close of *The Tempest* to the rising rhythms of Gonzalo's speech must repress what one critic has termed the mood of 'collapsed spirits' in which Prospero repeatedly refers to his impending retirement but repeatedly defers it. 'Four times, beginning with "our revels now are ended," he bids farewell to his art and island, and prepares to leave (IV.i.148; V.i.29, 34, 64). Four times he reminds Ariel that he will soon be free (IV.i.261; V.i.5, 95, 241). On three different occasions he promises to tell his story later (V.i.162, 247, 302), which is a way of attenuating the absoluteness of the break, and extending the experience into the future.'⁸ The final act is suffused with the awareness, culminating in the epilogue, that Prospero's efforts at romance-making may have somehow failed but may yet be amended by one last fling.

Yet such a demystifying approach to the romance ending of the play, while it directs our attention to ironic elements that have been traditionally overlooked, cannot be accorded the last word. Though Prospero is reluctant to abandon the art in which his power over others resides, the fact remains that he does abandon it and does so with an expressed awareness of its 'vanity' and 'roughness'. His vacillation, disenchantment, and eventual renunciation may even be said to constitute the romantic triumph of the play, even if they represent something of a break from the exultations of archetypal or conventional romance. After all, Prospero's attempts to protect himself behind a shroud of romantic wonder and project himself as a godlike source of power and wisdom, of masques of judgement and masques of mercy, had been an extension of his original squeamishness towards the mere worldlings whose baser motives he had never been entirely above, for all his masquing.

And if Prospero's exalted role-playing escapes the criticism of those in the cast whose capacity for high designs answers to his own, Caliban's irreverent insistence on his usurpation and tyranny serves at least to underscore the unattractive parallels between Prospero's situation and behaviour and those of the worldlings and groundlings he scorns. In the final act, his awareness of a common bond with the courtiers he has punished extends even to the meanest of the cast, to the darkest of the alter egos he had formerly repudiated but now acknowledges as 'mine'. In taking himself off his own pedestal and reappearing 'as I was sometime Milan', Prospero undergoes his own sea-change, a self-humiliation into humanity that goes far toward

---

⁸ Harry Berger, Jr, 'Miraculous Harp: A Reading of Shakespeare's *Tempest*', *Shakespeare Studies*, v (1969), 253–83 at p. 277. My own reading of *The Tempest* is deeply indebted to Berger's, one of the few essays to respond to the difficulties presented by the play rather than to the harmonies that the play, as a romance, is supposed to exemplify. Worth citing in this connection is Joseph H. Summers, 'The Anger of Prospero', *Michigan Quarterly Review*, 12/2 (Spring 1973), 116–35, in which the problem of Prospero's conduct is raised as a central issue only to be ceremoniously laid to rest, lest it upset orthodox interpretation.

redressing the imbalances of his earlier self-exaltation in art. The epilogue, in which he appears divested of his magic robe on the bare peninsula of the stage and utters a subdued plea for our indulgence, represents the final stage of this reformation, the mood of collapsed spirits, the intimations of failure paradoxically reinforcing the effect.

It is important to note, however, that this triumph of romance takes the form of a demystification of romance, a stripping away of illusion and a repudiation of art. We are at the furthest remove possible from the spells, magic, spectacle, and wonder of a naïve romance consciousness. All that coercive theatricality has, in fact, been explicitly repudiated by Prospero as the condition of a new ethical, if not political, integrity. It would seem that, far from returning to its source in religious awe and wonder, *The Tempest* has entered the realm of an ironic secularity, a world in which illusions of bravery are revealed as illusions and the social order is perceived not as a divine but an all-too-human and precarious construct. Yet even this final act of self-demystification on Prospero's part, and the demystification of romance it entails, must also and simultaneously be seen as a remystification, the building up of a new and potent illusion.

For Prospero has only exchanged one kind of magic for another, a naïve and literal for a sophisticated and figurative magic. He has even metaphorically fulfilled one of the primal dreams of human art at its most romantic: to create a man, i.e. himself. What is the effect, after all, of Prospero's deconstruction of himself as a mage and artist except his reconstruction, or as he might say, his new-creation of himself as a man? The cast-off role of omnipotent magician becomes a foil against which a fragile human self is defined by contrast. Of course this latest remystification of romance on Prospero's part is also subject, in turn, to further demystification. For it too is an act of illusionism; the human image that we are left with at the end is the product of a sleight of hand that can only represent the human and the real by the negative means of foils and contrasts, by showing what they are not rather than by presenting the thing itself.

The repudiation of art and magic in favour of 'humanity' and 'reality' that closes the play is thus only another version of art and magic; it renders Prospero's final act vulnerable to criticism as a form of slumming and mock humility; or, in the political terminology increasingly in favour nowadays, of colonialism. *The Tempest* remains true to its romance form only by acknowledging the artificiality and authoritarianism of its romance form. The play can neither reunite with its romance archetype nor leave it altogether behind, in much the same way that Prospero himself can neither remain the artist nor quite become the man, but defers his abandonment of art only to promise to return to it after the end of the play to re-tell his story to the cast. The play and its protagonist are caught up within an endless and dizzying dialectic between mystification and demystification for which no final or stable synthesis seems possible. It becomes increasingly clear that *The Tempest* can in no way be seen as a 'naïve' romance in Schiller's or Frye's sense but exhibits an ironic sophistication in relation to its romance models that is nothing if not 'modern'. The play is thus hopelessly displaced, by all the distance of theatrical self-consciousness that Prospero (and ultimately Shakespeare) bring to it, from the ritually sanctioned forms of romance espoused by Gonzalo.

If this example of naïve romance turns out not to be so naïve, however, what can be said of later examples of the mode? For according to the scheme of literary and cultural history we are examining, it is only with the Enlightenment that elements of irony, distance, and sophistication invade the pristine integrity of romance, and a major displacement from its origins in myth and ritual occurs. Only now does the joy of reunion with a mythic source become problematic or unavailable in its original purity. Even here, however, there is no suggestion of loss in Frye's work, especially by contrast with that of such romantic revisionists as Harold Bloom or Walter Jackson Bate, who share the same historical scheme, albeit more openly. After all, the dominant mode of modern literature, as we all know, is not romance but irony, and since all modes are, in Frye's view, created equal, there is no cause for alarm. Yet in his historical, as distinct from his theoretical, scheme all modes are *not* created equal since literature depends for its authority on its proximity and conformity to the religiously and culturally sanctioned source which is myth, and myth is not literature.

Literature, that is, cannot supply its own authority. Schiller and Schlegel at least felt the need to rescue romantic, that is, modern, literature from invidious comparison with ancient literature in a way that balanced acknowledged loss with gain. And more recently, Harold Bloom has developed the same historical view of Romanticism as a continuing process of revisionist displacement and, in a tonality of rich gloom, fixed the high cost of romantic belatedness in the dangers of solipsism or epigonism that beset the modern writer. The absence of a sense of loss in the work of a critic whose literary–historical scheme commits him a priori to a sense of loss can only suggest that Frye, at some level, does not accept the consequences of his own system. In this respect, Frye may be wiser than he might appear and a better literary historian than he is sometimes said to be. For Frye's historical equanimity reflects the undiminished admiration many of us retain, against all our own historicist training and bias, for a romantic tradition, that none the less rivals its Renaissance models even as it asserts its own belatedness and laments its own loss.

THE REMYSTIFICATION OF ROMANCE:
HEART OF DARKNESS

The distorting tendency of that older literary historicism which conditions our dealings with romance can be further illustrated if we turn to a great latter-day example of the mode. Conrad's *Heart of Darkness*, we are used to hearing, is an unrelieved 'night-journey', a quest romance turned upside down or perhaps inside out, the ultimate modernist ironization of the romance form it adopts.[9] Indeed, the tale opens with an

---

[9] The tendency to read the novella as a study of the psychological and cultural alienation of modern man was no doubt encouraged by T. S. Eliot's borrowing of the line, 'Mistah Kurtz—he dead', for the epigraph to 'The Hollow Men'. The influential work of Albert J. Guerard, *Conrad the Novelist* (Cambridge, Mass.: Harvard University Press, 1958), 32–43, discusses it as 'a *Pilgrim's Progress* for our pessimistic and psychologizing age'. Other critics have traced its ironic structural parallels to the descents into hell of the *Inferno* and the *Aeneid* as well as to medieval quest romance. See Bruce Harkness, ed., *Conrad's Heart of Darkness and the Critics* (San Francisco: Wadsworth, 1960). A valuable, though partial, attempt to de-ironize Conrad's fiction by disentangling it from prevailing notions of modernism and linking it with older traditions of romance and Romanticism is to be found in David Thorburn, *Conrad's Romanticism* (New Haven: Yale University Press, 1974), esp. 153–65.

extended analogy between the darkening flood of the Thames estuary, which will be the point of departure for Marlow's adventures, and the Thames of earlier days and brighter tales:

It [the Thames] had known and served all the men of whom the nation is proud, from Sir Francis Drake to Sir John Franklin, knights all, titled and untitled—the great knights-errant of the sea. It had borne all the ships whose names are like jewels flashing in the night of time, from the *Golden Hind* returning with her round flanks full of treasure, to be visited by the Queen's Highness and thus pass out of the gigantic tale, to the *Erebus* and *Terror*, bound on other conquests —and that never returned. It had known the ships and the men. They had sailed from Deptford, from Greenwich, from Erith—the adventurers and the settlers; kings' ships and the ships of men on 'Change; captains, admirals, the dark 'interlopers' of the Eastern trade, and the commissioned 'generals' of East India fleets. Hunters for gold or pursuers of fame, they all had gone out on that stream, bearing the sword, and often the torch, messengers of the might within the land, bearers of a spark from the sacred fire. What greatness had not floated on the ebb of that river into the mystery of an unknown earth . . . The dreams of men, the seed of commonwealths, the germs of empires.[10]

It is impossible, from this point on, not to view the movement of *Heart of Darkness* against a background of Renaissance travel literature—not only Drake's circumnavigation of the world but all those tall tales of exploration and discovery that so engaged the imagination of Coleridge, for one, and, further back, of Shakespeare himself in *The Tempest*.

That this is the narration of a spellbound or naïve romancer is clear from the unwitting disparities between the contemporary setting he has just described and the nostalgic paean he launches into. The 'knights-errant of the sea' who populate the gigantic tale of his recollection have been displaced on the darkening Thames by the bourgeois crew of company director, lawyer, and accountant aboard the cruising yawl *Nellie*; the single-minded vocation of Renaissance merchant-adventurers by the modern disjuncture of business and pleasure; the mythological splendour of the *Golden Hind* by the mundane domesticity of the *Nellie*. We are repeatedly struck by the narrator's apparent obliviousness to the ambivalence of his own language: 'Hunters for gold or pursuers of fame', 'bearing

[10] Joseph Conrad, *Heart of Darkness*, ed. Robert Kimbrough (New York: Norton, 1971), 4–5.

the sword, and often the torch', 'the germs of empires'. These opening ironies of situation and language do not bode well, to say the least, for the tale's chances of re-establishing continuity with the strong mythic forms of its source at a literary, a cultural or an ethical level.

The demystification of romance becomes even more explicit when Marlow takes up the narrative burden. His account of the Roman conquest of Britain is a further debunking of the first narrator's naïve account of the national past and, with it, all hope of a continuity or 'progress' of romance. For according to Marlow, not even the original or mythic form of romantic conquest ever existed in history but in 'the idea only'. In this respect, Marlow is a kind of 'new historicist' *avant la lettre*, calling attention to the material interestedness of the romance text, but also—portentously—to its potential for 'idealist' redemption or recuperation:

It [the Roman conquest] was just robbery with violence, aggravated murder on a great scale, and men going at it blind—as is very proper for those who tackle a darkness. The conquest of the earth, which mostly means the taking it away from those who have a different complexion or slightly flatter noses than ourselves, is not a pretty thing when you look into it too much. What redeems it is the idea only.[11]

Marlow, the middle-aged mariner and latter-day quester, presents himself to us—in contrast to the initial narrator, a Sunday sailor who has never left home—as a consciousness demystified from the start.

It is not that Marlow never shared the narrator's passion for gigantic tales but rather that he would seem to have outgrown them and left them behind:

Now when I was a little chap, I had a passion for maps. I would look for hours at South America, or Africa, or Australia, and lose myself in all the glories of exploration. At that time there were many blank spaces on the earth, and when I saw one that looked particularly inviting on a map (but they all look that) I would put my finger on it and say, When I grow up I will go there. The North Pole was one of these places, I remember. Well, I haven't been there yet, and shall not try now. The glamor's off . . . But there was one yet that I had a hankering after.[12]

---

[11] Joseph Conrad, *Heart of Darkness*, p. 7.   [12] Ibid., p. 8.

The mystified state of mind, the romance consciousness that Marlow implicitly claims to have left behind, he now identifies with childhood and, at several later points, with womanhood. His account of launching out into an actual Congo which 'had ceased to be a blank space of delightful mystery—a white patch for a boy to dream gloriously over' is presented from a ruthlessly demystified point of view. His appointment by the company is not the hand of providence or the calling of a divine mission but the 'glorious affair' of the chance killing of a 'supernatural being' named Fresleven and the intervention of an 'enthusiastic' aunt.

Significantly, not even the archetypically romantic figure of Kurtz holds any magic at this point for Marlow. 'Now and then I would give some thought to Kurtz. I wasn't very interested in him. No. Still, I was curious to see whether this man, who had come out equipped with moral ideas of some sort, would climb to the top after all and how he would set about his work when there.' It is only work, in fact, that escapes the unflattering glare of Marlow's present intelligence: 'I don't like work—no man does—but I like what is in the work—the chance to find yourself. Your own reality—for yourself, not for others.' The kind of work Marlow has in mind, dramatized in the gritty effort to repair his boat and keep it going up river, is the opposite of heroic. And yet his language invests this unheroic drudgery with something of the same purpose and value with which the more conventional heroics of earlier quest-romance have been endowed: a hard-won self-realization. It may be that the demystified state of mind Marlow claims to have achieved and seems to demonstrate in his narrative tone may itself turn out to be a mystification. With every ironic re-deployment of the language of romance, Marlow may actually be demonstrating the impossibility of ever leaving romance behind.

To leap to such a conclusion, however, would be premature, since the novella's work of demystification has at this point barely got under way. Just as the initial narrator had sounded naïve in contrast to Marlow, so Marlow seems naïve in contrast to Kurtz. For Kurtz has already been caught up in the same process of mystification and demystification in his own romantic quest as Marlow now is in his, only in a heightened and intensified—one is tempted to call it a mythic and archetypal

—form. In his descent upon the African darkness under the aegis of the 'International Society for the Suppression of Savage Customs', Kurtz has been cast as an apostle of European enlightenment, the latter-day counterpart to the romantic 'knights-errant' of the narrator's opening recollection. Far from being dead, the romance of commerce and Christianization, of the sword and the torch, is alive and well and living in the Congo—at least for a time.

For Kurtz has re-enacted his role in that romance on nothing less than a mythic scale. He seems less a character in a novel than a representative of Western culture in its late—missionary and imperialist—phase. Hence his utility for Eliot in his epigraph to 'The Hollow Men'. Marlow in fact demonstrates in genealogical detail that 'All Europe contributed to the making of Kurtz'. The myth he enacts had been in the making even before Columbus, for as Marlow points out, it is as old as imperialism itself. Kurtz's treatise on 'The Suppression of Savage Customs' aspires to the unself-questioning status of a sacred text, a myth not only in the sense of a story about a god but of a story *by* a god:

He began with the argument that we whites, from the point of development we had arrived at, 'must necessarily appear to them in the nature of supernatural beings—we approach them with the might as of a deity', and so on, and so on. 'By the simple exercise of our will we can exert a power for good practically unbounded', etc., etc. From that point he soared and took me with him. The peroration was magnificent . . . It gave me the notion of an exotic Immensity ruled by an august Benevolence. It made me tingle with enthusiasm. This was the unbounded power of eloquence—of words—of burning noble words. There were no practical hints to interrupt the magic current of phrases, unless a kind of note at the foot of the last page, scrawled evidently much later, in an unsteady hand, may be regarded as the exposition of a method. It was very simple, and at the end of that moving appeal to every altruistic sentiment it blazed at you, luminous and terrifying, like a flash of lightning in a serene sky: 'Exterminate all the brutes!'[13]

Kurtz's treatise—up to its lethal gloss—is a kind of anatomy of romance, and the impression it leaves on Marlow of 'an exotic Immensity ruled by an august Benevolence', an astute

---

[13] Conrad, *Heart of Darkness*, p. 51.

definition of the form at its most naïve. The historical—or is it mythic?—project out of which it grows, at once so topical and so anachronistic, of creating a brave new world of religion and commerce is of course a failure, one that recapitulates the previous failures of the Renaissance voyagers themselves: those men who, like Kurtz, had assumed the prerogatives of gods toward the natives they encountered, who fell often into practices more savage than those of the 'savages' themselves, and whose efforts at 'civilization', i.e., Christianization, lagged behind their efforts at colonial exploitation—the former being a pretext for the latter. The last irony is beautifully pointed in Marlow's comparison of Kurtz's head to an ivory ball.

But the crucial difference within Kurtz's repetition of past romantic texts and pretexts is his awareness of his failure to fulfil the prescribed pattern. That way madness lies. His encounter with an alien culture necessitates the examination of his own, but he cannot save himself from the maddening consequences of the relativism it entails. For Marlow, however, the encounter with Kurtz is a timely and saving confrontation with his own archetype. For Kurtz is a kind of vertical quester whose 'exalted and incredible degradation' precipitates an analogous, if less dangerous, demystification in the horizontal quester Marlow. It enables him to ironize his own earlier irony, to negate his unearned negations, and thereby recover a 'positive' goal for his questing: the goal of absolute demystification. Kurtz's self-convicted nihilism, expressed in his darkly lucid gloss and deathbed pronouncement of 'The horror! the horror!', carries for Marlow an authoritative clairvoyance that makes his own fugitive ironies seem frivolous and defines a further horizon of self-knowledge as the goal of his own quest.

It still appears, however, that in *Heart of Darkness* we are dealing with an ultimately ironic or demonic quest romance, the furthest displacement imaginable in literary–historical terms from the ideal vision of earlier quest romance. After all, Conrad's replacement of Christian revelation as the goal of romantic questing with that of a Nietzschean demystification, and the wisdom-figure of Christian hermit or tutelary spirit with that of a desperate nihilist, should result in the ultimate ironization of the mode itself. But a curious reversal has taken place, one that has been implicit from the outset. Like Dante, who moves through the deepest stage of his infernal descent only to discover that he has already begun his ascent, Marlow discovers in the nihilism of Kurtz a kind of affirmation:

I went no more near the remarkable man who had pronounced a judgment upon the adventures of his soul on this earth. The voice was gone. What else had been there? . . . If such is the form of ultimate wisdom, then life is a greater riddle than some of us think it to be. I was within a hair's-breadth of the last opportunity for pronounce-ment, and I found with humiliation that probably I would have nothing to say. This is the reason why I affirm that Kurtz was a remarkable man. He had something to say. He said it . . . He had summed up—he had judged. 'The Horror!' He was a remarkable man. After all, this was the expression of some sort of belief; it had candour, it had conviction, it had a vibrating note of revolt in its whisper, it had the appalling face of a glimpsed truth . . . He had made that last stride, he had stepped over the edge, while I had been permitted to draw back my hesitating foot. And perhaps in this is the whole difference; perhaps all the wisdom, and all truth, and all sincerity, are just compressed into that inappreciable moment of time in which we step over the threshold of the invisible. Perhaps! I like to think my summing-up would not have been a word of careless contempt. Better his cry—much better. It was an affirmation, a moral victory paid for by innumerable defeats, by abominable terrors, by abominable satisfactions. But it was a victory! That is why I have remained loyal to Kurtz to the last, and even beyond, when a long time after I heard once more, not his own voice, but the echo of his magnificent eloquence thrown to me from a soul as translucently pure as a cliff of crystal.[14]

Romance does not die so easily as Marlow—or the many commentators on this tale—seem to think. The progressive demystification of romance I have traced through *Heart of Darkness*, culminating in the dark end of the mythic poet—quester Kurtz, seems to have been in the service of a re-mystification of romance all along.

This counter-movement is implicit in Marlow's desire to set out for the Congo in the first place despite his foreknowledge that 'the glamor's off'; in his romanticization of the most unromantic kind of work; in his paradoxical recognition of Kurtz's 'exalted and incredible degradation'; and finally in his confrontation back in the 'sepulchral' city of Brussels with

---

[14] Conrad, *Heart of Darkness*, p. 51.

Kurtz's 'Intended'. Marlow has referred to her throughout—as to women in general—as inhabiting a benighted world of romantic illusions; so when he refers to her as 'a soul as translucently pure as a cliff of crystal', it comes as something of a volte-face. Yet when Marlow finally meets Kurtz's lady, that presiding figure of his romantic questing, the scene is far from one of unmitigated irony but of irony itself ironized to maintain the spell of romance! 'Bowing my head before the faith that was in her, before that great and saving illusion that shone with an unearthly glow in the darkness, in the triumphant darkness from which I could not have defended her—from which I could not even defend myself', Marlow once again turns romancer and 'lies'.

Not to do so would have been 'too dark—too dark altogether', a retreat from the level of enlightenment Marlow claims to have attained. To tell the simple truth would be to lie, to belie the experience of Kurtz into one of straightforward disenchantment when it has already been presented as a complex interplay of disenchantment and re-enchantment. Marlow none the less appears in the scene to claim an ironic advantage over the Intended and to include us in this dramatic irony. But Conrad is quick to ironize Marlow's irony and restore the balance of mystification through the Intended's naïve response: 'an exulting and terrible cry . . . of inconceivable triumph and of unspeakable pain'. The phrase in its thoroughgoing ambivalence is the truest response possible to Marlow's story, which is naïvely romantic and ironically sophisticated *at the same time*. It illustrates the inability of latter-day romance ever to regain its mythic form *or to shed that form completely*, to reunite with its source *or to leave that source definitively behind*. To consider *Heart of Darkness* as a 'myth of modernism' is to reveal at a certain level the mythic status of modernism itself.

REWRITING LITERARY HISTORY

In his *History of English Poetry* (1781), Thomas Warton asserts that during the Elizabethan age there still existed a 'degree of superstition sufficient for the purposes of poetry' and 'the adoption of the machineries of romance'; that 'the reformation had not yet destroyed every delusion, nor disenchanted all the strongholds of superstition', that 'Reason suffered a few demons still to linger, which she chose to retain in her service under the guidance of poetry', and that 'the national credulity, chastened by reason, had produced a sort of civilized superstition, and left a set of traditions, fanciful enough for poetical decorations, and yet not too violent and chimerical for common sense'.[15] Such a view of literary history since the Renaissance as a progressive demystification or displacement or ironization or secularization or internalization of romance is all but explicit in its condescension towards the Elizabethans. It is still very much with us and, as we have seen, conditions our criticism of romance and romantic texts alike.

Yet this historical scheme does not really fit the two extra-ordinary, but not unrepresentative, romances we have examined. Both *The Tempest* and *Heart of Darkness*, though separated by three centuries of literary and cultural history, enact a process of demystification and remystification of the romance mode common to them both and implicit at every point in their dramatic and narrative structures. In such phrases as 'Some vanity of mine art', 'this rough magic', 'this thing of darkness I acknowledge mine', and 'his exalted and incredible degradation', 'an exulting and terrible cry', phrases in which the full naïvety and the full irony of these texts are self-consciously present, the argument of this essay lies compressed. To place these great romances within an historical sequence of progressive demystification moving from myth to irony is to misread them, since each is demystified from the start. To do so is at once to underread the past by oversimplifying it and to overread the present by making it the locus of all complexity. The consequences of this procedure are not only bad literary history but bad literary interpretation, since the two are inseparable and interdependent.

---

[15] Thomas Warton, *The History of English Poetry from the Close of the Eleventh to the Commencement of the Eighteenth Century*, 4 vols. (London, 1774–81), iii. 490–7. See René Wellek, *The Rise of English Literary History* (Chapel Hill: University of North Carolina Press, 1941), pp. 192–4. Warton's successor among contemporary historians of literary modernism is Geoffrey Hartman, who invokes Warton in formulating his view that 'The history of English literature since the Renaissance suggests a continuous process of demystification.' See particularly his 'Romantic Poetry and the *Genius Loci*' and 'Toward Literary History', in *Beyond Formalism* (New Haven: Yale University Press, 1970).

3

'Tongue-tied, our Queen?':
The Deconstruction of Presence in
The Winter's Tale

> First, nothing exists; second, even if anything exists, it is
> unknowable; third, even if anything can be known, it
> cannot be communicated by language.
>
> (Gorgias, 'On Nature or Not-being', as reported by
> Sextus Empiricus)

MAKING THE MOST OF ABSENCES

In the first issue of a new journal on Shakespeare, self-mockingly
titled *The Upstart Crow*, the opening article offers a re-
interpretation of *Othello*. Where past critics have gone wrong, it
argues, has been in their failure to see that Desdemona has had
an affair with Cassio before the beginning of the play. Her
sexual appetite is, as her name clearly suggests, positively
'demonic', and altogether too much for the ageing Othello. Her
passivity toward the end of the play, so the argument goes, has
nothing to do with stoic self-dramatization, natural dignity, or
the virtue that suffers long and is kind. It is simply a matter of
her realization that she has been found out, and that the game is
up. The author of the article (who shall remain unnamed for
reasons by now apparent) shows restraint in not specifying
how many children Desdemona has had as a result of her
liaison with Cassio, if indeed she has had any. Having set
criticism of the play back on track, he is content to leave these
and related questions to the rest of us to answer in due course.[1]

In introducing the present essay on *The Winter's Tale*, I cite
this article not to follow its lead and pursue its method, but to

---

[1] I am grateful to *The Shakespeare Newsletter*, 29 (April 1979), ed. Louis Marder, for
having brought this inauspicious inaugural to my attention.

raise through an extreme or limiting case a perennial problem of criticism. The problem I have in mind arises for the audience or interpreter whenever a work of literature makes reference to prior or off-stage or, in the most general terms, unrepresented action. To what extent ought we to feel constrained in interpreting that which is not actually presented in the text, not actually 'there', as we say, before us? To what extent may we reasonably entertain such speculation as part of our larger attempt to interpret the text within which the unrepresented action occurs, or, as it were, fails to occur? What, so to speak, can one fairly make of an absence or a gap?

There is no escape from this problem. The traditionally mimetic ambitions of literature in general and drama in particular encourage us to consider its characters and plots as if they were actions performed by human beings with past and ongoing lives no less 'real' for being invisible or unavailable to us, and still in some sense 'there' while remaining unrepresented. Does our neighbour cease to exist when he disappears behind his front door? Short of voyeurism, how can we re-create his activities behind that door, given other knowledge of him? In this respect, is our perception of literary characters very different from our perception of our next-door neighbours? The strategic reference to a prior event or off-stage life is a repeated, characteristic, and highly effective device of that literature traditionally deemed 'realist'; of, that is, the nineteenth-century novel, or the drama of Ibsen and Chekhov.

Moreover, it may well be one of the devices by means of which the illusion of an actual world populated by actual people is achieved, albeit less systematically, in Shakespearean drama as well—Maurice Morgann asserted as much in the eighteenth century, initiating that tradition of characterology which turns only too easily into the sort of criticism with which we began.[2] Hence we must ask how far we can pursue this mode of criticism before our enterprise becomes misguided as well as

---

[2] Morgann writes: 'He boldly makes a character act and speak from those parts of the composition which are *inferred* only, and not distinctly shown. This produces a wonderful effect; it seems to carry us beyond the poet to nature itself, and gives an integrity and truth to facts and character, which they could not otherwise obtain'. Quoted from the *Essay on the Dramatic Character of Sir John Falstaff* [1777] by L. C. Knights in his now faded classic, 'How many children had Lady Macbeth?' in Knights, *Explorations* (London: Chatto, 1963).

anachronistic, before we ought to stop and remind ourselves that the work with which we are dealing is not only an Elizabethan text but, as we sometimes say, 'only a play', only artificial personages in a fictive construct whose 'life' consists only in representation. Did A. C. Bradley go too far? Or L. C. Knights not far enough? And how far do these same strictures apply to our speculations concerning the past or off-stage or invisible lives, even the inner or subjective lives in their ultimate opacity, of the people we know and gossip about in what we call— simply or simple-mindedly?—'real life' or 'life itself'?

In *The Winter's Tale*, at least as much as in *Othello*, we are faced in a stark and peremptory way with this problem of what to make of unrepresented events. For its action, as everyone knows, arises as a direct consequence of Leontes' wild surmise that his wife has been betraying him with his best and oldest friend during the nine months prior to the opening of the play. Shakespeare, that is, presents us with a principal character who stakes his reputation, his happiness, his realm, his selfhood— stakes nothing less than everything—on his interpretation of behaviour partly available and partly unavailable to him, and partly represented and partly unrepresented to us. In the conviction with which he presents his interpretation of events, Leontes is not altogether unlike the author of the article on *Othello* with which I began, perhaps not altogether unlike ourselves in our own efforts at interpretation.

Indeed, on what authority do we assume—and it is so confidently and unanimously assumed by critics of the play as never to my knowledge to have been raised as an issue—that Hermione is in fact innocent of Leontes' suspicions in the opening act? Why do we take for granted, as if it were a fact of nature, what can never be proved but only denied: that a king's wife has not had an affair with his best friend and nine months later given birth to an illegitimate daughter? How can we know that what has not been shown has not happened? In reaching the conclusion we have unanimously reached as critics of the play, we have proceeded, indeed been forced to proceed, in the absence of ocular or empirical proof—for how could there be ocular proof of what has not taken place? We have proceeded on the 'conventionalist' grounds delimited on the one side by Anglo-Saxon law (which presumes formal innocence until guilt is proved) and on the other by Pauline Christianity (which is based precisely on the evidence of things not seen).

THE ORACULAR PROOF

Let me reassure you at once that my purpose is not to argue that all commentators on the play until now have been wrong, and that Leontes is right in supposing his wife has betrayed him. It does seem worth pointing out, however, that in the negative nature of the case as Shakespeare has taken pains to set it up, neither Leontes nor we can ever know for sure, short of divine revelation. I mention divine revelation only because that is precisely what is at last represented to us on stage, what forces Leontes to change his mind, and what has prevented critics from doing to *The Winter's Tale* what the aforementioned critic did to *Othello* (though this last point must remain only conjecture). God—or at least Apollo—does speak in *The Winter's Tale*, and he speaks unequivocally: 'Hermione is chaste; Polixenes blameless; Camillo a true subject; Leontes a jealous tyrant; his innocent babe truly begotten; and the king shall live without an heir, if that which is lost be not found.'

How could the oracle have been any more explicit or unequivocal? After such knowledge, it would take a very wilful interpreter indeed to maintain Leontes' view of the matter. In the fact of that divine pronouncement, not even critics of Shakespeare have been so foolhardy. Now, I realize that I would be laying myself open to being considered more foolhardy than any critic of the play has yet managed to be, if I were not to let the matter rest there. But at the risk of bringing chaos into order, I want to question the definitiveness of the oracle's pronouncement and the basis for our happy consensus. Of course that is no more than Leontes himself does: 'There is no truth at all in the oracle. The sessions will proceed.'

Leontes, that is, seems suddenly to fall back on a mistrust of oracular pronouncements familiar enough in Renaissance as well as classical literature. Although this is the only point in the play where such a conventional mistrust is hinted at, it would seem to be well founded. The fondness of pagan oracles for ambiguity, obscurantism, equivocation, and verbal trickery is commonplace in Elizabethan literature. Shakespeare himself exploits the equivocations of pagan prophecy in *Macbeth*, where the unreliability of the witches' pronouncements is emphasized by contrast with the play's Christian milieu. Closer to the present context, the riddles of *Pericles* and the prophecies of *Cymbeline* are wholly consistent with this long-standing literary expectation of deceit from pagan sources. Both require considerable ingenuity to tease out their sense, in the latter case an interpretive strenuousness verging on interpretive self-parody, a wilful overreading comparable to anything in our learned journals.

The editor of the New Arden *Winter's Tale*, for example, contrasting the message of Jupiter with that of Apollo, calls the former 'Merlinesque', perhaps recollecting the similarly riddling and anachronistic prophecies of the Fool in *Lear*.[3] Yet here, in the deliberately pseudo-classical context of *The Winter's Tale*, Shakespeare presents us with a most plain-spoken and un-Delphic Delphic oracle: 'Hermione is chaste; Polixenes blameless; Camillo a true subject; Leontes a jealous tyrant;' etc. Only the last clause of the oracle's pronouncement could be said to be in the least Pythian or even pithy, and even there the meaning is, in context, clear to all concerned. It is significant, for example, that Coleridge has recourse to the more teasing language we expect from oracles in suggesting a supplementary phrase to adumbrate Hermione's destiny. He describes his

---

[3] *The Winter's Tale*, ed. J. H. P. Pafford (London: Methuen, 1966). p. lix. All quotations in my text are from this edition.

Among the ancients, Cicero mentions a lost collection of dubious oracular replies, or *kledones (Of Divination*, II.lvi). Shakespeare's older contemporary, Robert Greene, author of *Pandosto*, or *The Triumph of Time* [1588], Shakespeare's source for *The Winter's Tale*, puts just such a *kledon* into the mouth of the brazen head in *Friar Bacon and Friar Bungay* [1590]. There, the head's pronouncements—'Time is'; 'Time was'; 'Time is past'—are clearly of demonic inspiration. Milton shares Thomas Hobbes's lively contempt for 'the ambiguous or senselesse answers of the Priests at *Delphi*, *Delos*, *Ammon*, and other famous oracles' (*Leviathan*, I.xii), though on religious rather than rationalist grounds:

> What but dark,
> Ambiguous and with double sense deluding,
> Which they who ask'd have seldom understood,
> And not well understood as good not known?
> Who ever by consulting at thy [Satan's] shrine
> Return'd the wiser, or the more instruct
> To fly or follow what concerned him most,
> And run not sooner to his fatal snare?

(*Paradise Regained*, IX)

addition—'nor shall he ever recover an heir if he have a wife before that recovery'—as 'some *obscure* sentence of the oracle.'[4]

Given the pellucid prose in which this oracle pronounces himself—and Shakespeare makes even more explicit and un-equivocal the already clear pronouncement of his source—given this unwonted clarity, surely the matter must be considered resolved, our belief in Hermione's innocence proved beyond any reasonable doubt? Our consensus on this point is based, then, on nothing less than what in the world of the play is an unquestionable divine authority. We have, if not ocular proof, oracular proof, which should be at least as good. Or is it? I have already suggested that the clarity of the oracle does not deter Leontes from questioning and rejecting its validity in terms no less direct and absolute than the oracle's own: 'There is no truth at all i'th Oracle: | The sessions shall proceed: this is mere falsehood' (III.ii.140–1). But surely such scepticism, despite the tradition warranting it, cannot be allowed much force; after all, the death of Mamillius follows hard upon this latest blasphemy, and it is this news that finally shocks Leontes into recognition. How could Mamillius's death, in its precise timing and dreadful efficiency, be taken as anything other than clear evidence of divine design?

Yet even this apparent 'proof', with the strong sense it carries of Mamillius's death as portentous or exemplary, as bearing the signature of the archer-god who strikes from afar (Homer's and Sophocles' *hekebolos* Apollo), is not binding. The play offers a naturalistic or coincidental explanation of Mamillius's death as the result of an illness already under way in the second act: 'He took good rest to-night; | 'Tis hop'd his sickness is discharg'd' (II.iii.10–11). If Mamillius dies of mumps or measles, it does weaken, though admittedly it does not rule out, the case for divine intervention. In fact, yet a third diagnosis of Mamillius's decline is twice offered to us, a diagnosis that mediates between the naturalistic and the superstitious or religious explanations; namely, that the boy's disease is psychogenic: 'The prince your son, with mere conceit and fear | Of the queen's speed, is gone' (II.ii.143–4; see also

II.iii.12–16). We are thus invited, at several points, to view Mamillius's death as the result of natural rather than supernatural causes. If we choose to do so, the foundation on which both Apollo's divine authority over the action and the divine authentication of Hermione's innocence are based begins to weaken.

THE SUSPICION OF THE WORD

Now, just as Apollo's authoritative and authenticating presence within the world of the play is not quite so solidly 'there' as we might wish—I shall return to this point shortly—so Leontes' jealous and destructive passion is not quite so flimsy and fanciful, so unfounded and 'out of the blue' as is often casually assumed. Consider the tortured monologues in which Leontes discloses his jealousy to us. Since these are cast as commentaries on behaviour taking place before his eyes, and in the first instance before our eyes too, there must be some empirical evidence, as it were, for his suspicions, however slight it might be. Are the gestures of friendship that pass between Hermione and Polixenes 'too hot', as Leontes claims, or the 'paddling palms, pinching fingers, practis'd smiles, and heartfelt sighs' he enumerates as evidence (I.ii.108–18) as clearly adulterous as he suggests? These questions are also of course a matter of theatrical production; but unless we are ready to suppose a positively hallucinatory Leontes, gestures in some degree susceptible of such descriptions must take place in front of us.

So too must Hermione's 'Still virginalling | Upon his [Polixenes'] palm' (I.ii.125–6) shortly thereafter. (The impossibility of rendering theatrically the suggestive force of the word 'virginalling' must stand as a perennial caveat to those who maintain the primacy of performance over text and the conventionalism of theatre the 'key' to Shakespearean meaning.) And later in the scene, when his wife and friend have exited or are exiting, Leontes is presumably looking at something when he states: 'Go to, go to! | How she holds up the neb, the bill to him! | And arms her with the boldness of a wife | To her allowing husband!' (I.ii.182–5). Finally, the bill of particulars he cites to Camillo, while some of it may draw on the stock repertoire of stage or literary passion, compiles a lexicon of body language that, however conventional, also carries a direct appeal to empirical observation:

> Is whispering nothing?
> Is leaning cheek to cheek? is meeting noses?
> Kissing with inside lip? stopping the career
> Of laughter with a sigh (a note infallible
> Of breaking honesty)? horsing foot on foot?
> Skulking in corners? wishing clocks more swift?

> (I.ii.284–9)

Leontes' suspicions, while they may end in speculation, do none the less begin in perception: 'Ha' you not seen, Camillo . . . or heard? . . . or thought?' (I.ii.267–71). This is why it is impossible to ascertain just what basis there is for Leontes' jealousy, the degree to which what he describes is a distortion of an enacted reality, or the relative balance between perception and imagination in his account of what goes on. We see enough to know it has some basis, but not enough to say how much. We are from the outset in a world of interpretation—Leontes', the producer's, and our own—where nothing can be either wholly dismissed or wholly believed, and nothing can be known for certain.

The condition of interpretive uncertainty I have been describing arises, in the case both of Hermione's conduct with Polixenes and of Apollo's control over events, as a consequence of Shakespeare's choice to leave both actions unrepresented, or, at most, only partly represented. In this respect, Apollo's status in the play as a kind of *deus absconditus* is paradigmatic and crucial. We have already seen that he is not really or fully 'present', that is, not presented to us on stage, and only represented in the world of the play through the mediating forms of his written pronouncement and a verbal description by Cleomenes and Dion. Despite its extraordinary clarity and definitiveness, the pronouncement turns out, as we have begun to realize, to be disturbingly difficult to verify or validate. Since it is supposed to be itself a validation, there is nothing left to fall back on when its validity is questioned, other than Cleomenes' reported awe.

The god's language without the god to back it up is a bit like paper currency without any gold—or anything else—behind it. It becomes unstable, subject to the vagaries of special interests and private speculation, with all their devaluing effect. Once cut off from the presence of their divine speaker, with his univocality of meaning and intent, Apollo's words enter the realm of the human, the fallible, the ambiguous: in sum, the interpretable, where they can be contradicted or dismissed, for all we know, with impunity. The point seems to me worth emphasizing, because Shakespeare's divorce of the god's words from the god's presence marks a change from his dramatic practice in the two earlier romances, *Pericles* and *Cymbeline*, both of which include theophanies. (Even in Greene's *Pandosto*, Apollo speaks, whereas in *The Winter's Tale* his speaking is reported.) By separating Apollo's words from their sacred and authenticating voice, Shakespeare adumbrates a larger problem of interpretation, one that bedevils the world of the play from the outset.

The problem to which I refer might be termed the problem of linguistic indeterminacy. If the language of the oracle is remarkable for its clarity and explicitness—while still leaving the issue of divine control in doubt—the language of the Sicilian court is no less remarkable for its slipperiness and ambiguity. It would be reassuring if the doubts Shakespeare has left attached to Hermione's behaviour on and off stage, since they cannot be cleared away by looking closely at what she does—her body language as it were—could be cleared away by listening carefully to what she says, to her actual words. In fact, the opposite is the case. The more carefully we attend to what she says, the more the verbal evidence, as much as the visual, seems inconclusive, and only increases our—and Leontes'—uncertainty:

> Th'offences we have made you do, we'll answer,
> If you first sinn'd with us, and that with us
> You did continue fault, and that you slipp'd not
> With any but with us.
>
> (I.ii.83–6)

> Cram's with praise, and make's as
> Fat as tame things . . . You may ride's
> With one soft kiss a thousand furlongs ere
> With spur we heat an acre.
>
> (I.ii.91–6)

> I have spoken to th'purpose twice:
> The one, for ever earn'd a royal husband;
> Th'other, for some while a friend.
>
> (I.ii.106–8)

So much of what Hermione says may be construed either within or outside the conventions of royal hospitality and wifely decorum. Her emphasis on greater warmth in persuasion may signify flirtation; the indefinite antecedents of her royal pronouns, self-incrimination; her earthy wit, bawdry; and her rhetorical juxtapositions of 'husband' and 'friend', a fatal identification of the two. 'This entertainment', as Leontes himself points out, 'May a free face put on, derive a liberty | From heartiness, from bounty, fertile bosom, | And well become the agent' (I.ii.111–14). Yet these same words—'entertainment', 'liberty', 'fertile bosom'—may refer, as Leontes also makes clear, to behaviour anything but innocent.

The more closely we attend to the language of Polixenes and Hermione, the more we may detect in it (like Leontes again) a whisper of sexual innuendo. Can Polixenes' comparison of himself to 'a cipher | Yet standing in rich place' (I.ii.6–7) be taken as a sniggering allusion to his 'standing-in' for Leontes? So it seemed to—of all critics—Nevill Coghill.[5] What about Hermione's comment that Leontes presses his friend 'too coldly', or her reference to Polixenes' 'limber vows' (I.ii.46)? So they seem on scrutiny—I am almost ashamed to confess it—to me. Once our suspicions are aroused—and there is at least some language in these scenes that cannot help but arouse them—they become, like Leontes' own suspicions, promiscuous and contagious, tainting with doubt and duplicity all that passes between Hermione and Polixenes. For it is not only sexual innocence, idealized by Polixenes as a pastoral state belonging to childhood, that has been lost, but a kind of verbal innocence as well.

This latter loss might be described as a fall into a condition of

---

[5] In 'Six points of Stage-craft in *The Winter's Tale*', in *Shakespeare Survey*, xi, ed. Allardyce Nicoll (Cambridge: Cambridge University Press, 1969), 33: 'Who can fail to wonder whether the man so amicably addressing this expectant mother may not be the father of her child? For what other possible reason can Shakespeare have contrived the conversation so as to make him specify nine changes of the inconstant moon? These things are not done by accident.'

multivocality or equivocation, a new helplessness to avoid discovering or projecting a certain duplicity in what is said, meanings that may or may not have been intended. This loss of verbal innocence is evident in all the courtly banter over the force of the word 'verily' (I.ii.46–56); it appears again in Hermione's laboured distinction between 'saying' and 'swearing'; in the compromising implications of subsequent guilt, picked up by Hermione, in Polixenes' monologue itself on childhood innocence; in Leontes' worried retraction of the word 'neat' with the recollection that 'the steer, the heifer and the calf | Are all call'd neat' (I.ii.124–5); in his querying whether Hermione has 'never' spoken to better purpose and, if not never, then when? It is to be heard again in the reluctant and riddling revelations of Camillo to Polixenes: 'How, dare not? do not? Do you know, and dare not?'; 'A sickness caught of me, and yet I well?' (I.ii.376, 398).

It would not be difficult to multiply examples, for this loss of verbal innocence with its discovery of ubiquitous verbal dupli-city permeates the linguistic texture of the opening act. There, its rhetorical consequences are unavoidable, taking the form of quibbles, intended and unintended: 'Satisfy? | Th' entreaties of your mistress? satisfy?' (I.ii.233–4); of circumlocution: 'Nine changes of the watery star' (I.ii.i); of curious, archaic, and esoteric diction: 'the *gest* | Prefix'd'; 'The *mort* o'th'deer' (I.ii.42–2, 118); and resulting in a pervasive euphuism and syntactical contortion ambiguous to the point where the prin-cipals themselves, not to mention the audience, sometimes have trouble understanding what is said or implied or meant (I.ii.220 ff.).

This is not the place to enumerate all the instances of extraordinary—even by Shakespearean and Elizabethan norms—tortuousness in the language of the opening scenes. Suffice it to say that Leontes' suspicion of the word thrives upon the verbal mannerism, sophistication, even preciosity that dominates the language of Sicilia from the play's initial dia-logue, and that works to obscure as much as it reveals. From the moment Camillo refers to a long-standing affection between the two kings, 'which cannot choose but branch now' (I.i.23–4)— the most often noted of the scene's many *double entendres*—we are in a realm where a speaker's apparent meaning can turn or

be turned into its antithetical sense, where the medium for
defining human reality is so problematic as to render that
'reality' precarious at best. In the linguistic milieu of the
opening scenes of the play, nothing is but what, in a fundamental way, is not.

THE SUPERSTITION OF THE WORD

It is, of course, Leontes in whom this fall from verbal innocence,
which I have been struggling (in the nature of the case) to
describe, is most gravely figured. But it is also Leontes who
displays the keenest insight into, and offers the nicest formulation of, his own unhappy condition:

> Affection! thy intention stabs the centre:
> Thou dost make possible things not so held,
> Communicat'st with dreams;—how can this be?—
> With what's unreal thou coactive art,
> And fellow'st nothing: then 'tis very credent
> Thou may'st co-join with something; and thou dost,
> (And that beyond commission) and I find it . . .

(I.ii.138–44)

The passage is itself a notoriously difficult one, termed by one
critic the 'obscurest' in Shakespeare, and having attracted no
less than five pages of commentary in the New Variorum
edition. Leaving its own verbal difficulties aside for the moment,
the speech prompts two considerations that bear directly on the
cluster of problems with which we are concerned.

Leontes grasps, as we have begun to grasp, that the instability
of meaning and uncertainty of reference he is experiencing first-
hand—what I have termed linguistic indeterminacy—is not a
function simply of expression but of interpretation as well. It
arises, that is, not only out of an imperfection in the medium or
the speaker's use of it, but out of the radical subjectivity of the
listener or interpreter. For this reason, it is doubly inescapable,
a condition that prevents us from ever arriving at certain or
complete communication in human affairs, not to mention final
or definitive interpretations of literary texts. Leontes, that is,
seems to be aware that all he sees and hears is filtered through
his own affective state and is to that extent created by it. The

imagination operating under 'strong emotion' has the power to transform something into nothing, or nothing into something; a bush into a bear, or that which is subjectively felt into that which seems objectively there.

This poetics of self-projection is familiar enough from a number of Shakespearean contexts; and the Leontes of the opening scenes has more than a touch of the lunatic and lover, the roles with which Shakespeare most closely associates that engrossing subjectivity which prevents our arriving at unanimity in our interpretation of the evidence of our senses, or even at agreement as to what constitutes such 'evidence'. But Leontes' monologue on 'affection' raises a further problem, one that bears as directly upon our interpretation of the play as Polixenes' later, more familiar, and oft-invoked monologue on nature and art. The problem is one of which Leontes himself seems to be aware, albeit in the perverse way of seeking a wilful and premature solution to it. I am referring to his assertion of the power of the imagination to 'make possible things not so held', to create a world of its own that may or may not refer to any prior or primary reality. In his formulation of the problem, Leontes reveals as much a touch of the poet and contemporary critic as of the lunatic and lover.

Of course his account of the matter, as has often been observed, is not quite logical. If an unfaithful Hermione may be imagined who does not correspond to any conventional reality ('things not so held', 'dreams', 'what's unreal'), it is also possible that an unfaithful Hermione does exist. Indeed, it is perfectly plausible, 'credent' as he puts it, that such an imaginative construct corresponds to something in reality; in fact, he goes on to conclude, such a creature exists, and he has found her out. In these last illogical steps, the lunatic–lover has of course taken over from the poet–critic. Leontes' insistence that his subjective state has an objective correlative—despite his awareness of the problems involved—dominates the first two acts, and culminates in his stunning self-contradiction at the trial:

HERM.   You speak a language that I understand not:
My life stands in the level of your dreams,
Which I'll lay down.

LEON. Your actions are my dreams
You had a bastard by Polixenes,
And I but dream'd it!

(III.ii.80–4)

What begins as a just recognition of the autonomy of the imagination turns into a wilful insistence on its referentiality.

In his uneasy transition—by way of a psychological projection he suspects but cannot escape—from a poetics of difference to a poetics of reference, Leontes enacts in a mad, parodic form a characteristic drift of European literary criticism: a superstition of the word that endows it with the power to conjure its referent into being. The tensions between poesis and mimesis, between the formal and referential functions of literary language, are already present in Aristotle. By the time of Sidney's *Apology for Poetry*, those tensions have developed into something verging upon outright contradiction:

There is no art delivered to mankind that hath not the works of Nature for his principal object, without which they could not consist, and on which they so depend, as they become actors and players, as it were, of what Nature will have set forth. Only the poet, disdaining to be tied to any such objection, lifted up with the vigour of his own invention, doth grow in effect another nature, in making things either better than nature bringeth forth, or, quite anew, forms such as never were in nature, as the Heroes, Demigods, Cyclopes, Chimeras, Furies, and such like: so as he goes hand in hand with Nature, not enclosed within the narrow warrant of her gifts, but freely ranging only within the zodiac of his own wit.[6]

On the one hand, poetry is like all human art in being bound to nature as its object; that is, it represents that which already exists. On the other, the poet is endowed with the power to bring a rival nature into existence by 'freely ranging only within the zodiac of his own wit'; poetry, that is, is an autonomous, generative, and self-enclosed system. To the extent that the two, poetry and nature, are heterogeneous, they are clearly incommensurate. If poetic language is orphic and autonomous, it can never quite be referential; if it is referential, it cannot be completely autonomous and orphic.

Yet Sidney's language here, unlike that of Leontes' mono-

[6] Reprinted, with modernized spelling, in W. J. Bate, ed., *Criticism: The Major Texts*, 2nd edn. (New York: Harcourt Brace Jovanovich, 1970), 85.

logue on 'affection', is cool, sophisticated, and self-aware. To judge from the construction of the passage, Sidney, unlike Leontes, seems to know that he is verging on self-contradiction, and his language plays on that knowledge. To make something 'better' than nature is not the same as to make something 'other' than nature, since the former process idealizes nature while the latter replaces it. But it is Sidney himself who alerts us to this distinction, to the potential frustration of representation by the self-enclosure of the formal systems that mediate it. Then, too, Sidney repeatedly employs a vocabulary of presence to assimilate the poetic process to the natural. Such phrases as '*grow* another nature', '*set forth* the earth', '*deliver* a golden', '*delivering them forth* in such excellence'—such phrases lay claim, in the name of poetry, to nothing less than a fullness, presence, and immediacy analogous to that of the sensory world, a kind of ultimate or perfected mimesis in which the mediation of language disappears or is transcended.

Yet all this 'growing into', 'bringing forth', 'delivering', and 'setting forth' is itself only a linguistic process of invocation and comparison, and is in this respect no more than a substitute or stand-in for the second nature being invoked. Moreover, that second, golden nature is identified with a world of religious myth and poetic fiction, a world of dream and desire which is in a fundamental sense, not there, no longer or never existent. Sidney's language of presence is motivated by, and oriented towards, a world of absence, a paradise lost that can be represented but not regained through poetic language, figured forth' but not literally delivered. The large claims Sidney makes for poetry are thus qualified by the very language in which they are made. As if this continuous qualification were not enough, there is the framing anecdote of the horseman Pugliano on horsemanship with which Sidney begins his *Apology*, a caveat that puts the entire work as it were into parentheses or inverted commas by warning us 'that self-love is better than any gilding to make that seem gorgeous wherein ourselves are parties'.[7] Beware the power of subjective self-interest to distort the object under scrutiny: in sum, beware of poets on poetry.

We find at play in Sidney's *Apology*, then, the poetic will to

[7] Ibid., p. 83.

endow airy nothing not only with a local habitation and a
name, but with an objective existence as well—a tendency not
unlike the one we have seen at work in Leontes' more tortured
but no less wilful or poetic speeches in *The Winter's Tale*. As a
recent commentator puts it, Sidney offers a vision of poetry as
'the direct representation of the best', and 'the creation . . . of a
world of golden presence.'[8] Yet Sidney, as we have also seen,
simultaneously implies that this present perfection towards
which poetry longs cannot, in the nature of the linguistic case,
be attained. The actual language of *The Apology*, that is, is in
tension with the theory it expresses; but not because it is written
in a self-deceived language of presence. If anything, it is written
in the self-aware language of absence we know as fiction, but
which we habitually, almost compulsively, wish to make over,
in our reflections on it, into a language of presence.

What simultaneously emerges from *The Apology* is the nostalgic or wishful longing for poetry to become a second creation, at
least as full, as present as immediate as the fallen and brazen
first, and the cool awareness that its very secondariness as
representation, mediation, and artifice prevents it from ever
achieving this status. The idea of a restored poetic perfection is
imaginatively entered into and entertained by Sidney; but it is
not unequivocally affirmed—'the poet, he nothing affirms, and
therefore never lieth.' Entertaining is to affirming what representation is to presence. The very idea of 'direct representation' is recognized by Sidney, if not by his latest commentator,
as oxymoronic, as self-consciously so as the 'absent presence'
he invokes in Sonnet *106* of *Astrophil and Stella*.

FROM NAÏVE TO SOPHISTICATED REALISM

How, then, do these observations bear upon the particular
interpretive problems with which we have been concerned in
The Winter's Tale or, indeed, upon the more general and theoretical problem of unrepresented action with which we began? To
take up the latter question first, I would suggest that the
example of Sidney serves to remind us of something obvious
and familiar, yet something that we—like Sidney himself, not

---

[8] Murray Krieger, 'Poetic Presence and Illusion: Renaissance Theory and the
Duplicity of Metaphor', *Critical Inquiry*, 5/4 (Summer 1979), 603.

to mention his recent commentator—seem only too ready to ignore or repress in our dealings with literature: namely, that all literature—not just the off-stage events of *The Winter's Tale*, or Cassio's negotiations with Desdemona, or the domestic history of the Macbeths, but *all* literature—is, in an important sense, unrepresented, or, rather, *under*represented action: 'underrepresented', in the sense that in its very nature as representation, as figurative language, the literary text is never really 'there' or fully present, and the actions and transactions it generates are always mediated actions, action estranged by the linguistic medium in which it has its existence.

I realize that to say this is to say something as self-evident as that fiction is not history and words are not things; indeed, I may well be saying only that. The discovery that language is a formal, self-contained system of arbitrary signs heterogeneous in relation to the world is as old as the pre-Socratics. That literature is a system based upon the prior system of language, and to that extent a representation of the reality of language rather than a present language of 'reality'—these character- istically 'modern' discoveries in no way negate the power of the sign to refer, to constitute a world of reference. Yet this world of reference, as we have begun to see in *The Winter's Tale*, has finally no objective reality or ontological stability, but recedes into an infinite play of signs and deferral of affirmative or authoritative meaning. Poetic reference is saved, but only at the high cost of interpretive incertitude.

The referential dimension of language, of poetic or literary language *a fortiori*, changes its nature to be sure, but does not suddenly disappear when we realize that language is funda- mentally problematic. Reference is never quite presence, yet it is not quite absence either. The world of the text and the text of the world, once securely because dogmatically defined, now become indeterminate because overdetermined. And once having occurred, this fall into textual instability cannot be reversed—since it is not the text but our perception of the text that has radically altered—despite the impatience of some to regain the security of a lost certitude by identifying literary reference with one myth of presence or another. Thus, L. C. Knights tried to pull us back from that which certainly cannot be known—the inner and off-stage lives of Shakespeare's characters—to that which he contended could be known—the dramatic world of 'the words on the page'—when neither can be known with any assurance. More recently, the 'play in the theatre' was supposed to secure Shakespearean meaning against the instabilities of textualist interpretation—as if producers did not have to begin with a text and theatre was not a mode of interpretation.

When Sidney wrote in 1580, poetry stood in need of defence against the attacks of those who would have crudified it into a form of lying. Since then, it seems to me, it has more often needed defence against its would-be defenders, those who also violate poetry's tantalizing reserve in order to crudify it into a more or less outspoken form of truth-telling. *The Winter's Tale*, with a self-understanding extraordinary even for Shakespeare, dramatizes not only the precariousness of its own linguistic enterprise but the unhappy consequences of our positive incapability of accepting such precariousness as the condition of fiction and indeed of reality. 'Is it true, think you?' (IV.iv.267) asks Mopsa of Autolycus's ballad of a usurer's wife 'brought to bed of twenty money-bags at a burden'. 'Very true, and but a month old,' the balladeer replies: 'Why should I carry lies abroad?' 'True', too, is his ballad of a woman transformed into a fish 'for she would not exchange flesh with one that loved her', at least according to Autolycus:

AUTOLYCUS: The ballad is very pitiful, and as true.
DORCAS: Is it true too, think you?
AUTOLYCUS: Five justices' hands at it, and witnesses
more than my pack will hold.   (IV.iv.282–5)

Autolycus's ballads re-enact in a grotesque or surrealist form not only Leontes' opening fantasies of illicit pregnancy and condign punishment, but his—and our—eagerness for verification, for grounding what must forever remain linguistic and poetic possibility in historical fact or empirical truth. Autolycus resolves the problem of truth of reference—'Is it true, think you?'—by appeal to the testimony of a midwife named 'Mistress Taleporter, and five or six honest wives that were present,' as well as the authority of 'Five justices' hands at it, and witnesses more than my pack will hold'. That parody of judicial, indeed oracular, authentication may be enough to satisfy the naïve realism of the rustics, but no such simple confirmation—or disconfirmation—is to be found for Leontes' sophisticated fantasies, not even, as we have seen, in the Delphic oracle itself. In Leontes' case, validation is unavailable, a resting-point for reference repeatedly deferred and finally lost in the precariousness of language and the absence of an authoritative divine voice. The simple act of referring has turned into an endless process of deferral.[9]

Yet paradoxically it is this very deferral of reference, this problematization of language, on which the 'realism' of *The Winter's Tale* depends. By foregrounding the fallen nature of human speech and backgrounding any divine or redemptive 'reality' to which it refers, Shakespeare dramatizes, in linguistic terms, the condition of secularity within which we all, wittingly or not, inescapably dwell; language being, in Heidegger's pregnant phrase, 'the house we live in'.[10] In *The Winter's Tale*, the backgrounding of the divine referee—in *Pericles* and *Cymbeline*, we should recall, it has been foregrounded—becomes the condition for a new and extraordinary realism, a realism with which Shakespeare has been increasingly credited in this play, as distinct from the earlier romances, by critics as divergent in outlook as F. R. Leavis and myself.[11] Perhaps we are not so divergent after all.

It is worth noting, too, as a corollary of my argument and a condition of the play's 'realism', that the linguistic problems

---

[9] The astute reader will have recognized a certain resonance between my reading of *The Winter's Tale* and Jacques Derrida's critique of Western logocentricity. Derrida might almost have been commenting on this play when he writes that 'the center could not be thought in the forms of a being-present . . . but a function, a sort of non-locus, in which an infinite number of sign-substitutions came into play. This moment was that in which language invaded the universal problematic; that in which in the absence of a center of origin, everything became a system where the central signified, the original or transcendental signified is never absolutely present outside a system of differences. The absence of the transcendental signified extends the domain and the interplay of signification *ad infinitum*' ('Structure, Sign and Play', in Richard Macksey and Eugenio Donato, eds., *The Languages of Criticism and the Sciences of Man: The Structuralist Controversy* (Baltimore: Johns Hopkins University Press, 1970), 249).

[10] See Martin Heidegger, 'Letter on Humanism', in *Basic Writings*, ed. David Farrell Krell (London, 1978), 193. My use of Heidegger's inspired metaphor for language does not imply agreement with his larger view of poetry as a mode of being-present.

[11] See F. R. Leavis, 'The Criticism of Shakespeare's Late Plays', in *The Common Pursuit* (London: Chatto, 1952), 175 ff. My own earlier view of the play, radically revised here, is set out in H. Felperin, *Shakespearean Romance* (Princeton: Princeton University Press, 1972), 211–45.

foregrounded in the opening act of *The Winter's Tale* are never, because they cannot be, solved—not even in the exquisite transfigurations of the last. There, the language of art employed by Paulina is every bit as incommensurate and incompatible with the 'nature' it attempts to define as was the language of presence employed by Leontes to identify what was only imagination. The problem of language has been resolved in the sense of having been accepted and transcended; resolved, that is, by fiat or on faith. Paulina's description of the 'resurrection' of the last scene repeatedly adopts the language of miracle, magic, and madness at the same time that it repudiates miracle, magic, and madness.

Yet the superstition of the word that Mopsa and Dorcas exemplify in the sheep-shearing scene, and that lingers on in Paulina's account of Hermione's 'resurrection', is only the other side of the suspicion of the word exemplified in the first act by Leontes, much as Leontes' jealousy had been not the absence but the dark side of his faith. Because suspicion and superstition, jealousy and faith, thrive alike on the evidence of things not seen, they depend alike on the distancing and darkening property of language. The very opacity that had been such a problem in the language of the opening act becomes, in the closing act, the means of resolving that problem. If we cannot know except through the dark glass of language, we might as well accept what is a necessary limitation on our knowledge. Like Leontes yet again, we may even relax and enjoy it, and come to welcome this uncertainty as the ground for belief: 'If this be magic, let it be an art | Lawful as eating'; 'No settled senses of the world can match | The pleasure of that madness.'

The faith Paulina appeals to us to awaken, like the applause Prospero in his epilogue to *The Tempest* implores us to give, is the outcome of a sophisticated, as distinct from a naïve, realism. Such a realism understands, accepts, and above all *foregrounds* the inescapable mediacy of language, the radical difference between presence and reference, and the ultimate subjectivity of all interpretation. In sum, the fallen and incorrigible nature of language—of which the casual duplicity of the pun, Shakespeare's fatal Cleopatra, is only the most familiar symptom—paradoxically enables it in Shakespeare's hands to become the perfect medium for defining human reality. This foregrounding of linguistic difficulty in the interests of a sophisticated realism suggests that the larger relation between poetic and ordinary language is one of figure to ground, poetic language—whether that of Renaissance drama or modern lyric poetry—emerging as a problematic of ordinary language, a making explicit, indeed conspicuous, of the undeclared difficulty of everyday speech.[12]

[12] For a valuable working-through of this view in the case of modern poetry, see Gerald L. Bruns, *Modern Poetry and the Idea of Language* (New Haven: Yale University Press, 1974).

4

The Dark Lady Identified:
Or, what Deconstruction can do for Shakespeare's *Sonnets*

About anyone so great as Shakespeare, it is probable that
we can never be right; and if we can never be right, it is
better that we should from time to time change our way of
being wrong.

(T. S. Eliot, 'Shakespeare and the Stoicism of Seneca')

POETIC MONUMENTS

Is there any text, or group of texts, in the literary canon that so
invites exploration of the absences and indeterminacies of
textuality itself as Shakespeare's *Sonnets*? More specifically, is
there any pre-modern text better suited to serve as a test case
for deconstruction? For despite its universalizing claims, this
general theory of literary language has largely confined its
hermeneutic practice to post-romantic texts. And despite the
vast body of scholarship on the *Sonnets*, with its unending quest
for the positive identifications, biographical and historical,
that supposedly explain them—perhaps as an unintended
consequence of all that busy and contradictory scholarship—
the *Sonnets* might well seem to have been cunningly constructed,
Shakespeare's prophetic soul dreaming on things to come, with
the idea of deconstruction in mind.

The invitation to a deconstructive reading of the *Sonnets*
proceeds from a congeniality anterior to the inbuilt discontinu-
ity of the sonnet sequence as a genre or the failure of an older
historical scholarship to reach consensus on the identities and
relations of their protagonists. It arises from the peculiar nature
of Shakespeare's *Sonnets*—as distinct from Sidney's or Spenser's
or Elizabethan sonnet sequences in general—as a text that calls

attention to its own literal textuality, its mode of existence as a printed book remote, displaced, orphaned from whatever authorial intentions or autobiographical retentions it might have been expected, in the light of conventional practice, to register.

The title-page of the 1609 Quarto bears none of the idealized or acronymic sobriquets for its protagonists or theme common in Elizabethan sequences, only the cryptic glorification of its 'onlie begetter'. The absent presence of this dedicatee has tempted and frustrated identification with the fair youth of the sequence, whoever that might be, while certain bibliographical anomalies have led scholars to propose numerous re-orderings of the sequence to force its latent narrative out of the closet. This despite the fact that the poems are, on the whole, well printed. Yet after all these attempts at identification and rearrangement, only A. L. Rowse has arrived at a confident conclusion, a scholarly consensus of one.[1] The positivist yearnings of an older historical scholarship to pin down the personal experience of their author are thus bound up with the dream of reconstructing an authoritative text of the *Sonnets*. Both projects were baffled from the outset by the uncooperative aloofness of their unusually free-standing textuality.

Given the positivist incapability of an older biographical and bibliographical scholarship to fill the gaps in its own construction of the *Sonnets*, what followed was not a new negative capability in subsequent dealings with them. What followed was the displaced positivism of new-critical and proto-structuralist analysis, content to make do with the text as it stands but not quite content to relinquish the quest for unified and stable meaning within it. For Northrop Frye, such problems as what people and events in Shakespeare's life his sonnets record were effectively dissolved, if never quite resolved, when the poems were regarded as expressions of a distinctively literary language. To the vexed question of whether some of the sonnets celebrate homosexual love, for example, Frye advances a uniquely modern answer: it doesn't matter. When read in terms of the conventions of Elizabethan sonneteering, within which mistresses are invariably female and fair, Shakespeare's

[1] For his 'solution', see A. L. Rowse, *Shakespeare's Sonnets: The Problems Solved* (London: Macmillan, 1973) and *Shakespeare the Man* (London: Macmillan, 1973).

sonnets offer no less than two masterly variations, two un-precedented moves in the ongoing game, by introducing two presiding mistress–muses, a 'lovely boy' and 'a woman coloured ill'.

The *Sonnets* have less to say, that is, about 'experience', particularly Shakespeare's own, than about poetry and its conventional, archetypical, and ever-recyclable subject matter. We find in the *Sonnets* 'the authority of Shakespeare behind the conception of poetry as a marriage of Eros and Psyche, an identity of a genius that outlives time and a soul that feeds on death'.[2] Yet Frye's elegant invocation of 'the authority of Shakespeare' raises as many problems as it resolves, particularly at a moment in the history of criticism—and of culture—when the 'authority' of a distinctive literary language or a privileged authorial consciousness is very much in question. In what does Shakespeare's 'authority' consist, and by what is it conditioned? How can the powerful rhetoricity of his *Sonnets* be said to work itself free of the broader Elizabethan discursivity which supports and permeates it?

In the interest of economy, we might do well to focus initially on a single sonnet, one that raises explicitly the question of poetic authority. Such sonnets are of course not hard to find in Shakespeare's sequence, and I have settled on 55 for my point of departure. As one of the poetic 'highs' of the *Sonnets*, asserting as it does in the most unequivocal terms its power to confer a special status on its author, its object, and itself, 55 has always attracted critical attention:

> Not marble nor the gilded monuments
> Of princes shall outlive this pow'rful rhyme,
> But you shall shine more bright in these contents
> Than unswept stone, besmeared with sluttish time.
> When wasteful war shall statues overturn,
> And broils root out the work of masonry,
> Nor Mars his sword nor war's quick fire shall burn
> The living record of your memory.

---

[2] Frye, 'How True a Twain', in *Fables of Identity* (New York: Harcourt Brace, 1963), 106.

'Gainst death and all oblivious enmity
Shall you pace forth; your praise shall still find room,
Ev'n in the eyes of all posterity
That wear this world out to the ending doom.
     So, till the judgement that yourself arise,
     You live in this, and dwell in lovers' eyes.[3]

Clearly, the authority Shakespeare envisions and claims has something to do with rhetoric, the linguistic dimension of the will to power, though just as clearly, the sonnet is not rhetorical in any such simple sense as that it is not logical, or that it has practical designs on its object and readers, or that it uses a repertory of devices for effecting those designs—though all these senses do in fact apply.

The project so confidently proclaimed in 55 seems closer in its rhetorical mode to that described by Paul de Man and Roland Barthes as 'performative'. Barthes defines a 'performative' utterance, adopting the term from J. L. Austin, as 'a rare verbal form (exclusively given in the first person and in the present tense) in which the enunciation has no other content (contains no other proposition) than the act by which it is uttered—something like the *I declare* of kings or the *I sing* of very ancient poets'.[4] Though not exactly cast in present tense, and without giving up all practical designs on its object and audience, Sonnet 55 seems very close to this performative mode in its aspiration to a royal or orphic bringing into being of its object, to making itself good and itself flesh in something like the eternal present of its utterance.

It might seem tempting at this point to try to account for the triumphant poetic authority of Sonnet 55—as opposed to the more limited authority of any number of its Elizabethan congeners—as a function of this performative quality: in terms, that is, of the consistency and integrity with which it maintains the self-projection of its performative mode. Such an approach would at least have the advantage of re-inscribing the poem within the post-authorial poetic advanced by Barthes, among

---

[3] *Shakespeare's Sonnets*, ed. Stephen Booth (New Haven: Yale University Press, 1977), 48–51. All subsequent quotations from the *Sonnets* are to this edition.
[4] Roland Barthes, 'The Death of the Author', in *Image, Music, Text*, trans. Stephen Heath (New York: Hill and Wang, 1977), 145–6. See also Paul de Man, *Allegories of Reading* (New Haven: Yale University Press, 1979), 18.

others, within which '*writing* can no longer designate an operation of recording, notation, representation, "depiction" (as
the Classics would say) and every text is eternally written *here*
and *now*'.[5] But there is an obstacle to identifying the claim of 55
to poetic perdurability with its performative status as intransitive writing, or, in Barthes' term, 'inscription'.

Far from abandoning the notions of 'recording, notation,
representation, "depiction" (as the Classics would say)' in
favour of present, intransitive, and non-instrumental 'inscription', Shakespeare's *Sonnets* generally, and 55 particularly, continue to press their mimetic and practical claims, their designs
upon a pre- or non-linguistic 'reality', in order to fix and
perpetuate it. How could it be otherwise, when Renaissance
poetics are invariably mimetic in principle and seem to know
no other way in which to think of themselves, to theorize poetic
practice? In contrast to Barthes' 'modern scriptor', for whom
the intransitive autonomy of writing is to be welcomed with a
sense of relief at least, of pleasure or bliss at most, the Shakespeare of the *Sonnets*, particularly of the first half of the sequence,
consistently regards his writing transitively, as deriving whatever autonomy it may claim from an original, albeit
heightened, referentiality of the kind that 55 projects. Very like
a monument indeed. This is not to suggest that the Shakespeare
of the *Sonnets* is unaware of the paradox of this project and
cannot imagine the mimetic failure of his art, its defectiveness
or breakdown as representation. He does so often in the
sequence. But when he does, the inadequacy of writing is
always measured against a presupposed mimetic norm or ideal.

SPEAKING PICTURES

Before considering Shakespeare's distinctive variations on the
paradox of 'writerly' representation, let us look first at Sidney's
more conventional formulation of it. Sidney's defence of the
capacity of poetic language to represent a sensory world from
which it has for ever taken leave is cast precisely in terms of its
supposed difference from the mere 'black ink' of writing in
general and its supposed affinity with the visual arts. Contrasting the poet's representation of 'concrete universals' with

[5] Barthes, 'The Death of the Author', p. 145.

the particulars of historiography and the precepts of philosophy, Sidney contends that

he [the poet] giveth a perfect picture of it [the general precept] . . . *A
perfect picture I say*, for he yieldeth to the powers of the mind an image of
that whereof the philosophers bestoweth but a wordish description:
*which doth neither strike, nor possess the sight of the soul so much as that other
doth.*

For as in outward things, to a man that had never seen an elephant
or a rhinoceros, who should tell him most exquisitely all their shapes,
colour, bigness, and particular marks, of a gorgeous palace the
architecture, with declaring the full beauties might well make the
hearer able to repeat, as it were by rote, all he had heard, *yet should
never satisfy his inward conceits with being witness to itself of a true lively
knowledge*: but the same man as soon as he might see those beasts well
painted, or the house well in model, should straightways grow,
without need of any description, to a judicial comprehending of them:
so no doubt the philosopher with his learned definition—be it of
virtue, vices, matters of public policy or private government—
replenisheth the memory with many infallible grounds of wisdom,
which, notwithstanding, *lie dark before the imaginative and judging power,
if they be not illuminated or figured forth by the speaking picture of Poesy.*[6]

The language in which Sidney maintains the classic claim of
poetry, as distinct from other modes of writing, to the status of
pictorial representation, is strikingly similar to that of the most
sanguine of the *Sonnets*. For both Sidney and the Shakespeare of
55, poetry does not so much 'speak' as 'perform' its object. It is a
'perfect picture' that bears 'witness to itself of a true lively
knowledge'; it 'illuminates' or 'figures forth' what lies 'dark
before the imaginative and judging power'. How close we are to
the proclaimed 'power' of 55 to make its object 'shine bright'
and 'pace forth' in times to come! And once again, this enunciation of visual and sensory immediacy is made in spite of the
abstraction and distancing, also acknowledged, inherent in the

---

[6] Sidney, 'An Apology for Poetry' in W. J. Bate, ed., *Criticism: The Major Texts*, 2nd
edn. (New York: Harcourt Brace Jovanovich, 1970), 89 (my italics). See also Henry
Peacham, *The Garden of Eloquence* (London, 1953), sig. A.iii: 'By figures he (the speaker)
may make his speech as cleare as the noone day: or contrarywise, as it were with cloudes
and foggy mists, he may cover it with darkness: he may stirre up stormes, and
troublesome tempests, or contrariwyse, cause and procure, an quiet and sylent
calmnesse, he may set forth any matter with a goodly perspecuitie, and paynt out any
person, deede or thing so cunninglie with these coloures that it shall seeme rather a
lyvely Image paynted in tables, then a reporte expressed with the tongue.'

'wordiness' of its written medium. The paradox with which we began has not so much been resolved by Sidney as restated.

But not 'merely' restated, in so far as Sidney's own language is itself 'performative' or at least 'rhetorical'. The agency that confers on poetry a power of representation equal to that of the visual arts, despite the abstract wordiness of the written medium it shares with philosophy, is also the one Sidney employs: namely, rhetorical or figurative language. Such figures George Puttenham terms 'Sensable, because they alter and affect the mind by alteration of sense', i.e. they violate or disturb conventional usage and therefore the *naturalized* relation of sign and signification.[7] The very phrase with which Sidney concludes his account of poetry's superior power of imaging its object illustrates the operation it describes. The phrase 'speaking picture' is first and foremost a metaphor, albeit a metaphor that has lost, through its repetition as a commonplace, the root meaning that Puttenham, Englishing the nomenclature of classical rhetoric, ascribes to the figure of 'transport': the transfer of the qualities of one thing—here the human voice—to something similar yet distinctly different—here a mute visual image.

Yet the comparison of poetry to its 'sister' art of painting, Renaissance commonplace that it is, again raises as many problems as it resolves. Poetic representation is far more indirect and mediated than iconic representation, in so far as its arbitrary and conventional system of verbal signs requires a more complex decoding and displaced concretization of the signified object. Our decipherment of poetic language is always already belated and occurs at a temporal and spatial remove from its putative object. Even then the concretization that results is itself inescapably subjective, a filling-out of textual indeterminacies always dependent on prior beliefs, assumptions, and ideologies that vary from reader to reader and are never fully specifiable. For the contextual norms that might secure our reading of texts

[7] George Puttenham, *The Arte of English Poesie* [1589], facsimile edn. (Menston, Yorks.: Scolar Press, 1968), 133, 148, 150, 189. Puttenham defines 'figurative speech' generally as 'a noveltie of language evidently (and yet not absurdly) estranged from the ordinarie habite and manner of dayly talke and writing . . . giving them ornament of efficacie by many manner of alterations in shape, sounde, and also in sence, sometime by disorder, or mutation' (pp. 132–3). Similarly Peacham, for whom rhetorical figuration is a means of 'tournying from the common manner and custom of wryting and speaking' (sig. B.i).

are themselves a kind of text that requires a further, ultimately elusive, determination.

Writing, by decontextualizing its putative object, also puts it into a radical abeyance from which it can never be reliably or fully redeemed in any particular readerly concretization. As a second-order system of representation neither deployed nor deciphered in the presence of its objects, or of concrete images of them, writing begins and remains on their far side, remote and alienated from them while continuing to aspire, at least in classical and Renaissance accounts, to *re*-present them. All the major Elizabethan sonneteers—Sidney, Spenser, and especially Shakespeare—recognize within their sequences the manifold difficulties involved in representing an object conventionally or actually 'fair' in so unlikely, estranged, and unverisimilar a medium as the 'black ink' of writing, while nevertheless claiming to pursue that mimetic ambition. Yet it is only Shakespeare, as we shall see, who at once apprehends the full difficulty of that project and attempts a fully modern and writerly solution to it, which is to say, a dissolution of it.

THE PUN MADE FLESH

The performative potential of rhetoric thus promises, by altering the customary internal relations of language, to overcome its comparative disabilities in the foreign affairs of representing a sensory world quite alien to it. The *Sonnets*, of course, offer countless examples of this kind of performative language—later to be critically termed 'enactment'—in which the normal linguistic relations between signifier and signified, sound and sense, form and meaning, are altered in what Puttenham terms 'figures of disorder'. One of the most basic ways of thus opening an appeal from language to nature, to which Roman Jakobson has recently recalled attention, is onomatopoeia, Puttenham's 'new-namer'. Perhaps the most familiar poetic device through which sound approximates sense, it represents a classic example of the kind of language through which the difference between sign and referent that defines language as a system is apparently foreclosed.[8] Indeed, if Jakobson had analysed *55*, he would

---

[8] See Roman Jakobson and Laurence S. Jones, *Shakespeare's Verbal Art in 'Th' Expence of Spirit'* (The Hague: Mouton, 1970).

certainly have noticed the high incidence of alliteration on 'm',
'p', and 's' in its first strophe, as well as its repetition in the third
strophe. While it is clear that Shakespeare 'affects the letter'
in these strophes, and that they are thereby linked at the
phonetic level, it is by no means clear that this alliterative
linkage is in the service of onomatopoeia, and hence, of 'performance'.

What performative power could this purely formal linkage
confer upon the sonnet's 'contents'? Here a linguist like
Jakobson can be of little help, taking, as he notoriously does,
'content' for granted, or deriving it from the received ideas of
other commentators. In terms of his analysis, the most that can
be made of alliteration is that it offers an earnest of poetic
power, alerting us that some extra-communicative intention
may be at work; in itself, it cannot be a source or explanation of
that power. Occurring as it does within a semantic field the
alliteration does not itself generate, the function of alliteration
cannot be causal or integral to signified meaning. Rather, it
operates here as what Puttenham would call a figure of 'ornament' of the kind Shakespeare designates and illustrates as
such in the previous sonnet ('O how much more doth beauty
beauteous seem, | By that sweet ornament . . .'). As ornament or
decoration, alliteration bears the same superficially striking
but inessential relation to the verse as 'gilt' does to the 'monu-
ments | Of princes' mentioned at the outset. Gilding is to
monumental sculpture as alliteration is to the sonnet.

This analogy, if we allow it to guide our reading, would make
the sonnet itself a kind of monument or tomb containing the
earthly remains of a prince or nobleman. Indeed, there is much
to suggest, and nothing to deny, just such a reading. Several of
the *Sonnets* similar to 55 in form, theme, and diction explicitly
compare themselves, as monuments to the beloved, triumph-
antly or unhappily to 'tombs of brass' (*107*.14) and 'a tomb |
Which hides your life' (*17*.3–4). The editor of the most intelli-
gent recent edition of the *Sonnets*, glossing the phrase 'in these
contents', plausibly suggests that the word *in* and the idea of the
poem as a receptacle make the phrase ominously reminiscent of
monuments: 'the phrase carries a suggestion "in this coffin", a
suggestion given scope by the vagueness and imprecision of
these contents as a means of expressing "this poem" or "these

lines".[9] The suggestion gathers even greater force with the third and fourth strophes, in which the beloved object is said to 'pace forth' and 'still find room' by analogy with a Christian or Christological resurrection through which the confinement of the tomb is transcended.

The implicit depiction of the sonnet as a coffin or tomb, with the beloved as the body it contains, is an example of the figure Puttenham loosely terms 'icon, or resemblance by purtrait, and ymagerie'. Even without an Elizabethan tradition of emblem poetry refined to a high art by Jonson, Donne, and Herbert to encourage the perception of such resemblances, the foursquare block of print presented by the sonnet on the page would assimilate it to the form of a box. Given this rough resemblance, Shakespeare's opening paraphrase of Horace works to carve it more finely into a verbal icon of the poem as mausoleum or sarcophagus. The economy of inflection lends to Horace's Latin—*exegi monumentum aere perennius*—something of the epigrammatic concision of an epitaph such as might actually appear inscribed on the base of a monument or the lid of a sarcophagus, a pointedness that is of course much harder to attain in the uninflected 'wordiness' of English.

Yet this syntactical structure—the 'Not . . . nor' or 'nor . . . nor' construction that Shakespeare also employs in *107* and at several other points in the *Sonnets*—may well be an attempt to reproduce in English something like the epigrammatic symmetries of Latin by translating its classic 'nec . . . nec' construction. This impression of latter-day latinity may be further reinforced within the 'nor . . . nor' clause of line 7 by the inclusion of a latinate metonymy ('Nor Mars his sword'), whereby the name of the Roman war-god and its archaic genitive is paralleled with its modern English equivalent ('nor war's quick fire'). These latinate usages suggest a kind of double resurrection at work. At one level, Shakespeare's pseudo-latinity lends his sonnet something of the quality of an epitaph proclaiming the resurrection of the body contained

[9] Booth, ed., *Shakespeare's Sonnets*, p. 228. The 'tomb/tome' pun, through which the printed book defeats its own project of immortalization by becoming a mausoleum, is recurrent in the *Sonnets*. Its case is argued by T. Walter Herbert, 'Shakespeare's Wordplay on Tombe', *Modern Language Notes*, 64 (1944), 235–41, and supported by Booth, *Shakespeare's Sonnets*, p. 283.

within the mausoleum or sarcophagus of the sonnet itself. On another, it performs a resurrection of the dead language of Latin poetry into the life of a modern European vernacular.

The effect is analogous to that produced at the climax of *Julius Caesar*, a play dense with reference to monumental sculpture, when Caesar breaks into Latin at the moment of death— '*et tu Brute*'—only to return to English, but an English cadence closely modelled in its dying fall upon that patch of Latin— '*Then fall Caesar*'. The lapse into Latin and relapse into English dramatize the time-transcending claim made earlier by the play's co-carver of Caesar's fate, Cassius, that their bloody scene will be re-enacted 'in states unknown, and accents yet unborn' (III.i.113), a claim not unlike that of *55*, and one similarly dependent on the performative potential of the poetic medium to reproduce a 'living record'. 'When you entombed in men's eyes shall lie', Shakespeare writes in *81*, 'Your monument shall be my gentle verse, | Which eyes not yet created shall o'er-read, | And tongues to be your being shall rehearse'. In so far as the monumental statuary, mausoleums, and sarcophagi of the classical world have been mimed in the phonetic and syntactical units of the sonnet itself, they have been literally textualized, rendered into a 'speaking picture'.

And if such a project of performative re-appropriation is at work in the poem, is it entirely fanciful to read the transition from its third quatrain—in which the beloved is envisioned as about to 'pace forth' and 'find room'—to its closing couplet— in which a last judgement of Christian resurrection is foreshadowed—as enacting the change of state promised at the outset, the release of the beloved from imprisonment in the tomb of history into the liberty of textual 'freeplay'? Is it entirely fanciful to read the final couplet as a turning of the hinges of the poem, an unsealing of the tomb or opening of the coffin-lid through which the youth is released from the box of the sonnet's quatrains in order to live and roam abroad, even increase and multiply, in the free, lively, and endless reflection of the 'lovers' eyes' that will read the poem? Indeed, is this entire exercise in reading the sonnet as a sustained attempt at performative vivification—as a substantiation of the claim of poetic language to equal mimetic power with the visual arts

through its own carving of phonetic and graphic materiality—
no more than an exercise in metaphor-making, a fallacy of
imitative form, however seriously encouraged and underwritten
it may be by Elizabethan poetics?

Indeed, even as it attempts to transcend the residual materiality of its own utterance, 55 simultaneously voices a certain
consciousness of its own mimetic embarrassment and defeat,
an awareness that the breath in which it is spoken and the
paper on which it is written are, in their very perishability, an
ironic denial of its claim to a transcendent and perdurable
'supermimesis'. The sonnets that follow actually foreground
the contradictions of this supermimetic project by granting
Time his full tyrannical due over every nook and corner of
material reality, including those of breath and paper:

> Since brass, nor stone, nor earth, nor boundless sea,
> But sad mortality o'ersways their power,
> How with this rage shall beauty hold a plea,
> Whose action is no stronger than a flower?
> O how shall summer's honey breath hold out
> Against the wrackful siege of batt'ring days,
> When rocks impregnable are not so stout,
> Nor gates of steel so strong but time decays?
> O fearful meditation; where, alack,
> Shall time's best jewel from time's chest lie hid?
> Or what strong hand can hold his swift foot back?
> Or who his spoil or beauty can forbid
>   O none, unless this miracle have might
>   That in black ink my love may still shine bright.
>
> (65.1–4, 9–14)

The great 'ruins poems' that dominate the decade of the 60s in
Shakespeare's sequence may be read as a dark postscript to the
bright promise of 55.

If 55 triumphantly substitutes, by a masterly if narcissistic
sleight of hand, its own transcendent textuality for its mimetic
object, thereby defeating time, these subsequent sonnets envision Time as himself a master-artificer of self-consuming
artefacts, a kind of action-sculptor or action-painter gone berserk. For Time's fine frenzy climaxes in that master-stroke of

his 'cruel hand' which is the self-destruction of his own great works; his 'transfixing' (*60*.9) of 'the flourish' he himself has 'set on youth' means not permanence but murder, and would have to be countered by a 'strong hand' indeed. The struggle for immortality is now cast as a poetomachia, in which Time himself is seen by Shakespeare as a powerful rival, with the outcome quite uncertain as to which will prove *il miglior fabbro*. The ringing Horatian and Ovidian diction of *55* is still invoked, but the boast of a poetry written in black ink on yellowing paper to outlast Time's own favoured media of brass and stone now requires the 'might' of a 'miracle' to make itself good; here in *65* a most subjunctive 'might'.

THE FLESH MADE PUN

In recalling attention to the unlikely nature of 'black ink' as a medium of representation—'His beauty shall in these black lines be seen | And they shall live, and he in them still green' (*63*.13–14)—Shakespeare returns, and returns us, through this radical defamiliarization of his medium, to the questionable mimetic potential of writing in comparison to that of the plastic and visual arts. The paradox that haunts all performative accounts of poetic language, Elizabethan and modern, is that the means of recovering a lost univocality is a further linguistic disturbance, a shattering of internal linguistic relations that can be re-codified at a higher rhetorical level but never re-unified with a referential world outside language. Rhetorical figuration, far from repairing the rift between sign and meaning, becomes only an anatomy of linguistic dislocation which, when applied in practice, simply re-enacts it. This paradoxical condition cannot be resolved from within the logic of a performative poetics. Defect cannot be made up by more defect, by what Puttenham classifies as 'figures of disorder' and 'figures of default'.

It is just such an interrogation of the adequacy of any rhetorical or poetic programme to reproduce its object that lies at the core of Shakespeare's sequence, the poems from *76* to *106*, and that issues in the partial 'answers' of the rival poet and the dark lady herself. At this stage, the sequence turns what must

be termed 'metamimetic', questioning from within itself the
capacity of its rhetorical repertory—'What strained touches
rhetoric can lend' (*82*.10)—to represent the youth at all. The
problem is now conceived as twofold: not only is the youth's
beauty so transcendent as to strain to the limit the resources of
Shakespeare's own rhetoric, but the inadequacy of that rhetoric
has been revealed by its having been imitated and exceeded at
the hands of rival poets, 'As every alien pen hath got my use, |
And under thee their poesy disperse' (*78*.3–4). Sexual puns
aside, a rhetoric that derives its performative capability from its
transgression of conventional usage has itself become conventional usage, thereby requiring a further transgression to
maintain its mimetic advantage.

This heightened awareness of rhetorical limitation is doubly
difficult to overcome, since what has been revealed to Shakespeare is at once 'How far a modern quill', despite the eager
ingenuity displayed around him, 'doth come too short' (*83*.7)
and the essential poverty of his own rhetorical invention, its
inability to overgo itself and thereby overgo his imitators and
rivals: 'Why is my verse so barren of new pride, | So far from
variation or quick change?' (*76*.1–2). In these sonnets, Shakespeare comes up against the paradox of a self-superseding
modernity: 'Finding thy worth a limit past my praise, | And
therefore [am] enforced to seek anew | Some fresher stamp of
the time-bett'ring days' (*82*.5–8). If rhetoric, as Hopkins
remarked, is the 'teachable' part of poetry, then some new and
unprecedented rhetorical resource beyond the present state of
the art must continually be found.

Shakespeare meets this double dilemma with a two-pronged
strategy. He bequeaths to other poets 'What strained touches
rhetoric can lend' (*82*.10), pre-eminently to that red herring of
biographical research, the 'rival poet' (the dark lady being its
Loch Ness monster). Such a rhetorical fullness and power he
himself no longer claims to have, or to have any use for ('Was it
the proud full sail of his great verse?' *86*.1). For rhetoric misses
the mark in any case, however seductive it may be. Instead, he
pursues a new and self-conscious minimalism in his own
writing, which now cuts between plain speech and tongue-tied
silence, and claims to hit the mark precisely because of its
acknowledged inadequacy:

This silence for my sin you did impute,
Which shall be most my glory, being dumb;
For I impair not beauty, being mute,
When others would give life, and bring a tomb.
    There lives more life in one of your fair eyes
    Than both your poets can in praise devise.

(*83*.9–14)

Truth needs no colour with his colour fixed,
Beauty no pencil, beauty's truth to lay;
But best is best, if never intermixed?
Because he needs no praise, wilt thou be dumb?
Excuse not silence so, for't lies in thee [the muse]
To make him much outlive a gilded tomb,
And to be praised of ages yet to be.

(*101*.6–12)

But this Neoplatonic or Keatsian approach—heard melodies are sweet, but those unheard are sweeter—has its own inbuilt handicap and, as Shakespeare fully recognizes, a certain potential defeatism. In setting up the rhetorical eloquence of the rival poet as a foil to his own understatement, Shakespeare does not so much transcend the problem of rhetorical defect as defer it: 'Where art thou, muse, that thou forget'st so long | To speak of that which gives thee all thy might?' (*100*.1–2). The ingenious solution of abjuring rhetoric and 'speaking in effect'—'Then others for the breath of words respect, | Me for dumb thoughts, speaking in effect' (*85*.13–14)—turns out to be no solution at all, in so far as it is still speaking and still rhetoric, albeit a self-deprecating or self-denying rhetoric of understatement. What Shakespeare has done in this phase of the sequence is to exchange one rhetorical programme for another, a rhetoric of presence, fullness, immediacy, and enactment—now ascribed to and personified by the hypothetical rival poet—for a rhetoric of difference, deferral, and indirection.

This latest rhetorical programme of 'counter-enactment' involves a new set of dominant figures—those Puttenham terms 'figures of default'—and generates a new set of thematic oppositions and contrasts: between himself and his rivals, poetry and its object, past and present poetry. Its rationale is that of *reculer pour mieux sauter*, that rhetorically less is mimetically more, as if a fault in the medium of representation can still be made fortunate. The earlier project of reproducing through a poetics of performance and enactment the fullness of 'great creating nature' set out in the initial 'procreation sequence' with a 'second nature' that rivals and replaces the first, fallen one has now been inverted. It remains questionable, however, whether this latest programme of 'speaking in effect' can recuperate the performative project, can make effective, let alone perfect, the 'defect' in which it seems to be founded, or whether its new promise of enactment is haunted by linguistic bad faith from the beginning.

For this latest turn in Shakespeare's search for rhetorical adequation, as the phrase that names it suggests, seems to be rooted in nothing more than a pun. 'Speaking in effect' can mean either 'speaking effectively' or 'speaking by default, or defectively,' i.e., 'not speaking at all.' In this new programme of defective speech, it is not so much 'ellipsis' as 'syllepsis', Puttenham's 'figure of double supply', or perhaps 'paranomasia', his 'nick-namer', on which so much now depends. What with its demonumentalization of fixed or 'natural' meaning, Shakespeare's wordplay—what would later be termed his 'puns' and 'quibbles'—would seem to be the ultimate 'figure of disorder'. From the viewpoint of a performative poetics, it would appear to be counter-productive in the extreme, a denial and demystification of the lofty claims to poetic monumentality advanced in 55.

If anything, the pun seems to play into the hands of the enemies, devouring Time and Death. It does so not only in the structural sense that it undermines the monumental integrity of the word, fractures its meaning and thereby 'roots out the work of masonry', but also in the historical sense that the connotations it activates, particularly its lower connotations, are often of a local or colloquial nature—as with the Elizabethan 'spirit' (= 'sprit' = 'erect phallus')—and therefore likely to be lost on posterity, while its root, etymological meanings are often already lost on all but the most historically and philologically erudite, as modern readers of Shakespeare's comedies will attest. The cult of etymology and etymological puns in the Renaissance as a favoured means of concentrating present meaning by recovering supposed origins can counter-productively turn the poet, as in the case of its foremost practitioner Spenser, into a poet's poet at best and a scholar's poet at worst—a destiny quite the opposite of the timeless and universal immediacy projected by any performative poetics.[10]

Yet Shakespeare notoriously puts his performative poetics at risk by cultivating the pun, and often the etymological pun. There is no better example of a sonnet rooting out its own masonry and counteracting its own enactment than *107*, already cited as a companion piece to *55* in its monumental theme and its ringing 'Not . . . nor' opening. Let us leave aside the radical wordplay of 'the mortal moon hath her eclipse endured,' with its all but infinite variety of reference—does the phrase not epitomize the restlessness of reference itself, the ebb and flow of phonetic and semantic flux?—and proceed to the third quatrain, in which the triumph of writerly 'freeplay' over historical flux is asserted:

> Now with the drops of this most balmy time
> My love looks fresh, and death to me subscribes,
> Since spite of him I'll live in this poor rhyme,
> While he insults o'er dull and speechless tribes.
> And thou in this shalt find thy monument,
> When tyrants' crests and tombs of brass are spent.

Though more provisionally than in *55*—for here the poem refers to itself as a 'poor' rather than 'powerful' rhyme, whose monumental status is no longer self-evident—the triumph over Time and Death is none the less proclaimed.

More remarkably still, it is proclaimed as having been wrought with their own weapons. For the etymological puns on 'subscribes' and 'insults' revivify the old Latin senses of those words, which work to reinforce their more modern and abstract meanings. Death 'subscribes' to Shakespeare not only in the abstract sense of 'submits' or 'enters into agreement' but in the concrete, enactive sense of writing one's name at the bottom of a document, in this context a lease on life or treaty of surrender, and he does so with the 'drops' of Shakespeare's own ink! After such a defeat, the only victory remaining for Death is a hollow one over hypothetical 'speechless tribes'. These he will continue

---

[10] See Martha Craig, 'The Secret Wit of Spenser's Language', in Paul Alpers, ed., *Elizabethan Poetry* (Oxford: Oxford University Press, 1967), 447–72.

to 'insult'—in the older sense of 'leap against' or 'assault' and in the later sense of 'verbally abuse'—without any possible comeback on their part. By re-activating through wordplay these decayed senses and pressing them into the service of his writing, Shakespeare imagines himself defeating Time and Death at their own war-game, arresting the linguistic shifts that undermine poetic masonry, and fixing these words permanently in place within his own poetic monument.

It seems that even the most potent weapon of verbal destabilization, the pun, can be pressed into the service of poetic presence, and victory snatched from the jaws of devouring Time himself. Indeed, the very next sonnet ('What's in the brain that ink may character') self-consciously celebrates, through a series of writerly puns, just such an improbable victory:

> So that eternal love in love's fresh case
> Weighs not the dust and injury of age,
> Nor gives to necessary wrinkles place,
> But makes antiquity for aye his page,
>> Finding the first conceit of love there bred,
>> Where time and outward form would show it dead.
>
> (*108*.9–14)

If puns—and these lines contain several: on 'case,' 'injury', 'age', 'antiquity', 'aye', 'page', 'conceit', 'would'—particularly etymological puns, are the wrinkles carved by Time on the clear face of meaning, what Shakespeare has done is to inscribe them upon his own work in such a way as to pre-empt decay and obsolescence. 'Wrinkles' may be a biological necessity in the progress of nature towards death, but by assigning them a place in his work he denies them priority or pride of place.

This was his practice as far back as *18*—'Nor shall death brag thou wand'rest in his shade, | When in eternal lines to time thou grow'st'—though here in *108* it has become fully and self-consciously foregrounded. Lines of living become lines of verse; classical antiquity, the freshly written page; the tomb or coffin of the love-sonnet, the tome from which love rises afresh to the reading eye for aye. The most astute modern reader of the *Sonnets* is surely—and quite uncharacteristically—under-reading this sonnet, when he demurs over earlier editors' paraphrasing of its closing strophes as a 'continuation of the discussion of literary invention in lines 1–8', suggesting that it 'exaggerates the purposefulness and continuity of *this secondary train of thought*'.[11] Only by maintaining the priority of the sonnet's, indeed the sequence's, autobiographical and mimetic over its writerly and metamimetic enterprise could Booth relegate this train of thought to a 'secondary' status.

THE DARK LADY IDENTIFIED

It is precisely the abandonment, I am arguing, of the super-mimetic project of reproducing the beloved object for all time that makes possible Shakespeare's metamimetic foregrounding of the flaws and tricks of his written medium. It makes room, that is, for another performative project, but performative with a difference, and still necessarily mimetic. Since signs must signify something, signification—though it can be complicated, multiplied, and embarrassed—can never be made to cease, not even in 'nonsense' verse or symbolist poetry, and certainly not through the poetic figures of defect or default we have been discussing. But this latest project, which occupies the last fifty or so sonnets of Shakespeare's sequence and carries the processes of writerly self-consciousness we have been tracing to an uneasy cadence, is not only mimetic with a difference, but mimetic *of* a difference. For this is the fully metamimetic project of representing nothing other than linguistic difference itself. Its object is language in the act, always imperfect or defective, of representing, and it depends on precisely that hyperactivity of the sign epitomized in the pun and such related figures as irony, litotes, and ellipsis, all of which share a constitutive capacity to mean more than they say.

If Shakespeare's scepticism towards the mimesis of the youth in so unlikely a medium as 'black ink' has generated a new rhetoric, or counter-rhetoric, of disability and default, it also generates a new object better suited to metamimetic representation. That is, if the medium of black ink cannot ultimately be appropriated to its conventionally 'fair' object, one potential solution—the only one remaining to be explored—is to appropriate the 'object' to the defective medium. Why not a

[11] Booth, *Shakespeare's Sonnets*, pp. 250–1 (my italics).

'figure' whose physical complexion, being dark, would make her as representable in the medium of ink as any traditional 'fair' might be in the media of paint or marble? But while this 'solution' may restore a certain superficial similarity between medium and message, it cannot compensate for the more profound defects in the linguistic medium that the sonnets of the 70s and 80s have already uncovered. After such self-consciousness, there can be no return to a naïve realism that presupposes the mimetic adequacy of language. But even that problem can be met by making the lady's character as shady as her complexion, indeed as dark and defective as the characters that describe it. What more writerly address to the problem of the difference of writing than to have writing generate its own best—or worst—object, a 'figure' as darkly different as writing itself?

Yet this fanciful figuration of a writerly dark lady, visual and moral negative to the countless colourless fairs of sonnet convention, does not finally resolve the problem of mimesis. For the projection of a dark lady is still a function of rhetorical duplicity, of an ironical figuration or negative comparison ('My mistress' eyes are nothing like the sun') that foregrounds the impostures of prior convention, the 'false compare' of all verbal art. Even this audacious figure cannot make up the difference of the written medium in relation to its object and deliver a dark and unlikely presence. But if this new object cannot be presented any more directly than the old object, a still newer and more truly congenial object can be represented through her: the duplicity and discrepancy, infidelity and betrayal of poetic representation itself:

> In the old age black was not counted fair,
> Or if it were it bore not beauty's name.   (*127*)

> Why should my heart think that a several plot,
> Which my heart knows the wide world's common place?
> Or mine eyes, seeing this, say this is not
> To put fair truth upon so foul a face?
>   In things right true my heart and eyes have erred,
>   And to this false plague are they now transferred. (*137*)

Therefore I lie with her, and she with me,
And in our faults by lies we flattered be.   (*138*)

My thoughts and my discourse as madmen's are,
At random from the truth vainly expressed;
    For I have sworn thee fair, and thought thee bright,
    Who art as black as hell, as dark as night.   (*147*)

O me! what eyes hath love put in my head,
Which have no correspondence with true sight?   (*148*)

For I have sworn thee fair: more perjured eye
To swear against the truth so foul a lie.   (*152*)

What is striking in these late sonnets is not just how openly
Shakespeare confesses the mimetic inadequacies of his art in
order to claim a certain metamimetic validity for it, but how
fully these confessions of poetic misrepresentation have been
re-thematized in the moral misprision of the dark lady's and
the poet's interactions. An untrustworthy textuality and an
untrustworthy sexuality now mirror one another in the perfection of defect of the pun on 'lie': 'Therefore I lie with her, and
she with me, | And in our faults by lies we flattered be.' It is no
longer possible to tell which has chronological or ontological
priority, language or action; which 'mirrors' which, the betraying pun or the betraying flesh; or which is the signifier and
which the signified, dancer or dance in this old gavotte. The
relations now represented—or are they generated?—are as
unstable, polymorphous and perverse as the language which
represents or generates them.
    Whether the lady in question is fair or dark, morally
irreproachable or reprehensible, a wrinkled Hermione or a
wrinkled Cleopatra, her perfect representation in the medium
of black ink would seem to be impossible. Even in the latter set
of cases, she can be represented only at the metamimetic level of
the pun, and that is to foreground defect and defeat perfection:
'Therefore I lie with her, and she with me, | And in our faults by
lies we flattered be.' The point cannot be made too strongly,
however, against those textualists, disciples of Barthes and de
Man, who would like to proclaim the end of representation,
that representation does not, because it cannot, cease. What
ceases is the dream of univocal representation, which now gives

way to a multivocal representation in something of the way the Roman Empire does not so much cease as become Europe.

The foredoomed project of univocal representation, based in a performative poetics and aspiring to a perfect realization of its object, has yielded to a multivocal representation arising from the hyperactivity of the pun and generating numerous objective correlatives. It is no longer possible to disentangle the erotic and ethical duplicities and disloyalties represented in the later sonnets, because the language in which they are represented so openly acknowledges its own duplicity and disloyalty. But neither is it possible to deny that anything is being represented at all. For the Shakespeare of the later sonnets, unlike Leontes in *The Winter's Tale*, this condition of multivocality is neither a nightmare of anxiety nor a utopia of bliss. The characteristic tone of these poems can only be described as one of detached or reluctant engagement towards the extremes of raw 'experience' they at once encapsulate and distance. Their own bemusement at the irrepressible power of their language to work as it were overtime, to keep on signifying beyond any particular significance, has been met by our continuing embarrassment and frustration before an overplus of signification that cannot be exhausted in any act of interpretation, either positive and historicist or negative and deconstructive.

But not even Shakespeare's metamimetic art, which tells us in one and the same breath that univocal representation and definitive interpretation are impossible, can prevent us from trying to restore the monumentality of the printed sign, so apparently stable and permanent on the page, to full mimetic integrity and univocality. The modernist authenticity of the *Sonnets*, as distinct from their traditional mimetic authority, arises precisely from Shakespeare's ongoing exertions, against the grain of his medium and against his foreknowledge of ultimate frustration, to test to the limit of its potential monumentality the figurative power of language, in particular of writing. We, in our turn as readers, go directly against their acknowledgement of imperfection and betray the authenticity of this acknowledgement by attempting to re-monumentalize his writing through the systematic reification of it we name interpretation.

Shakespearean interpretation in particular represents one of the more extreme cases of that cultural repetition-compulsion which attempts, over and over again, to discover within or project on to his poetry a mimetic coherence it has already acknowledged it cannot have—as I have just done in the foregoing interpretation. Or perhaps it is just such a foreknowledge on Shakespeare's part of the vain efforts at interpretive re-monumentalization his text will occasion that enables his equally vain claim of poetic monumentality in the first place. Perhaps he resembles none of the figures projected in his own sonnets so much as those of Spenser's *LXXV*, whose fair lady rebukes her poet's repeated attempts to inscribe her name in sand: 'Vayne man, sayd she, that doest in vaine assay, | A mortall thing so to immortalize.' Yet it is only because of this work of compulsive, frustrated, but irrepressible re-monumentalization through the repeated reifications of reading across history that Time, the destroyer of the gilded monuments of princes, can become the ally and preserver of the printed monuments of poets.

5

Contextualizing the Canon:
The Case of Donne

> No wonder he [man] later always discovered in things
> only that which he had put into them! . . . And even your
> atom, messieurs mechanists and physicists, how much
> error, how much rudimentary psychology, still remains in
> your atom!—To say nothing of the 'thing in itself,' that
> *horrendum pudendum* of the metaphysicians! The error of
> spirit as cause mistaken for reality. And made the measure
> of reality! And called God!
>
> (Nietzsche, *Twilight of the Idols*)

THE TEXT IN ITSELF

No issue in contemporary critical theory is more topical, or
more contentious, than that of 'the text in itself'. Doubtless, its
newly questionable status is one effect of the paradigm-shift
from liberal humanism to politicized post-structuralism that
literary studies are now experiencing. Such paradigm-shifts are
like seismic movements in the strata that support the landscape
of knowledge; in the course of their slippage, institutional
constructs of long standing may teeter and collapse, the ground
they stand on sink and disappear, and hitherto invisible tracts
suddenly emerge to be surveyed and built up. In the current
tremor, the familiar concept of 'the text in itself' seems to be
one of the more serious casualties.[1]

---

[1] The recent symposium on 'The Text in Itself', *Southern Review*, 17/2 (July 1984), is
my point of departure. It is significant that, despite the wide range of contextualist
positions represented in that exchange, not one of the symposiasts defends the kind of
textualism once so familiar in new and practical criticism, or advances any other. Such
remarkable—and somewhat alarming—agreement within apparent diversity marks, I
am arguing here, the imminent replacement of one critical orthodoxy by another. On
institutional paradigms and paradigm-shifts in general, see of course Thomas S. Kuhn,
The Structure of Scientific Revolutions (Chicago: University of Chicago Press, 1962).

The quasi-objectification of 'the text in itself' performed a crucial function within the development of the paradigm of liberal-humanist literary study during the last century. The study of classic literature—'the best that has been thought and known in the world'—was to serve as the replacement for a failing religion and the alternative to an ascendant science. The classic text, re-defined by the end of the century to include the modern vernacular classic, seemed to offer something of great and permanent value that religion no longer could, and science never would, provide. Call it a meaning for existence. Though that meaning was now man-made, cultural and personal rather than God-given, it was still inspired and redemptive, put into the work by an author analogous in his creative activity to God. So something of the healing, even saving, power of religion remained latent in the literary text. The future of poetry, in Arnold's view, was immense.[2]

But a further move was necessary if the humanist project of institutionalizing high European culture as the means of secular salvation was to succeed. It still had to compete with science on the latter's own demystified ground. The meanings of literature, while filling the demand left by religion for a reliable source of value and belief, needed the appearance of objectivity, of having been arrived at through something like disinterested enquiry, if they were to hold their own against the proliferating discoveries of science. Generated out of the incongruous congress of religion and science (one dying, the other rapidly coming of age), the humanist paradigm came to project the classic text as a kind of superior material object, its dual birthright demanding for its proper study a kind of abstracted passion, or in Arnold's phrase, 'disinterested love'. Arnold's metaphor of the classic text as 'touchstone', the rigorous test of value through which an authentic 'criticism of life' could be established, was only the first of many subsequent attempts to objectify the text within the humanist paradigm.

For the great, canonical text was now supersaturated with a

[2] The crucial influence of Matthew Arnold, some of whose best-known pronouncements I have been quoting, upon the formation of academic English at the turn of the century, and its subsequent development at the hands of Eliot, Leavis, and the new critics has come in for renewed attention of late. See especially Chris Baldick, *The Social Mission of English Criticism 1848–1932* (London: Oxford University Press, 1983) and John Fekete, *The Critical Twilight* (London: Routledge and Kegan Paul, 1977).

fullness of meaning, universally valuable and eternally negotiable, a meaningfulness perdurable as gold. This rich concentrate, once extracted, was hard currency even in times and cultures remote from its own; it could be drawn on as occasion demanded, provided only that the demand was sufficiently earnest and assiduous to overcome such contingent differences and get to the metaphysical heart of the matter. If the First World War made the critical earnestness and assiduousness demanded by the humanist paradigm look more like aestheticism, religiosity, or pedantry, that only meant that a new tightening and toughening up was needed. And even in its latest, technocratic phase of development in American new criticism, the religious as well as the scientific genealogy of the 'text in itself' was not forgotten. The text was now a 'well-wrought urn' and a 'verbal icon', still a material object to be sure, but one that continued to trail clouds of transcendental glory and a sacred, even Christological, aura.

Nor was the procedure now required to unpack its precious and ever-present fullness of meaning merely a technical analysis of form and figure. Yes, criticism presupposed a necessary 'hypostatization', a stabilization of the substance under study akin to that of empirical science; but the term is also theological and connotes an incarnation, the words on the page made flesh.[3] Form always turned out, in the analysis, to be organic, and the rhetorical discontinuities of irony, paradox, and ambiguity to be bound together in a higher metaphysical unity. Even the new-critical banishment of authorial intention from the study of the text did not rule out the presence of its own immanent intentionality and transcendental authority. For each reading of patterns of imagery, subtleties of texture, and complexities of structure was in effect a displaced argument from design, only confirming the authority of the text, however depersonalized it now might be. The tale could still be trusted, if no longer the teller.

---

[3] The term is W. K. Wimsatt's, and is strategically deployed in what may be the most influential pronouncement of new-critical theory, 'The Intentional Fallacy', in *The Verbal Icon* (Lexington: University of Kentucky Press, 1954).

THE TEXT IN QUESTION

The beginning of the end for the text in itself came with the structuralist revolution, when everything in the cultural universe—kinship, cuisine, dress, the unconscious, even literary 'works'—was democratically declared so many 'texts' to be systematically analysed on the model of language. In the beginning—and in the end—was the text. This wholesale textualization of culture entailed upon the 'work' of literature a massive devaluation in prestige and centrality. Where the 'work' was, there shall be the text. With everything now a text, those once privileged 'texts in themselves' lost that intrinsic distinction which had given them a special claim to attention. Worse yet, the structuralist move from 'work' to 'text' also detranscendentalized at a stroke the personal author, since its meaning could no longer originate in his unique biography or hagiography—for that, too, was only another text. Nor was its meaning a function of the sacred labour he had put into it, but of the way it functioned in society through the systematic and conventional codes, rules, and grammars on which all language depends. What a falling-off was there!

But if structural analysis had detranscendentalized the apparently free-standing text by uncovering its linguistic and cultural support systems, it also inadvertently transcendentalized those support systems. Though relocated from content to form, from substance to system, or from inside to outside, the meaning of the text was still assumed to be ascertainable through a new kind of processing. The quest for what Derrida termed a 'transcendental signified' had not ceased after all. It remained for deconstruction to pose the question of textual meaning, not as a 'what' or a 'how', but as a 'why' or even a 'whether'. This project entailed the strenuous re-thinking of a host of anterior questions, hitherto repressed, concerning the most general conditions of textual construction, and involving such basic concepts as 'iterability', 'difference', and 'decidability'. The language of literary and philosophical texts turned out to be not a rule-bound fabric of grammaticality but a loophole-riddled patchwork of rhetoricity. No longer a substantial object, nor even a framing structure, the text came to seem more like a force-field of drifting particles, the 'inside' and 'outside' of which are not clearly delimitable.[4]

Having been softened up by these preliminary manœuvres, the 'text in itself', sometime stronghold of authoritative meaning, was now open to political takeover from all sides. 'The birth of the reader', wrote Roland Barthes in the heady political climate of 1968, 'must be at the cost of the death of the author.'[5] And at the cost too, of texts in themselves and their extension into the canon 'in itself'. From the moment the text came to be regarded no longer as the source of a prior meaning, put there by the god-like author and sanctioned by the dominant culture, but 'a site on which the production of meaning—or variable meanings—takes place',[6] its expropriation or appropriation in the name of any group or movement seeking to advance its own political cause became inevitable. These assimilations of texts to contexts have been carried out under various, and sometimes opposed, banners, ranging from radical individualism and conservative receptionism to several distinctive Marxisms and any number of feminisms. Political differences notwithstanding, all such readers share the hermeneutic assumption that the text is always already infiltrated or saturated by its context. In the recent work of such politically diverse theorists as Stanley Fish and Tony Bennett, the text disappears altogether into the 'interpretive communities' and 'reader formations' that dictate its meanings.[7]

THE NEW CRITICS AND THE NEW HISTORICISTS

Within the range of emerging contextualisms, one school in particular is making a mark upon the canonical texts—mainly Elizabethan poems and plays—on which it has focused its non-

[4] See Paul de Man, 'Semiology and Rhetoric', in *Allegories of Reading* (New Haven: Yale University Press, 1981) and Jacques Derrida, 'Signature Event Context', in *Margins of Philosophy*, trans. Alan Bass (Chicago: University of Chicago Press, 1982).

[5] Roland Barthes, 'The Death of the Author,' in *Image, Music, Text*, trans. Stephen Heath (New York: Hill and Wang, 1977), 148.

[6] Tony Bennett, *Formalism and Marxism* (London: Methuen, 1979), 178.

[7] Stanley Fish, *Is there a Text in this Class? The Authority of Interpretive Communities* (Cambridge, Mass.: Harvard University Press, 1979); and Bennett, 'The Bond Phenomenon: Theorising a Popular Hero', *Southern Review*, 16/2 (July 1983).

or anti-canonical readings. It consists of a number of younger critics currently termed 'new-historicists'. That label, though broad, is not inaccurate; their work is not emphatically or relentlessly theoretical, but a kind of applied theory that draws somewhat eclectically on contextualist principles formulated in the writings of Michel Foucault, Raymond Williams, Clifford Geertz, Jacques Lacan and Mikhail Bakhtin—as well as on the textualist practices of such deconstructionists as Barthes, Derrida, and de Man. My present purpose, however, is not to trace genealogies or identify affiliations, but to draw attention to a radical contextualism that is changing the way we read the Renaissance texts that constitute so much of the canon and the curriculum.

The new-historicist project has been to re-read these canonical, and generally idealized, Elizabethan texts in a defamiliarizing and demystifying way: as not for all time but of their age, as the articulations of a historically specific system. This is to regard such texts as culturally 'other' and 'coded' and to develop techniques for 'cracking' the otherness of the codes in which they are written: what one new historicist terms, with something of Miranda's breathlessness before a brave new world, 'a poetics of culture'.[8] Its concerns would 'prevent it from permanently sealing off one type of discourse from another or decisively separating works of art from the minds and lives of their creators and their audiences'.

Here, for example, is Arthur Marotti summing up his conclusions on the flowering and deflowering of the Elizabethan sonnet:

The analysis of the sonnet fashion in late Elizabethan England in a sociopolitical context points to challenging critical problems—of explaining the culture-specific encoding of literature, the nature of literary change, and the arrangement of a society's hierarchy of genres: singly and collectively, the various genres of Elizabethan or Jacobean literature served as the symbolic language that articulated the complex character of the social system and expressed the criticisms that were part of the cultural dialectic. In examining works from any historical moment we need finally to recognise that not only are we in the process of discovering the relationships between verbal artifacts

[8] Stephen Greenblatt, *Renaissance Self-Fashioning: From More to Shakespeare* (Chicago: University of Chicago Press, 1980), preface.

and their sociocultural context, but also we are attempting to define the institution of literature itself—not ahistorically, but in a way proper to a specific period.[9]

The oppositions at play here, of 'verbal artifacts' to 'their sociohistorical context' and of an 'ahistorical' to a 'period-specific' definition of 'literature', signpost the institutional context within which this new historicism is to be read, and its own oppositional orientation within that context. The new historicism is to be read and weighed against the new criticism.

The choice of Donne as one of the poets to whom this new historicism repeatedly returns is itself strategic within the American institutional context.[10] The hegemony of the new criticism, within which the new historicists were trained and against which they are reacting, had effectively canonized Donne's poetry into the type of literature itself. Through a rhetorical virtuosity that enabled it to combine a vernacular immediacy with a depersonalized, often erudite, wit, the 'metaphysical' poetry of Donne and his 'school' (the adoption of this seventeenth-century term in the new-critical currency was no accident) epitomized precisely those qualities valued by a contemporary anti-romantic poetry and a new university-based criticism with significant mutual interests to legitimate and promote. They were not of course represented as such, but as the eternal constituents of poetic language.

Before returning to the new-historicist reading of Donne—and its own contextually generated interests—it is worth pausing to re-examine the interests of the new criticism. For if the contextualists are right, the former cannot be understood independently of the latter. As we have already begun to see, the new criticism in America, rather like practical criticism in England somewhat before it, was embedded within a specific

[9] Arthur F. Marotti, 'Love is Not Love': Elizabethan Sonnet Sequences and the Social Order', *English Literary History*, 49 (1982), 421–2.

[10] Exemplary new-historicist readings of Donne include those of Marotti, 'John Donne and the Rewards of Patronage', in Guy Fitch Lytle and Stephen Orgel, eds., *Patronage in the Renaissance* (Princeton: Princeton University Press, 1981), 207–33, and Jonathan Goldberg, *James I and the Politics of Literature: Jonson, Shakespeare, Donne and their Contemporaries* (Baltimore: Johns Hopkins University Press, 1983), ch. 5. For a reading of Donne along parallel lines in Australia, see David Aers, Bob Hodge, and Gunther Kress, *Literature, Language and Society in England 1580–1680* (Dublin: Gill and Macmillan, 1981), ch. 3. See also Thomas Docherty, *John Donne, Undone* (London: Methuen, 1986) and Marotti, *John Donne: Coterie Poet* (Madison: University of Wisconsin Press, 1986).

cultural and institutional formation. Arguably, a major ingredient in that formation was the changed role and composition of the universities during the years following the Second World War. Crucial in precipitating these changes were the Butler Education Act in Britain and the GI Bill in America. The opening of the old elitist universities in Britain and America to a broader social cross-section, both economic and regional, coincides with the growth in prestige and influence of English literature within the curriculum.

English studies, formerly elitist and amateur in both countries, were to become newly professionalized in the face of a more diverse student body, and would ultimately require a new academic clerisy to teach them. The Anglophone nationalism that fuelled the growth of English studies in Britain preceding and following the First World War—here the Newbolt report was the crucial political catalyst—was giving way by the time of the Second World War, with the full entry of America into world politics, to what might be termed a new Anglophone imperialism and internationalism. The future, not just of English, but of European, culture was now at stake, and what better way to ensure its survival, indeed its continuing dominance, than to extend the institutionalization of its study as far as possible? The result was a new attention on both sides of the Atlantic to that 'great tradition', particularly (though not exclusively) to that major part of the tradition written in English, and the institutionalization of it in a 'core curriculum' of canonical texts. What had the Second World War been fought for, after all?

This demographic broadening of the universities, which brought a new lower middle class into contact with high culture, also invited the democratization of its pedagogical transmission in the form of a new equality before the text, the 'words on the page'. The possession of 'culture' now consisted not in the ownership of its material productions, in the form of first editions, original paintings and artefacts—its actual well-wrought urns—but of its reproducible essence, its words and ideas, now more widely available than ever, owing to the technological innovations of cheap paperback editions and anthologies, of prints and slides, ultimately even of microfilm, photo-printing and copying, all enabling the education of large numbers of students of limited means. No longer was it necessary to be of the same privileged social class as one's father and grandfather to gain access to 'culture' and a place in its institutions. Both the technicist professionalism of new criticism and the cultural elitism of practical criticism were newly meritocratic, and in so far as they were in principle open to all, potentially democratic.

The ownership of the means of cultural production—and I am talking here of 'high' culture—had passed from the hands of aristocrats and amateurs into the hands of professionals. Within the politics of newly professionalized literary study in this century, the rise to prominence of Eliot and Pound can be partly explained by their enactment of these wider cultural shifts. Their poetic careers, moving as they had from the provincial periphery to the metropolitan centre, exemplified the imperial extension of high Anglophone culture under the *pax americana*. Cleanth Brooks and Robert Penn Warren enacted an analogous career within the American university system, linking the vernacular South—Brooks wrote his Ph.D. thesis on Louisiana dialects—with one of the traditional centres of aristocratic New England culture.

But this redrawing of the world-cultural map also put into question the very idea of a 'centre', of a stable source of values and reliable point of reference to anchor the cultural system. Hence the new-critical need and anxiety to reclaim a 'centre' out of post-war cultural displacement, a totality out of fragmentation, a tradition capable of accommodating the emerging individual talents to whom a *carrière* was now *ouverte*. And hence the new-critical rhetoric, much of it supplied by Eliot, of 'organic unity', 'unified sensibility', 'tradition and the individual talent', as well as the resurrection of such older concepts as Johnson's *discordia concors* and Hegel's 'concrete universal', as the distinguishing features of literary language. As all of these crucial and recurrent terms suggest, new and practical criticism effectively re-situated literature in all its component parts within a unified field, what Frank Kermode (following Eliot) has called 'the classic' vision.

Within the re-defined *romanitas* of the classic vision,

vernacular outposts retain an organic relation, across history and geography, to an imperial centre and totality.[11] The metaphysical poets were especially valuable in this enterprise, both to the modernist poets who promoted them and to the professional critics who disseminated knowledge of their work through publication and pedagogy. (The connections between literary modernism and the new academic professionalism have yet to be closely inspected.) After all, the 'metaphysicals' were intellectually difficult, flaunting their curious learning and scholastic logic, thereby demanding the services of professional academics (recall the 'school' of Donne); yet their vernacular Englishness and moderate Anglicanism could be pressed into the service of a new Anglophone imperialism supposedly continuous with the *romanitas* of classical and medieval Europe—as opposed to the more apocalyptic, nonconformist, and introspective visions of Milton and the romantics.

Metaphysical poetry was supposed to exemplify a restored univocality of the sign, termed at the time 'enactment' or 'realization'. In such new-critical commonplaces as 'for Donne and the metaphysicals thought and feeling were experienced as one', or 'the poem is an instance of the doctrine which it asserts . . . both an assertion and a realization of that assertion,'[12] the longing becomes apparent for that recovered fit between signifier and signified which might now be derided as a version of 'logocentric self-presence', but which was then supposed to have obtained before the 'dissociation of sensibility' set in with the Civil War and the rise of empirical science in the seventeenth century. The historical breach of this post-metaphysical fall from grace was at last to be repaired; from the one side, by a new poetry which would recover the metaphysical condition of univocal meaning, and from the other by a new criticism which would make that older univocality available in the present by teaching its continuity with that of the new poetry.

The study of these past masters was thus meant to reveal, again in Eliot's phrase, the 'simultaneous existence' and 'simultaneous order' of a European tradition within which the scattered and democratic present could find a place.[13] As his terms suggest, the spatialization of literary history was crucial to its idealization. At the same time, a new imperial history of types and prefigurations—not altogether unlike those of the 'Tudor Myth' itself—which emphasized the continuity of past with present, came to rival if not quite replace an older empirical historicism in which the difference and alterity of the past had been foregrounded. Such seminal works of canon-formation as *The Great Tradition* and *The Well-Wrought Urn*, while preserving a chronological sequence, treat the texts they take up as exemplary and eternal, as if they were written yesterday under the sign of an eternal present.

Yet the new-critical contraction of context to text and history to tradition, whatever its own contextual motivations, was not performed without the co-operation of its chosen texts. For example, Cleanth Brooks's reading of Donne's 'Canonisation', through which he reconstructs the history of English poetry into a self-contained, well-wrought language of paradox, finds ample pretext in the poem's construction of Donne's personal history. It goes by no means against the grain of the text, which wilfully substitutes hagiography for biography and textuality for history:

> We can die by it, if not live by love,
> And if unfit for tombs and hearse
> Our legend be, it will be fit for verse;
> And if no piece of chronicle we prove,
> We'll build in sonnets pretty rooms;
> As well a well-wrought urn becomes
> the greatest ashes, as half-acre tombs,
> And by these hymns, all shall approve
> Us canonised for love.[14]

Here is a 'transcendental reduction' if ever there was one, a radical bracketing-off of consciousness from the surrounding buzz of worldly activity.

'The Canonisation', like 'The Sun Rising', 'The Good Morrow', and the *Songs and Sonnets* generally, posits a self-

[13] See T. S. Eliot's 'Tradition and the Individual Talent', in *Selected Essays*, 3rd edn. (London: Faber, 1951).
[14] My text throughout is *The Elegies and the Sonnets*, ed. Helen Gardner (Oxford: Clarendon Press, 1965), with spelling and punctuation modernized.

transcendentalization analogous to the new critics' activity of canon-formation, and an exclusion of the *faits divers* that history or biography might be expected to include. However, such mundane considerations are not entirely excluded from the poem, only demoted in prominence. They are mentioned explicitly in the business of getting 'a place', a royal audience, money; in the evocations of plague, wars, legal process, tombs —but only to be downgraded or dismissed just as explicitly. 'And if no piece of chronicle we prove,' as Donne neatly sums up his sublimation of the biographical to the literary–amatory self, 'We'll build in sonnets pretty rooms.'

The poetic 'contraction' of 'the whole world's soule' into a 'pattern' and 'epitome' thus prefigure what Brooks and the new critics have done with the poem. Even in those poems, such as 'A Nocturnal upon St Lucy's Day', in which the theme is despair rather than triumph, the transcendence of history and biography is still the explicit project, in this case a negative transcendence, as Donne transforms himself into 'every dead thing | In whom love wrought new alchemy'. 'His art'— Donne's as well as Love's—'did express | A quintessence even from nothingness . . . and I am re-begot | Of absence, darkness, death; things which are not.' Why Donne should be driven to such desperate measures is not made clear in the new-critical account, any more than it is in the poem. What does emerge clearly is the will to dehistoricize and decontextualize the self, which provides the pretext and justification for the later new-critical project. The new critics were nothing if not attentive readers.

THE CONTEXT IN ITSELF

What the new historicists have done is to find and foreground a historical and psycho-biographical context to explain Donne's disposition to construct the text of the self and the self of the text in this manner. And they find it in the system of social and literary patronage within which Elizabethan love poetry is inscribed. The sonnet—so the argument runs—matures slowly in Tudor England, but comes to its climax with the posthumous publication of Sidney's *Astrophil and Stella* in 1591, which begat no fewer than twenty sonnet sequences by the end of Elizabeth's reign. Throughout this development, the language of frustrated love became a highly refined and intricate language for the encoded expression of frustrated ambition, which for political reasons could not be expressed directly. An elaborate vocabulary of 'desire', 'languishment', 'rivalry', 'favour', 'banishment', and 'disappointment' served to link apparently distinct spheres of activity, sexual and social, in a common discourse.

'In the thematics of the sonnet sequence,' as Arthur Marotti epitomizes the new-historicist argument, 'erotic desires for the sexual favours of a Petrarchan mistress (whose conditions for loving explicitly forbid such yielding) is the amorous analogue of the poet's political wilfullness.'[15] The expressive potential of the sonnet sequence thus depends on a system of cultural connotation very different from the prelapsarian univocality dreamed of by the new critics. The sonnet's capacity to resonate in different social registers at one and the same time is brought to a fine state of tune by Sidney, a minor aristocrat whose failure to enhance his social position through marriage becomes the unstated, but eloquent, subtext of *Astrophil and Stella*. But it is in the poetry of Donne and Shakespeare that the 'heteroglossia' characteristic of the sonnet-form finds its realization.

In the case of Donne, what the new historicists discover is not a unified sensibility but a disintegrated personality. A talented and ambitious child of the middle class, Donne had been educated as a Catholic, and was thereby excluded from public office. Having overcome this obstacle to his social advancement by adopting the Church of England, he became secretary to Sir Thomas Egerton. He then made the disastrous error of marrying his patron's niece without his consent, indeed, against his will. Thus began a ten-year period during which he repeatedly tried and failed to regain aristocratic and court favour. 'I died ten years ago', he wrote in a letter, employing a phrase that will remind all readers of the *Songs and Sonnets* of one of the more notorious Elizabethan sexual puns. But in Donne's case this pun is eminently accountable, and its account is the *Songs and Sonnets*, written during the period 'in the wilderness' before Donne regained office, but only, in accordance with James's own sense of poetic justice, within the Church.

[15] Marotti, 'Love is not Love', p. 404.

What was 'background' has been upgraded to 'foreground' and what was 'context' has infiltrated the 'text'. Within the context of the breakdown of patronage—equivalent within Donne's psychology to the breakdown of the self—his love poetry takes on a hitherto unsuspected mordancy and pathos. And viewed in the light of his failed public career, the 'universal monarchy of wit' over which Donne rules as poet–lover becomes a compensatory fantasy, a fulfillment in the poetic realm of a will to power frustrated in the social realm. Denied position within the system of patronage, Donne responds by deconstructing in verse the constitutive oppositions of that system and inverting their implicit privilege. In such poems as 'The Canonisation', 'The Sun Rising', and 'The Good Morrow', the conventionally inferior terms in the oppositions 'Public/private', or 'business/pleasure', now constitute a poetic and erotic subjectivity set over and against the terms of the court and mercantile world. The success of Donne's rhetorical project of 'self-fashioning', to adopt Stephen Greenblatt's term, is inversely proportional to that of his social project. Yet Donne's rhetorical demotion of the public world remains clearly determined by it, albeit negatively determined.

Alternatively, Donne sometimes expresses the personal consequences of his 'ruined fortunes' and social marginalization in a rhetoric of self-negation verging on psychopathology, as in 'A Nocturnal upon St Lucy's Day' or 'Twickenham Garden'. This low note, this sense of utter and complete worthlessness, is also sounded in his religious poetry, his sermons, letters, and voluminous treatise on suicide. On the one hand, 'She is all states, and all princes, I; | Nothing else is,' and on the other, 'I am re-begot | Of absence, darkness, death; things which are not.' These contradictory mentalities succeed one another in a psycho-poetic process that finds no new synthesis or re-integration—not even in his religious poetry, where analogous feelings of hope and hopelessness similarly alternate. Undone indeed.

As must already be apparent, the new-historicist reading of Donne's poetry attempts to supply the motivation missing from the new-critical account of it by re-inscribing the poetry within a distinctly Elizabethan context. Yet paradoxically, this new-historicist move illustrates not so much that politicized model of interpretation, in which different communities of readers constitute different texts through their respective reading practices, as it does the model of 'citational grafting' advanced by Jacques Derrida, in which the same text becomes endlessly re-interpretable by offering itself for unlimited re-contextual-ization.[16] I say this, because there is little disagreement in this case between new critics and newer historicists over what they perceive the text to be and to be up to, at least at the level of its manifest content. For both schools, the *Songs and Sonnets* display a virtuoso performance of paradoxical wit, through which the self is effectively replaced by a fiction. It is only when this self-textualization is 'cited', in Derrida's term, 'grafted' into a context, that disagreement arises over its meaning.

The disagreement arises not because they are reading differ-ent texts—in fact, they see the same operations at work in the text—nor even because they employ different 'strategies' of reading—for both have made the move of contextualization—but because of the particular contexts into which the text has been grafted in each case, and the different meaning it acquires in consequence. This last point may be obvious in the case of the new historicists, who announce themselves as contextualists from the beginning, but it is no less true, if less obvious, in the case of the new critics, who regarded themselves, and are still widely regarded, as textual puritans who derive the meanings of the texts they read only from the 'words on the page'. Yet the constellation of those classic texts into the canon or great tradition of English and European literature, the 'simultaneous order' hypostatized by Eliot, was itself a contextualization, albeit one that concealed its own historical motivations from itself in the interest of an imperializing timelessness and uni-versality. It is only from within this 'textualist context' as it were—the humanist and idealist construct that the new critics called 'tradition'—that the motivation for Donne's construction of himself as monarch of wit remains unexamined or invisible.

The very congruence between Donne's will to universalize himself and the new critics' will to do the same for his poetry is precisely what prevents them from recognizing, or even seeing, the ideological nature of both constructions. The undeniable

---

[16] Derrida, 'Signature Event Context', pp. 312–21.

rhetorical mastery Donne displays in his project of self-sublima-
tion entails a rhetorical violence (clearly perceived, though not
explored, by Dr Johnson in his famous definition of metaphysical wit) that the new critics, engaged upon their own
imperialist project of yoking heterogeneous objects by violence
together, were not in a position to notice, precisely because it
was their own position. Enclosed as they were within a humanist
essentialism—the 'simultaneous order' of text and tradition—
that remained pre-Freudian, pre-Marxian, and pre-
Nietszchean, the new critics had neither a will nor a way to
name the violence that all such rhetorical mastery—Donne's
and their own—entails and conceals, let alone to explain it.

The new historicists, as beneficiaries of the paradigm-shift
called post-structuralism, are in a position to regard Donne's
self-textualization as a recurrent dream, and the new critics'
transcendentalization of it as a kind of repetition-compulsion.
For just as the love poet is compelled to go on producing himself
as monarch of wit by exercising that mastery in the discourse-
domain of love which had been denied him in the public
domain, so the new critics are doomed by their enclosure within
the system of the text to reproduce its operations at the level of
critical ideology. The new historicists do not deny the manifest
content of Donne's recurrent dream, but treat it as part of a
larger system that includes the motives and interests that
generate it. The latent content of a repressed and traumatic
personal history now becomes its primary meaning, and for a
time of political opposition or scepticism, its present, if not its
'real', meaning.

The rhetorical mastery—and violence—of Donne's self-
textualization into the free and autonomous subject that in a
historical and biographical sense he most certainly was not
becomes the compensatory, inverse expression of that socially
sanctioned violence of which Donne was the object. By interpreting Donne from outside his constructed system—though
very much from inside another system—the new historicists
are in a position to attend to what he does not and cannot say
and to explain how that moves him to say what he does. Or, to
put the matter another way, to understand how what Donne
does not and cannot name—the precarious system of
Elizabethan patronage—at once says and unsays Donne. In

any case, context now ventriloquizes text; Elizabethan social relations speak Donne; his meaning is its meaning; the illusion of the text in itself—or of the 'self' in itself for that matter—has dissolved back into the historical context in itself that generated it in the first place.

THE CONTEXT IN QUESTION

But which 'context in itself' are we discussing? The context of production or the context of reception? Where does Donne's context end and the interpreter's begin? For surely by the principles of new-historicist analysis the culture within which the text was produced, like that in which it is received and read, is itself constituted by many overlapping contexts, whose discourses now blend in complex counterpoint, now clash, now resonate, in a veritable harmony—or is it a hum?—of heteroglossia. Which of these do we identify as the authentic historical context, or the appropriate discursive formation, of the text in question? How do we go about recognizing it? And what contextual forces determine our selection and construction of that historical context? I am not trying to make things any more difficult than they are, or to invent problems where none exist, by raising rhetorical or academic questions. Every one of these questions must be decided at some level before any contextual interpretation could ever take place, in order that it can take place.

So how are they decided? At least in part by the text. For at this point the text, recently repressed by its context, pipes up again, and whispers some clues as to which discursive context we might be wise to attend to. It is the text that suggests, through its own words and phrases ('my ruined fortunes flout'; 'get you a place'), the court discourse outside it with which it is in one-sided dialogue, and back into which it can be reinserted to foreground meanings hitherto relegated to the 'background' of the poem or the footnotes at the bottom of the page. It is the text that up to a point still determines, indeed *overdetermines*, the question of which reconstructible context it can be inserted into to produce multiple meanings. The uncanny productivity of the text may thus turn the tables on every attempt to restrict its meaning to that of a single, allegedly privileged or authentic context—be it that of the new critics or that of the new historicists.

This is an effect of what Derrida terms the 'iterability' of the signifier and the infinite potential for 'citational grafting' that follows from it:

This is the possibility on which I wish to insist: the possibility of extraction and of citational grafting which belongs to the structure of every mark as writing even before and outside every horizon of semiolinguistic communication: as writing, that is, as a possibility of functioning cut off, at a certain point, from its 'original' meaning and from its belonging to a saturable and constraining context. Every sign, linguistic or nonlinguistic, spoken or written (in the usual sense of the opposition), as a small or large unity, can be cited, put between quotation marks; thereby it can break with every given context, and engender infinitely new contexts in an absolutely nonsaturable fashion. This does not suppose that the mark is valid outside its context, but on the contrary that there are only contexts without any center of absolute anchoring.[17]

Lest this insistence on the infinite recontextualizability of the text seem to contradict Derrida's more characteristic insistence on an arch-textualism that knows no outside, it should be pointed out that 'context' is here subject to the same process of recontextualization that conditions the 'text'. The statement that 'there are only contexts without any center of absolute anchoring' is perfectly consistent with his more notorious dictum that 'there is nothing outside the text',[18] since any attempt to cite or construct a context is to regard or render it as a text.

But surely Derrida's rigorous insistence on the limitless capacity of the text to be meaningfully recontextualized is, like so much of his thought, counter-intuitive in the extreme. Are there no cultural and historical, i.e. contextual, limitations on this capacity? Can all meanings be possible at any particular moment? It is precisely to limit this infinite 'freeplay', this radical flotation of the signifier, that some means of policing interpretive practice has always been felt necessary. For the new critics the criterion of valid interpretation had been the

[17] Derrida, 'Signature Event Context', p. 320.
[18] Derrida, *Of Grammatology*, trans. Gayatri Chakravorty Spivak (Baltimore: Johns Hopkins University Press, 1976), 158.

text itself, the words on the page; only those interpretations that could be referred back to their arbitration, and be justified by them, would be considered valid. For succeeding contextualists, the constraints are to be found rather in the institutional and cultural norms and practices always already in place, within which a given meaning would take or be rejected by the body politic, like a transplanted organ.

Thus Tony Bennett proposes that Derrida's principle of the 'iterability' of the text be renamed its 'inscribeability', thereby suggesting the resistance in the form of an historical formation always already in place, into which the text has to be cut in order to make its mark, and which may reject its imprint or implanting.[19] Similarly, Terry Eagleton, while thinking he disagrees with Bennett on the existence of the text in itself, is in complete agreement with him that prior social conditions and constraints make certain textual meanings more or less viable, if not more or less possible, than others:

We can choose to see *Macbeth* as being about Scottish kingship or Manchester United, but we cannot choose to see the Arden edition of the play as a wombat, unlike some other culture which totemised its text. Some of our interpretations are so entrenched as to be for the moment ineluctable—not in the sense that we cannot decide to violate or transgress them, but in the sense that we cannot at present escape their force in the very act of doing so.[20]

In positing such a choice in order to reject it, Eagleton may seriously underestimate at once the resourcefulness of textual interpreters and the multiplicity of contextual determinations in place at any given moment. Eagleton—and Bennett as well—write from within what Derrida terms the 'horizon of semiolinguistic communication', *as if that horizon were fixed and untranscendable and effectively exhausted all interpretive options in the present.*

But the history of interpretation suggests that this is not quite the case—dominant interpretations *do* change suddenly and drastically—and Derrida has theorized why it is not. In posing his alternatives for interpreting *Macbeth*, Eagleton puts forward two options that would be culturally possible and one that would be impossible. Yet Eagleton himself can

[19] Bennett, 'The Bond Phenomenon', p. 221.
[20] 'The Text in Itself', p. 118.

imagine a cultural context—that of Australian Aborigines, for example—within which the Arden edition of *Macbeth* might just signify a wombat. This context is not much harder to imagine than that of, say, Craig Johnston reviewing a performance of the play in *Soccer Today*, and seeing *Macbeth* as an allegory of Manchester United. In the wake of John Kennedy's assassination, *Macbeth* was in fact reproduced as *Macbird* and re-interpreted to be about the assassination, with great box-office success. As for 'Scottish kingship', it is true that some old historicists have thought the play to be about it, but I doubt whether many new historicists would pursue this option. The *English* kingship of Shakespeare's time—which, at the moment of *Macbeth* was also Scottish—seems a more likely candidate. The most likely contextual option of all is the one that enables us to recognize in the text a figuration of our own historical and cultural situation, as any producer of *Macbeth* for the Royal Shakespeare Company is bound to attest.

For this is precisely what the non-canonical, as distinct from the canonical, interpretation of the canonical text is always about. It goes against the grain of prevailing notions of the cultural or institutional context that work to constrain its reading, 'the semiolinguistic horizon of communication', and grafts the text into a context that might well seem at the time novel, counter-intuitive, or downright improbable but was, at least in retrospect, always already available. After all, today's nonsense is tomorrow's common sense, and vice versa. This is, of course, precisely what Derrida has done on an extravagant scale—this is what paradigm-shifts are about—and what the new historicists have done more modestly. They have constructed a 'new' historical context, a post-structuralist version of the politics and psychology of Elizabethan patronage, to replace the older new-critical context of a simultaneous order in which wit and love, thought and feeling, were one; and by grafting Donne's poetry into this newly constructed context, made that poetry newly meaningful.

The important point for our own purposes—and for Donne's poetry—is that this new historical context is not, as some of those who wield it might maintain, discovered as some pre-existing, authentic, indeed 'real', set of conditions newly brought to light, but is decidedly *constructed*, and constructed in response to a *contemporary* cultural climate quite different from the one in which the new critics constructed their own interpretive context. For the new historicists are working on the other side of the historical slope from the new critics. They are reinterpreting the canon within the breakdown of a world-historical order that reached its height in the *pax americana* that followed the Second World War. That order threw up its own patronage system in the form of the newly expanded and professionalized university system within which the new critics flourished and the canon, the 'great tradition', was finally and fully established.

For the past two decades, coinciding with the rise of poststructuralist theory, that older ideology of cultural imperialism and its system of academic patronage have arguably been breaking down, and with them their construction of the canon. It is difficult for younger academics to read the canon of English literature in anything like the same spirit as their new-critical teachers, as if this latest *translatio imperii* and the ideology of what might be termed 'Anglophonocentrism' that supported its idealist readings were still securely in place. Instead, they have constructed a new interpretive context for literary study that vibrates sympathetically with their present sense of increasing precariousness and marginality, cultural and institutional. This could not have been done without the help of the decentring and demystifying techniques of post-structuralist methodology, itself the by-product of that institutional and cultural breakdown. Love may not be love, any more than Scottish history is Scottish history, but neither are they merely *Elizabethan* matters.

6

Marlowe our Contemporary

Nor can we ever rid ourselves entirely of our own time and
personality. As soon as history approaches our thinking
and working selves, we find everything more 'interesting'.
In fact it is we who are more interested.

(Jacob Burckhardt, *Reflections on History*)

THE OLD HISTORICISM AND THE NEW

My point of departure is a recent essay by Stephen Greenblatt
entitled 'Marlowe and the Will to Absolute Play', a strong
reading of Marlowe's plays and a strong showing in the current
struggle for the repossession of Renaissance literature in the
name of a new historicism.[1] In spite—indeed because—of
its strength, and that of the movement it spearheads, I want
to take issue with Greenblatt's reading and with the new-
historicist understanding that supports it. I hasten to point
out that the present essay is not meant as a corrective to
Greenblatt's, either at the level of interpretation or at that of
theory. I am not suggesting, that is, that Greenblatt has taken a
wrong turn within his approach to the plays—though this may
seem to be the case at a certain point—or a wrongheaded
approach to them from the outset. My purpose is not to
invalidate Greenblatt's new historicism or its application to
Marlowe but to deprivilege it; or more precisely to dispute its
own covert claim to interpretive privilege by revealing the
repressions necessary to enable that claim to be made.

So the following observations are offered more as a supple-
ment than as a corrective; they attempt to articulate the

[1] See Stephen Greenblatt, *Renaissance Self-Fashioning: From More to Shakespeare*
(Chicago: University of Chicago Press, 1980). Something of the historical background,
critical practices, and institutional implications of the new historicism is sketched out
by Jean E. Howard, 'The New Historicism in Renaissance Studies', *English Literary
Renaissance*, 16/1 (Winter 1986), 13–43.

shadow-side of a sympathetic, even shared, enterprise: what Greenblatt saw without seeing and knew without being able to take into account, the 'unspoken other' of his discourse.[2] That 'other' is, as we shall see, a political as well as a philosophical matter, and in attempting to uncover it here, I admit to a political motive of my own: to make room within the spreading institutional hegemony of the new historicism for a different kind of reading, one only too often regarded from within this latest regime as ideologically unsound and politically suspect. That is a pity, to say the least, because the new historicism, in both its American and British manifestations, still has much to learn from its deconstructive 'other'.

Hence the need to question the principles and practices on which the new historicism is proceeding before they have the effect of proscribing every alternative, particularly more openly 'metaphysical' readings of Renaissance texts. Such readings, I shall argue, are not only no less philosophically valid than their own but play a conscientious and productive institutional role in relation to them. The particular reading of Marlowe I have in mind, for which the present essay is meant to clear the way, stands in just such a dialogic relation to Greenblatt's reading. It is entitled 'Marlowe and the Will to Authentic Being'. In the difference between 'absolute play' and 'authentic being' as the object of the Marlovian will and the project of his plays, my entire argument with Greenblatt's new historicism is fore-shadowed, and an appeal opened from an historical and cultural to a more philosophical criticism.

Now, having charged Greenblatt with illicitly privileging his new-historicist reading of Marlowe, I am bound to account for my revision of his title and re-naming of Marlowe's project as something other than a wilful or arbitrary inversion of Greenblatt's reading, with its own implicit and no less illicit claim to privilege. For neither of us is permitted by the logic of our respective post-structuralisms to believe in interpretive privilege, in the inbuilt advantage of one interpretive strategy over another in disclosing a 'real' or 'authentic' textual meaning hitherto obscured to our blind and blundering predecessors—not even (especially not) when the strategy and meaning in

[2] The concept is Mikhail Bakhtin's. See Katerina Clark and Michael Holquist, *Mikhail Bakhtin* (Cambridge, Mass.: Harvard University Press, 1984), 197–211.

question are our own. This is not by virtue of any particular personal modesty, false or sincere, of the kind expressed in acknowledgement pages ('we are pygmies standing on giants' shoulders'); nor is it by reason of any liberal-democratic belief in the value of individualism or pluralism in interpretation ('all interpretations have a right to exist, and are to that extent more or less right—let a thousand flowers bloom').

It is the case, rather, because post-structuralism, in both its contextualist (or new-historicist) and its textualist (or deconstructive) versions, is not, philosophically speaking, a 'realism' at all, but a 'conventionalism'.[3] That is to say, post-structuralism does not posit as its object of knowledge a text whose meaning exists independently of our terms and methods of inquiry into it, or in current parlance, of our construction of it. In this respect, post-structuralism is fundamentally different from such epistemological and methodological 'realisms' as scientific empiricism and historical Marxism on the one hand, and also from the more extreme 'conventionalism' of structuralist poetics and cultural semiotics on the other, whose textual dealings are entirely definitional and aprioristic.

Post-structuralism, by contrast, proceeds on the understanding that language is, and hence all texts are, multivocal, plurisignificant, polymorphous, so that any attempt to restrict textual productivity to a single meaning, claimed to be 'real' or 'true', 'authentic' or 'autonomous', arises not from the side of the text but from that of its interpreters or the interpretive communities that take it up. Such interpretive claims are always a function or illusion of a will to power over the text, even when they are made by the author him/herself. The shifting into place, under historical pressures, of a new set of collective presuppositions, a change of institutional ground rules and interpretive grid, changes the object of knowledge according to the new conventions of inquiry. It throws different texts into and out of scrutiny and esteem, and makes visible previously unseen or unforegrounded meanings in the same texts. But because of the very historicity of this process of

---

[3] For a rigorous discrimination of 'conventionalism' from 'realism' and 'empiricism', see Terry Lovell, *Pictures of Reality: Aesthetics, Politics, Pleasure* (London: British Film Institute, 1980), 9–28.

becoming visible, thinkable, and sayable, those meanings may well be new but can never be 'true' or 'real', 'authentic' or 'autonomous', in any transhistorical sense.

All such claims to privilege are made, and sometimes enjoyed, by grace and power of the ruling or dominant paradigm that made them thinkable, which changes soon enough from that of the context of production of the text to those of its contexts of reception. The very notion of a 'will to absolute play', or for that matter a 'will to authentic being', as the project of Marlowe's plays would have been unthinkable and unspeakable to Marlowe and his contemporaries, not because such concepts are from an Elizabethan viewpoint shameful or even heretical—this might well have recommended them to Marlowe—but because the discursive formation, the conceptual framework, within which such terms might have made sense to him did not yet exist. So the question arises, what is a new historicist like Greenblatt doing when he anachronistically foregrounds 'absolute play' as the Marlovian project? Or for that matter, what is a deconstructionist like myself doing when he urges a shift of focus to its 'other', something so apparently contrary, but no less anachronistic, as 'authentic being'?

What we are certainly not doing, and should not delude ourselves that we are doing, is identifying either of these notions as the 'real' or 'authentic' meaning of Marlowe's plays, in the sense of an *historical* meaning, either that which Marlowe intended to convey through them or that which contemporary audiences and readers might have found in them. That is what the 'old historicism' was about. Operating as a late, empirical development of nineteenth-century hermeneutics, it identified the meaning of the literary text with the author's intention and his historical culture's understanding of it, the adequation of the one to the other being assumed in a successful work. For the old historicism language presented no problem; or, more accurately, it presented only philological problems, in so far as these were perceived as arising, not from a fundamental semiotic slippage, multiplicity, or excess, but from the contingencies of historical distance and alterity. Language itself was not yet conceived as intrinsically problematic above and beyond historical languages, and was in principle transparent to the point of invisibility. Problems concerning authorial intention, later to trouble literary criticism, were thus radically contained by this assumption of linguistic transparency.

Intention, the goal of the old historicism, was pre-textual and extra-linguistic, since it was located in the mind of the author, on which the text was potentially a transparent window once the operations of its historical idiom were mastered and knowledge of his historical situation acquired. Even when intention was not clearly accessible in the text or was a matter of contention, it could still be corroborated or triangulated by comparing other historical and biographical evidence—the author's letters, his annotations of his sources, his other writings, or those of his contemporaries. Thus confined and stabilized within the enclosure of an historical culture's self-presence, or an historical mind's self-understanding, confined, that is, within the presumed coherence of this perfect circle of communication, the meaning of the text could be exhumed and established once and for all time through the painstaking methods of empirical research. Reliable, positive knowledge of the literary past, like that of the historical past with which it was contiguous, could be built up and filled out bit by bit, until it was complete.

For the old historicism, unlike the new, *was a 'realism'*; its object was a knowledge that, once ascertained, was supposed to be independent of its methods of inquiry, which were modelled, after all, as closely as possible on those of nineteenth-century empirical science. Its methods, that is, were objective, so it could yield authentic knowledge of the other, of the other *as* other, untransformed and unappropriated by the language of the self. For such knowledge was based on objective evidence, the best of which was the author's actual writings; what would correspond in empirical science to direct sense-data gleaned from the phenomenon under investigation. This was primary and carried, naturally enough, the greatest weight and authority.

But a great deal of secondary evidence, ranging from contemporary allusions and anecdotes to other accounts—put together by analogous means—of the political, intellectual, and social history of the time, was also admissible, once duly analysed and weighed, as it bore upon intention and meaning. For anything close to the author in time and place was potentially meaningful, or metonymic of meaning, proximity to the work's point of origin in the mind of its author being the overriding criterion of value and validity, in a word, of 'authority'. Through its act of approximation across time and distance to this supposed point of origin, historical criticism could then appropriate to itself something of the same authority to support its claim to interpretive validity and privilege. It was 'true', at least 'truer' than any other interpretation, because it was historical.[4]

Now some new historicists, pre-eminently Greenblatt, recognize the hermeneutic hybris of attempting to maintain this privileged position and the hermeneutic hazards that beset any attempt to make contact with, or even approach, the text's point of origin in the past. This is the case for two fundamental reasons, both of which Greenblatt raises directly. One is the problem of present appropriation we have already touched upon, of accessing the other in the language of the self without turning it into the self. 'If cultural poetics is conscious of its status as interpretation', he writes, 'this consciousness must extend to an acceptance of the impossibility of fully reconstructing and re-entering the culture of the sixteenth century, of leaving behind one's own situation . . . The questions I ask of my material', he goes on to realize, 'and indeed the very nature of this material are shaped by the questions I ask of myself.'[5]

Having identified, but without fully addressing, the problem of 'these impurities', Greenblatt raises the second, equally serious problem, what might be termed the problem of past elusiveness:

Each of these texts is viewed as the focal point for converging lines of force in sixteenth-century culture . . . Their significance for us is not that we may see *through* them to underlying and prior historical principles but rather that we may interpret the interplay of their symbolic structures with those perceivable in the careers of their

[4] I am doubtless oversimplifying the 'old' historicism, for the purposes of exposition, by reducing it to a basically Schleiermachian position. The full range of positions and operations bequeathed by the tradition of German hermeneutic philosophy, particularly as they pertain to literary criticism, is usefully unfolded by Richard E. Palmer, *Hermeneutics* (Evanston: Northwestern University Press, 1969); see also E. D. Hirsch, *Validity in Interpretation* (New Haven: Yale University Press, 1967).

[5] Greenblatt, *Renaissance Self-Fashioning*, p. 4.

authors and in the larger social world as constituting a single, complex process of self-fashioning.[6]

At this point the full conventionalism of the new historicism, as distinct from the realism of the old, becomes almost explicit. Greenblatt does not imagine himself seeing *through* the text 'to underlying and prior historical principles', in other words to that which is objectively, independently, and 'really' there, but seeing in the text 'symbolic structures' whose relation to other symbolic structures in the life and society of the author (whose mode of existence is also presumably textual) is not one of direct correspondence or perfect coherence but one of 'interplay'.

Greenblatt's syntax here, uncharacteristically and significantly, is less than transparent, but he seems to be saying that his encounter with historical texts yields not real authorial intentions or cultural meanings but 'constructions' built upon some prior and deeper and ultimately unknowable reality and more or less incoherent among themselves. These symbolic structures, that is, are always already divergent and detached from what they symbolize, at 'play' with it and with one another, and thereby requiring further interpretation. Their relation to 'underlying and prior' historical principles—which may not be available or ascertainable at all—is elusive and untrustworthy, in something like the way rhetoric is in relation to logic, or ideology is *vis-à-vis* history, or manifest to latent dream-content is traditionally conceived. For as in the case of each of these analogues, such structures may well be cunningly, or unconsciously, contrived by author and culture to conceal a deeper, potentially threatening, knowledge from others—or even from themselves.

Such methodological circumspection is only to be expected from a historicism too well read in modern social and psychoanalytic theory to view historical cultures as fully transparent or coherent articulations of data and documents to be read off unproblematically; and one at the same time too well read in modern critical theory, too attuned to the duplicities of language, power, and ideology, to make bald claims for its own historical certitude and interpretive authority. For this is a

---

[6] Greenblatt, *Renaissance Self-Fashioning*, pp 5–6.

'hermeneutics of suspicion' if ever there was one. The new historicist, at least this one, may know all this, but such knowledge does not prevent him from going about his business of interpretation as if he did not, and from staking his own claim to interpretive privilege, albeit covertly, in the process. 'I do not shrink from these impurities', Greenblatt writes, 'but I have tried to compensate for the indeterminacy and incompleteness they generate by constantly returning to particular lives and particular situations, to the material necessities and social pressures that men and women daily confronted, and to a small number of resonant texts.'[7]

'Shrink' he most certainly does not from the 'impurities' of method and material he openly acknowledges. But the compensation offered for 'the indeterminacy and incompleteness they generate' may still leave something to be desired, may remain an unfulfilled, indeed unfulfillable, promise. For this 'constant return' to 'particular lives', 'particular situations', 'material necessities', and 'social pressures that men and women daily confronted'—to things that may well seem in their obvious concreteness to subtend or pre-exist textuality altogether—and hence the indeterminacy and incompleteness of textuality—would reinstate a claim to engage with a 'real' historicity prior to and deeper than that which any mere textualism, by Greenblatt's own principles, could ever have made. The return to such pre-textual specificities would certainly be the compensation and corrective necessary to counter the hermeneutic scepticism that he himself feels and acknowledges. The problem is that such specificities are not a pre-textual but still very much a textual matter, and such a 'return', however constant, is not really a return at all. It is rather, as we shall see, a projection, albeit a back-projection.

GREENBLATT'S MARLOWE

The essay on Marlowe richly exemplifies this pattern of proclaimed return to the other and unwitting relapse into the self. Greenblatt begins, according to his promise and usual practice, with a particular life and situation—that is, with a text—in this

---

[7] Ibid., p. 5.

case an eyewitness narrative of an incident that occurred on the West African coast in 1586. The narrator is an English merchant named John Sarracoll. Greenblatt lets him 'tell his own story':

> The fourth of November we went on shore to a town of the Negroes . . . which we found to be but lately built: it was of about two hundred houses, and walled about with mighty great trees, and stakes so thick, that a rat could hardly get in or out. But as it chanced, we came directly upon a port which was not shut up, where we entered with such fierceness, that the people fled all out of the town, which we found to be finely built after their fashion, and the streets of it so intricate that it was difficult for us to find the way out that we came in at. We found their houses and streets so finely and cleanly kept that it was an admiration to us all, for that neither in the houses nor streets was so much dust to be found as would fill an egg shell. We found little in their houses, except some mats, gourds, and some earthen pots. Our men at their departure set the town on fire, and it was burnt (for the most part of it) in a quarter of an hour, the houses being covered with reed and straw.[8]

Remote as it may initially seem from the topic of Marlowe's plays, the passage serves Greenblatt's purposes. With its careful notation of places and dates and matter-of-fact, diaristic style, Sarracoll's account seems to transport us, as it were, into the very presence of the past.

Sarracoll's account is, after all, 'his own story'. Moreover, the spontaneous destruction it reports, if not the tone of its reportage, has a distinctly Marlovian flavour. Well before Greenblatt cites Tamburlaine's burning of the town where Zenocrate dies and Barabas' poisoning of the nunnery that houses his daughter, the student of Marlowe will have brought to mind several analogous moments in the plays. Even the Deptford tavern where Marlowe himself was fatally stabbed a few years later seems, in this connection, uncannily close at hand, not just because it was located only a few miles from the docks at Gravesend whence Sarracoll had embarked, but because of the similarly undermotivated violence of the brawl that took place there, an event that seems in retrospect to have flared up out of almost nothing.

The effect is one of rapidly collapsing perspectives, as vast

---

[6] Greenblatt, *Renaissance Self-Fashioning*, p. 193.

gaps of geographical distance and historical time seem to close at a dizzying pace. 'Interpret me, if you can' is the hermeneutic imperative that cries out to us from between the reticent, riddling lines of Sarracoll's account across the cultural and psychological distance that separates us from it. 'Interpret me, in my radical alterity', it beckons, 'and you will also understand Christopher Marlowe.' After all, they are products of the same culture. Greenblatt can now extract from his hat the rabbit he has so deftly concealed there. 'If', he fancies, 'on returning to England in 1587, the merchant and his associates had gone to see the Lord Admiral's Men perform a new play, *Tamburlaine the Great*, they would have seen an extraordinary meditation on the roots of their own behaviour.'[9]

It is only fair to Greenblatt to acknowledge that getting down to those 'roots', to the heart of the deeply cultural understanding shared between these two Elizabethans, who might well have rubbed shoulders with one another in 1587 at the Theatre, is not in fact made easier or more straightforward by Sarracoll's account. In fact, traditional interpretive priorities are reversed. While he plays up the claim to contemporary actuality of Sarracoll's 'own story' and thus the potential hermeneutic advantage it seems to offer in reading Marlowe, an advantage prized by an older historicism, Greenblatt does not quite forget that it too is a text, and a rather opaque and puzzling one at that. Far from explaining or even illuminating Marlowe's plays by virtue of its temporal and cultural proximity, Sarracoll's account itself stands in need of explanation, for it raises more questions than it answers.

In fact, it is Marlowe who will ultimately be called upon to illuminate Sarracoll. Remarking on its 'casual, unexplained violence' as 'most striking', Greenblatt proceeds to interrogate the merchant's tale:

Does the merchant feel that the firing of the town needs no explanation? If asked, would he have had one to give? Why does he take care to tell us why the town burned so quickly, but not why it was burned? Is there an aesthetic element in his admiration of the town, so finely built, so intricate, so cleanly kept? And does this admiration conflict with or somehow fuel the destructiveness? If he feels no uneasiness at all, why does he suddenly shift and write not *we* but *our men* set

9 Ibid., p. 194.

the town on fire? Was there an order or not? And, when he recalls the invasion, why does he think of rats? The questions are all met by the moral blankness that rests like thick snow on Sarracoll's sentences. 'The 17th day of November we departed from Sierra Leona, directing our course for the Straits of Magellan.'[10]

It is characteristic of new-historicist criticism to pay the same kind of detailed attention to texts formerly considered mere historical background as used to be reserved for the 'literary' foreground. Yet this procedure does not resolve interpretive difficulties. Greenblatt's strategy of return, of letting the merchant 'tell his own story', yields something other than 'a concrete apprehension . . . of a specific form of power'; it yields a series of troubling, unanswered questions.

These questions are troubling, however, not simply becuse they are unanswerable but because they are rhetorical, because we think we know only too well their answers in advance. We certainly know where their answers are likely to be found and the general outline they would take. Where else but in the forestructure of prejudices—Heidegger's and Gadamer's *Vorurteile*—that conditions the expressive possibilities of Sarracoll's description of events, in the unspoken assumptions of the discourse he shares with his contemporaries that enables his utterances to make sense to them without his having to spell everything out.[11] That forestructure of understanding, and the disturbing answers it holds to Greenblatt's questions, he has already telegraphed to us even before raising them when he ironically refers to the 'atypical' absence in the passage of 'the bloodbath that usually climaxes these incidents', and terms it

---

[10] Greenblatt, *Renaissance Self-Fashioning*, p. 194.

[11] The concept of '*Vorurteil*' within the structure of hermeneutic understanding is developed by Martin Heidegger, *Being and Time*, trans. John Macquarrie and Edward Robinson (New York: Harper & Row, 1962), 194–5, and by Hans-Georg Gadamer, *Wahrheit und Methode* (Tübingen: Mohr, 1960). Whereas Heidegger employs the concept in the sense of 'pre-judgement', for Gadamer it takes on the more negative sense of 'prejudice'. While remaining a necessary and even welcome condition of interpretation, the inescapable existence of this forestructure of 'prejudice' changes the criterion of valid interpretation from that of historical authenticity to one of contemporary relevance. In the case of Sarracoll's interpretation of events, we are clearly dealing with 'pre-judgements' that are also very much 'prejudices'. For a critique of Gadamer's position, see Hirsch, *Validity in Interpretation* pp. 245–64; and for a defence of it against Hirsch's (among others') objections, see Joseph J. Kockelmans, 'Toward an Interpretative or Hermeneutic Social Science', *Graduate Faculty Philosophy Journal of New School for Social Research*, 5/1 (Fall 1975), 73–96.

'a reminder of what until recently was called one of the glorious achievements of Renaissance civilisation'.[12]

The 'casual, unexplained violence' that is so striking and the 'moral blankness that rests like thick snow on Sarracoll's sentences' turn out to be explicable before the narrative fact in terms of the prejudices that condition it. Sarracoll does not need to explain or even state these prejudices precisely because they could be taken for granted within the contemporary discourse of colonial and mercantile expansion already in place. One did not need to be a kind of Elizabethan 'snow-man' to think these things after these ways, in an almost Kafkaesque neutrality of tonal register; in fact, there were no Elizabethan snow-men. For many, if not most, of Sarracoll's contemporaries the motives for incinerating an African village, or even for decimating its inhabitants, are too evident to require explanation, as they inhere in the very structure of the discourse in which such events are described.

The village is the fabrication of creatures alienated from that divine authority in whose name English expansionism is carried out and justified. It is the work, that is, of creatures who are not fully human, subhuman at best and demonic at worst; and like the destruction of some prodigious ant-hill, its burning involves no transgression against kind; in fact, there is nothing 'unnatural' about it. Nor is it extraordinary in Elizabethan terms that the fine construction and cleanliness of the town does elicit extended comment from Sarracoll, for given the subhumanity of its builders and occupants, how could these qualities not have struck him as remarkable indeed? And within such a discursive field, is it really surprising that Sarracoll should think of 'rats'?

I have no wish to press this explanation of Sarracoll's narrative exclusions and of his matter-of-fact reserve. To press it much farther would be to fall into the same interpretive realism of which I am accusing Greenblatt. But I trust that he and other new historicists engaged in the archaeology of colonial discourse would not find it invalid, since it merely extends and applies the work they have done. Now, such an explanation must have its own forestructure of understanding, its own

---

[12] Greenblatt, *Renaissance Self-Fashioning*, p. 193.

discursive context. And that would have to be sought, not in the discourse of expansionism presupposed by Sarracoll but in that presupposed by us; not in the context of his production of the text but in our contemporary context of its reception. Greenblatt has already alerted us, after all, that 'the questions I ask of my material, indeed the very nature of this material, are shaped by the questions I ask of myself'. Sarracoll's account is striking and troubling to Greenblatt and to us in precisely the degree to which the forestructure of shared prejudices that condition and constrain its expressive possibilities, that define and permeate its discourse-domain, have changed radically over the past four centuries.

Few would even attempt nowadays to speak as Sarracoll speaks in a discourse of neutral tones; even if they attempted to do so, it would not strike others *as neutral*, any more than Kafka's narrative neutrality, that of *In the Penal Colony* for example, can be so regarded. Our twentieth-century—or *late* twentieth-century—discourse of colonial and mercantile imperialism no longer permits neutral tones, detached observers, or the absence of ulterior motives to exist in good faith within it. So thoroughly anthropologized, Marxified, and Freudianized has it become that whatever innocence, moral and political, it might once have possessed—if only by virtue of there being no alternative, non-Eurocentric discourse—has been lost to it. Or to put the matter the other way round, whatever ideological legitimations it might once have assumed or produced for itself—had it felt the need to do so—are no longer available to it.

More tellingly still, whatever innocence or justification it might once have had is now retrospectively denied to it, as the contemporary guilt of our discourse of imperialism—which can only be felt at the moment of its breakdown—is projected backward on to a past constructed (whether or not new-historicist critics are aware of it) in terms not of cultural alterity but of cultural continuity. Sarracoll troubles us because of our own guilty conscience, our sense of residual complicity with him and his enterprise: we are, after all, still enjoying its fruits. The very idea that there must be a deeper psycho-social structure of motive and meaning underlying Sarracoll's—and Marlowe's—utterances is a projection of the twentieth-century

forestructure of understanding we bring to bear on their utterances, but one not necessarily shared by them. The inescapable
shadow-side of Greenblatt's disarming candour about the questions he asks of his material is that the *answers* he finds in it are
the answers he has already found for himself—with the help,
needless to say, of a great deal of contemporary cultural
prompting.

So a present political motive begins to emerge as part of the
deeper structure of Greenblatt's reading, the tip not of an
iceberg but of a submerged volcano. A politics of decolonization
at once broadly cultural and more narrowly institutional conditions that reading both in its large methodological contours
and in its local exegetical details. Greenblatt does not explore
the submerged politics of his own reading, at least not its
cultural politics and certainly not explicitly—one of the curious
blindnesses of American new-historicist criticism in general.
But the very choice to begin the reading of Marlowe with a text
so understated and pedestrian, yet significant and pregnant for
these same qualities, is also politically strategic in an institutional sense:

> For despite all the exoticism in Marlowe—Scythian shepherds,
> Maltese Jews, German magicians—it is his own countrymen that he
> broods upon and depicts . . . If we want to understand the historical
> matrix of Marlowe's achievement, the analogue to Tamburlaine's
> restlessness, aesthetic sensitivity, appetite, and violence, we might
> look not at the playwright's literary sources, not even at the relentless
> power-hunger of Tudor absolutism, but at the acquisitive energies of
> English merchants, entrepreneurs, and adventurers, promoters alike
> of trading companies and theatrical companies.[13]

Whether or not such lateral attentiveness will achieve the
professed object of understanding, i.e. Marlowe's 'historical
matrix', it is driven by political motives quite remote from
those of Tudor England. The lateral attentiveness Greenblatt
recommends is expicitly opposed to the hierarchical fixation
that has dominated academic study of Elizabethan drama.
Not Marlowe's literary sources, not even the relentless power-
hunger of Tudor absolutism alone—these cynosures of
traditional attention are too bookishly or aristocratically aloof,

---

[13] Greenblatt, *Renaissance Self-Fashioning*, p. 194.

too exclusive, to comprehend the *discordia concors* and *concordia discors* of Marlowe's achievement within a 'historical matrix'.

So something of an inversion of the values and priorities assigned to texts within institutional practice, a programme of textual land-reform or levelling—already announced explicitly in Greenblatt's preface—is on the platform. The high textuality of literary sources and the high drama of Tudor absolutism—those once rich repositories for doctoral dissertations and BBC costume-series respectively—are demoted in hermeneutic privilege and such 'low' textuality as Sarracoll's mundane travelogue, promoted. Foreground becomes background, and background foreground. Or, more accurately in Greenblatt's case, both assume a more egalitarian standing within a reconsistuted ground of historical interpretation. This project of systematic inversion at the level of Greenblatt's own textual and institutional practice, its consistent redistribution of privilege, is, as we shall see, strikingly similar to, yet significantly different from, that deliberate inversion of Elizabethan social process which he discerns or projects in the form of the 'will to absolute play' at the heart of Marlovian drama.

RENAISSANCE CARNIVALESQUE

Common to both Elizabethan social process and the Marlovian inversion or subversion of it is the principle of relentless repetition. On the part of Tudor authority, this takes the form of a systematic deployment of didactic examples designed to secure the political, religious, and moral conformity of potentially wayward subjects. Its counterpart in the careers of Marlowe's protagonists is an equal and opposite display of 'constructive power' exercised in defiance of, or deviation from, those authoritarian structures and directed towards the establishment of an autonomous identity independent of them, 'as if a man were author of himself', as Greenblatt puts it, quoting one of Shakespeare's most Marlovian heroes. The 'repetition-compulsion', through which the Marlovian hero repeats his name and his actions over and over again in the course of his dramatic career, is a dialectical response to a culture in which literature and history are primary media for the inculcation of 'repeatable moral lessons' designed to maintain the reigning orthodoxy.

The theatre is crucial in this process, taking its place within an inescapable array of public spectacles ranging from homilies against rebellion appointed to be read in churches to public hangings and beheadings for a wide variety of offences. These include conspiracy, atheism, and sodomy, the activities through which Marlowe's heroes, and possibly Marlowe himself, enact their ringing reiterations of a difference that sets them above the 'base slaves', the men of common mould, who are defined by obedient subjection—in Marlovian terms, the abjection of not defining themselves at all. Whatever his own beliefs, proclivities, or activities, Marlowe's heroes derive their compulsive energy and project their outsize form in systematic opposition to the rigidity and closure of a social order that leaves little room for deviant or sceptical manœuvre, for what we might call 'self-expression'. It is not that deviance was unthinkable, but, as Greenblatt points out elsewhere, that it was thinkable only as the thought of another, of *the other*; thinkable, that is, surreptitiously, vicariously, or at a relatively safe distance.[14] Surely this is one reason for the exoticism of Marlowe's heroes and settings; closer to home, the 'other' was thinkable only in the mode of denunciation.

This profoundly perverse project, this negative labour of constructing the self in the name of a culturally forbidden and officially proscribed 'other', tacitly affirmed by virtue of its being so proscribed, Greenblatt terms 'the will to play' in Marlowe. And properly understood, the will to play is in no way a misrepresentation of that peculiar dynamic of Marlovian tragedy which underlies and motivates the more particular wills to power, pleasure, wealth, and knowledge that respectively characterize the careers of Tamburlaine, Edward II, The Jew of Malta, and Dr Faustus. The 'will to play' certainly takes us back to themes quintessentially Elizabethan; yet it has distinctly modern connotations as well. The 'will to play' promises to function as an interpretive link between Marlowe's

---

[14] Stephen Greenblatt, 'Invisible Bullets: Renaissance Authority and Its Subversion, *Henry IV* and *Henry V*', in Jonathan Dollimore and Alan Sinfield, eds., *Political Shakespeare* (Manchester: Manchester University Press, 1985), 19.

theatre and culture and our own, a necessary mediation between a Renaissance and a modern anthropology.

Indeed, nothing seems to have been more deeply ingrained in the texture, or more instinct with the structure, of Renaissance social existence than 'play'. As numerous studies have shown, play was elaborately institutionalized in the form of holiday rituals—'carnival', the 'feast of fools', and other saturnalian occasions—which enabled potentially anarchic or threatening energies within culture to be at once expressed and regulated. The point has frequently been made—and Greenblatt is well acquainted with such studies—that Elizabethan drama seems to reinscribe these ritual patterns—'through release to clarification', as C. L. Barber puts it—within its own structure.[15] 'If everyday were playing holiday,' Prince Hal reflects in a play in which such ritualized inversions are pervasive, 'To sport would be as tedious as to work.'

That is of course the social danger posed by Falstaff; and there is a sense in which Marlowe's heroes succeed where Falstaff fails in reversing the cultural priority of everyday to holiday and realizing the ever-present potential of play to overthrow repressive social norms. 'Through release to self-construction' might serve as their revolutionary slogan; for Marlovian monodrama, as Greenblatt and others have made abundantly clear, is also metadrama of a high order, theatre supremely alive to the idea of theatre and to its power to construct, rather than merely imitate or even mediate, 'reality'. So the idea of play, in an anthropological and a metatheatrical sense that are pre-eminently Elizabethan, seems a highly promising point of departure for a new-historicist understanding of the Marlovian project. Yet Greenblatt's reading of the 'will to play' in Marlowe is not confined within any accepted Elizabethan sense of these terms. It is a reading of the playwright not backwards towards his culture, as it claims and appears to be, but forwards towards our own.

And there is something in Marlowe's work, or in the relation between that work and our culture, that licenses this kind of reading. The idea of 'licence' is important here, because it is crucial to an Elizabethan understanding of play as culturally

---

[15] See C. L. Barber, *Shakespeare's Festive Comedy* (Princeton: Princeton University Press, 1959).

'licensed', albeit in a sense different at once from our own and from Marlowe's undertanding of it. For the Elizabethans, play is generally conceived as a licensed transgression of workaday norms, in the way that Shakespeare's plays were 'licensed' by the authorities and his fools are 'licensed'—allowed up to a point to voice the normally impermissible—by the authority-figures within those plays. Such limited licence seems to have been not only tolerable within an authoritarian, not to say totalitarian, social order, but, it has been plausibly argued, necessary to maintain and perpetuate it. Bakhtinian 'carnival' occupies a position more dialogic than revolutionary in relation to the conservative authority of church and state that permits it.[16] It may well have been as much a structural containment of potentially subversive energies, such as Aristotle, if not Plato, would have understood and approved, as an unleashing of them.

In all the major genres of Elizabethan drama—revenge tragedy, romantic comedy, and chronicle history—this same structural containment of the ludic or anarchic is repeatedly re-inscribed. A dazzling cast of metadramatic megalomaniacs—Richard III, Falstaff, Volpone, Iago, Vindice, to name but a few—are allowed to turn their worlds into a stage on which they strut and fret their histrionic and directorial fantasies until they are definitively silenced by rigid conventions of closure, which are theatrically, socially, and, in the end, theologically sanctioned. These non-Marlovian self-dramatizers are possessed of a demonic gusto similar to, if not quite the same as, that which Greenblatt attributes to their Marlovian counterparts:

cruel humour, murderous practical jokes, a penchant for the outlandish and absurd, delight in role-playing, entire absorption in the game at hand and consequent indifference to what lies outside the boundaries of the game, radical insensitivity to human complexity

---

[16] See Mikhail Bakhtin, *Rabelais and his World*, trans. Helen Iswolsky (Cambridge, Mass.: MIT Press, 1965). Bakhtin's seminal notion of the 'carnivalesque' has provoked much subsequent discussion of its subversive or revolutionary potential. See Peter Burke, *Popular Culture in Early Modern Europe* (London: Temple Smith, 1978), ch. 7; Barbara A. Babcock, *The Reversible World: Symbolic Inversion in Art and Society* (Ithaca: Cornell University Press, 1978); and, especially, Michael Bristol, *Carnival and Theatre* (London and New York: Routledge, 1988).

and suffering, extreme but disciplined aggression, hostility to transcendence.[17]

All this is contained in many, if not most, of the plays of the period, including Shakespeare's, and it is readily understandable within the dialectic of carnivalesque inversion of social norms elaborated by Barber and Bakhtin. In a fundamental sense it exists in the plays that contain it *in order that it may be contained*. It is shown to be a containable will to play or a will to contingent play, and as such it might well work to reinforce the order it defies by collapsing back into the dominant ideology of its age and culture.

THE RETURN OF THE REPRESSED

This is not exactly what we encounter in Marlowe; not the licensed, contingent, containable play that certainly tests but finally verifies the social order as its framing and grounding condition. Marlowe's is rather an uncontainable, unlicensed, and uncontingent play that works to undermine, even to de-realize, the dramatic societies that only succeed in extinguishing it after themselves having been revealed as an illusion, a mystification, a kind of play. Greenblatt recognizes this difference, and in order to accommodate it, he has to qualify—or more accurately, to *unqualify*—his notion of the 'will to play' in Marlowe in a way that also de-Elizabethanizes it:

The will to play flaunts society's cherished orthodoxies, embraces what the culture finds loathesome or frightening, transforms the serious into the joke and then unsettles the category of the joke by taking it seriously, courts self-destruction in the interest of the anarchic discharge of its energy. This is play on the brink of an abyss, *absolute* play.

[Marlowe] writes plays that spurn and subvert his culture's metaphysical and ethical certainties. We who have lived after Nietzsche and Flaubert may find it difficult to grasp how strong, how recklessly courageous Marlowe must have been: to write as if the admonitory purpose of literature were a lie, to invent fictions only to create and not to serve God or the state, to fashion lines that echo in the void, that echo more powerfully because there is nothing but a void . . . For the one true goal of all these heroes is to be characters in Marlowe's plays;

---

[17] Greenblatt, *Renaissance Self-Fashioning*, p. 219.

it is only for this, ultimately, that they manifest both their playful energy and their haunting sense of unsatisfied longing.[18]

In unqualifying the play-motive in Marlowe, in revising the terms in which it is cast from those of a 'will to play' to those of a 'will to absolute play', Greenblatt seems to move into an altogether more modern, decentred, and ungrounded realm than that of the Renaissance carnivalesque. For the displacement of Marlovian play from the matrix of Elizabethan culture to 'the brink of an abyss' and finally into 'the void' itself has the effect of turning it into a textual absolute, of cutting it loose from a Bakhtinian domain of contextual determination and launching it into a Nietzschean space of limitless differentiation.

There is a paradox here of such proportion that it requires some explanation. What Greenblatt states as an obstacle to our comprehension of the full force of Marlowe's achievement— 'We who have lived after Nietzsche and Flaubert may find it difficult to grasp how strong . . . Marlowe must have been'—is actually the very condition that makes our comprehension of it possible. It is of course impossible to know precisely what an Elizabethan theatregoer—John Sarracoll, for example—would have made of the 'high astounding terms' in which the Prologue to *Tamburlaine* announces that its hero will threaten the world. We know only that the play was a resounding box-office success, so Sarracoll and his ilk had to have made something of its force.

In one sense Sarracoll might have been more astounded— and threatened—than we by the terms of Marlowe's play. To witness a human being set himself above other human beings (emperors and kings at that) in something of the same way he had Eurocentrically set himself above the 'uncivilized' African natives—this must have been truly 'astounding', mind-boggling indeed. For such an act would have lain outside the system of relations that defined his culture, if not altogether outside his cognitive capability, in a way that the terms of Prospero's humiliation of the fishy Caliban or Artegall's of the barbarous Irish did not. But because it was so 'other', so alien to his cultural if not cognitive resources, he could not have comprehended it in anything like the clarity and depth that

[18] Ibid., pp. 220–1.

those of us who have lived after Nietzsche and Flaubert, not to mention Conrad, can. Greenblatt, in an important sense, understands Marlowe *better* than Sarracoll could have done, not simply because Greenblatt is smarter than Sarracoll, but because of the very historical distance, and the alternative discourses it has generated, that separate him from Sarracoll. The Elizabethan understanding of 'will' and 'play' can gain only a weak and limited purchase on Marlowe's project; it is only when those terms are endowed with something of their full Nietzschean and Derridean senses that Marlowe's project can be 'properly' understood in anything like its present force.

Greenblatt has gone a long way towards doing this, but he has done so at the cost of abandoning his residually historicist objective of telling the Elizabethans' story as their own, and of relinquishing the old and false claim to realist reconstruction that inheres in it. He has put words in their mouths, or, more accurately, put their words into a context that renders them 'metaphysical' in ways they could never have dreamed. Their words now echo and chime, not so much in the void, as within a time and tradition much more nearly ours than theirs. The 'metaphysics' of post-modernist and post-structuralist thought that many have tried to repress in the interest of renewed historical understanding—and Greenblatt is admittedly far less dogmatic in this project than some—has uncannily returned in the magnified form of 'the void' and 'nothing but the void'. It is a tribute to the honesty of its textual witness that Greenblatt's reading allows it to return without further attempts at futile repression.

For his faithful pursuit of the transgressive Marlovian will to its destination in the void has led him, willy nilly, into precisely that space where his strategy of constant return to historical particulars was supposed to prevent him from fetching up, and where it can certainly no longer help him: the utopian or dystopian 'nowhere' of ungrounded and unbounded structural displacement. His reading of Marlowe is, after all, a chapter in a book dominated by the thesis that Renaissance 'self-fashioning' —no matter how ardently or fearlessly pursued—finds itself inescapably re-inscribed within the very social structures from which it seeks deliverance. Self-construction, so Greenblatt consistently maintains, is always already social construction;

culturally prescribed and sanctioned positions are all there are; they alone determine, even if negatively, the discourse of the self, for all the ludic and rhetorical resistance it may throw up against them. But Marlowe's heroes turn out to be defined by discursive structures that are quite un-Elizabethan. For Greenblatt ends up where, by his own principles, neither Marlowe nor he has any right to be: in a void of purely textual 'freeplay', a culture-free 'noplace' that in contextualist terms should not exist.

No less remarkable than the Marlovian itinerary he traces is the tone of admiring incredulity that enters Greenblatt's own writing as he traces it. For Greenblatt is no snow-man either. That Marlowe's heroes—indeed Marlowe himself—can bring off the apparently impossible project of eluding the powerful reach of their own cultural norms, let alone that of Greenblatt's historicist thesis, seems to quicken his prose with a kind of wonder that is increasingly registered but remains unaccountable. Greenblatt's reading recognizes and responds to a heroic audacity in Marlowe's work that violates the very principles on which that reading proceeds. For all his Renaissance erudition, command of historical detail and local incident, and attentiveness to contemporary texts, it is his own culture Greenblatt broods on and depicts without realizing it. If we want to understand the historical nature of Greenblatt's achievement, we must look beyond the Renaissance to his own cultural and institutional context. And when we do, his new historicism turns out not be a historicism at all but its post-modern afterlife, what might be termed a 'post-historicism'.[19]

---

[19] I owe this apt coinage to Simon During. See his 'Postmodernism and Post-colonialism Today', *Textual Practice*, 1/1 (Spring 1987), 32–47.

7

Early Utopian Discourse

For a transitory enchanted moment man must have held
his breath in the presence of this continent, compelled into
an aesthetic contemplation he neither understood nor
desired, face to face for the last time in history with
something commensurate to his capacity for wonder.

(F. Scott Fitzgerald, *The Great Gatsby*)

HISTORICAL RELATIVISM AND HISTORICAL REALISM

In one of the strongest new-historicist re-readings of *The Tempest*
to date, Francis Barker and Peter Hulme express misgivings
about an alternative version of their own enterprise: the political
re-interpretation of early modern texts.[1] Their cultural-materialist misgivings are aroused by Tony Bennett's politicization of
Derrida's theory of 'citational grafting', and the change of focus
entailed by the resultant project of 'intertextual reinscription'.[2]
For Bennett's concern is less with the historical determinations
of the literary text at its moment of production—the traditional
domain of Marxist ideological critique and unmasking—than
with 'the diverse and changing structures which condition the
modes of its consumption', its reception and re-inscription.
Such retrenchments within Marxist cultural theory at its post-
structuralist moment cannot help but have consequences at the
level of critical practice.

Among these is the risk that the re-inscription of texts
along these lines offers little resistance to their conservative
recuperation by the very same means:

---

[1] Francis Barker and Peter Hulme, '"Nymphs and Reapers Heavily Vanish": The
Discursive Con-texts of *The Tempest*', in John Drakakis, ed., *Alternative Shakespeares*
(London and New York: Methuen, 1985), 191–205.
[2] Tony Bennett, 'Text and History', in Peter Widdowson, ed., *Re-Reading English*
(London: Methuen, 1982), 223–36.

The break with the moment of textual production can easily be presented as liberatory . . . This approach undercuts itself, however, when in the passage from historical description to contemporary rearticulation, it claims for itself a radicalism which it cannot then deliver. While a genuine difficulty in theorizing 'the text' does exist, this should not lead inescapably to the point where the only option becomes the voluntaristic ascription to the text of meanings and articulations derived simply from one's own ideological preferences. This is a procedure only too vulnerable to pluralistic incorporation, a recipe for peaceful co-existence with the dominant readings not for a contestation of those readings themselves.[3]

One consequence of following such a programme, then, is to open the text to appropriation by each and every community of interests with no means of validating or invalidating any of their interpretations: in a word, interpretive *relativism*.

The safeguard against such relativism, for Barker and Hulme, is to contest rival readings of the text directly, 'to read their readings . . ., to identify their inadequacies and explain why such readings come about and what ideological role they play', and to do so in the name of a 'no longer privileged but still crucially important *first* inscription of the text'. In the case of *The Tempest*, the dominant reading has been its editorial re-inscription by Frank Kermode, which Barker and Hulme proceed to discase of its late humanist idealisms and universal-izations in order to disclose Shakespeare's first inscription of the text as 'imbricated within the discourse of colonialism'. By returning to the canonical text at its moment of production they can thus lay claim to a validity for their reading that is denied to their rivals': 'After all, only by maintaining our right to make statements that we can call "historical" can we avoid handing over the very notion of history to those people who are only too willing to tell us "what really happened".'[4]

Thus the claim to validity they build into their reading is ultimately historical, but not historical in an empiricist or realist sense. It is not based, that is, on some account to end all accounts of 'what really happened'. The return to the 'first inscription of the text' as a means of discovering its 'real' or 'true' or 'definitive' historical meaning beyond recuperation or

[3] Barker and Hulme, '"Nymphs and Reapers Heavily Vanish"', pp. 192–3.
[4] Ibid., p. 194.

relativisation is not what Barker and Hulme have in mind. It is a return, not to the historical 'events' to which the text refers or corresponds, nor even to the historical 'meaning' of the text, but to the historical 'discourses' with and within which the text was articulated:

The operation of discourse is implicit in the regulation of what statements can and cannot be made and the forms that they can legitimately take. Attention to discourse therefore moves the focus from the interpretive problem of meaning to questions of instrumentality and function. Instead of *having* meaning statements should be seen as *performative* of meaning; not as possessing some portable and 'universal' content but, rather, as instrumental in the organisation and legitimation of power-relations—which of course involves, as one of its components, control over the constitution of meaning. As the author of one of the first modern grammars said, appropriately enough in 1492, 'language is the perfect instrument of empire' . . . Each individual text, rather than a meaningful unit in itself, lies at the intersection of different discourses which are related to each other in a complex but ultimately hierarchical way.[5]

The political and methodological necessity of returning to the 'first inscription' as the means of avoiding interpretive relativism has thus exposed another, opposite, danger, and one that Barker and Hulme are no less concerned to avoid: that of interpretive *realism*, the attempt to discover a stable historical meaning, a 'portable and "universal" content', in the text. This latter danger is to be avoided with the help of the notion of 'discourse'.

The underlying problem here, experienced by Barker and Hulme as pressure from opposite directions, is to establish a working relation, not just between 'history' and 'texts', but, more dangerously, between the 'historicity of the text' and the 'textuality of history'.[6] The reason why this problem must be

---

[5] Barker and Hulme, ' "Nymphs and Reapers Heavily Vanish" ', p. 197.

[6] The formulation is that of Louis Montrose: 'The poststructuralist orientation to history now emerging . . . may be characterised chiastically, as a reciprocal concern with the historicity of texts and the textuality of history' ('Professing the Renaissance: The Poetics and Politics of Culture', in H. Aram Veeser, ed., *New Historicism* [New York: Routledge, 1988]). The strongest form of post-structuralist historicism, i.e. of history as an intertextual construction, remains, in my view, that of Fredric Jameson: 'Only if [the issues of history] are grasped as vital episodes in a single vast unfinished plot: "The history of all hitherto existing society is the history of class struggles . . ." It is in detecting the traces of that uninterrupted narrative, in restoring to the surface of the

confronted and not simply left to take care of itself, is that these principles of 'historicity' and 'textuality', both fundamental to 'new' or post-structuralist historicism, are as antipathetic to one another as matter and antimatter. Unless treated with equal respect and kept out of each other's way, the consequences will be unfortunate. If, for example, the 'historicity of texts' is privileged above the 'textuality of history', 'history' is crudified into a naïve or vulgar realism, a positivist account of 'what really happened'; if priorities are reversed, 'history' is hollowed out, lightened, and relativized to the point where its study ceases to be a 'historicism' at all and becomes a kind of 'textualism' or 'conventionalism'. So there is definitely a problem here, even if it usually goes unrecognized.

DOMINANT DISCOURSES

Fortunately, there is also a solution, or at the very least a means of negotiating this antagonism between the 'historicity of the text' and the 'textuality of history': namely, the Foucauldian notion of the 'discursive con-text'. If 'discourse' refers to a cultural system or 'field' of signification, the contemporary texts that constitute it are its 'discursive con-texts'. 'The ensemble of fictional and lived practices', Barker and Hulme write, 'which for convenience we will simply refer to here as "English colonialism", provides *The Tempest*'s dominant discursive con-texts.'[7] The notion of 'discursive con-text' thus serves to establish the historicity of the text as a set of communal and conventional determinations within which its meanings are situated and constrained; that is, as something more than a mere 'fiction', an arbitrary or fanciful construct of the historian, but other than 'fact', a positive and unproblematic transcript of real meanings and events. Thanks to the notion of the 'discursive con-text'—without which there could be no 'new' historicism—it again seems possible to 're-insert' the text into history without reducing the former to the latter (as in an 'older' empirical historicism and vulgar Marxism) or dissolving the

text the repressed and buried reality of this fundamental history that the doctrine of a political unconscious finds its functions and its necessity' [*The Political Unconscious* (London: Methuen, 1981), 19–20].

[7] Barker and Hulme, '"Nymphs and Reapers Heavily Vanish"', pp. 196–8.

latter into the former (as in deconstructive or post-modernist textualism).

So 'discursive con-texts' are handy things to have lying about. The problem with the solution they provide—already signalled in the plural form in which Barker and Hulme consistently refer to them—is that there are altogether too many 'discursive con-texts' apposite to the text at hand to be found lying about; or more to the point, there are too many available discursive con-texts, precisely because they are not to be 'found' at all, and certainly not 'lying about'. For a no longer realist or empirical historicism, the discursive con-text cannot be an unchanging 'found object' given to hand by history, but is a 'made text', open to construction in every sense at the hands of an historical interpreter. Of making discursive contexts—or constructing discursive con-texts—there is potentially no end; like the 'textuality of history' it was meant to specify and stabilize for interpretive purposes, discursive contextuality is itself in need of limitation. For it too is, from the outset and in the final analysis, a text, and therefore an extension of the very same methodological problem—that of the textuality of history —it was meant to 'contain'.

The uninvited return of the textuality of history, however, is anticipated and, up to a point, met by Barker and Hulme. Their recognition of the danger posed by this potential embarrassment of discursive con-texts—for once again the effect would be to relativize any particular one—is registered not only in their consistent use of the plural and specific 'con-texts' but in their repeated play on 'dominant'. For the idea of 'dominance' would provide a principle of limitation on potential multiplicity:

To identify dominant discursive networks and their mode of operation within particular texts should by no means be seen as the end of the story. A more exhaustive analysis would go on to establish the precise articulation of discourses within texts: we have argued for the discourse of colonialism as the articulatory *principle* of *The Tempest*'s diversity but have touched only briefly on what other discourses are articulated and where such linkages can be seen at work in the play.[8]

While allowing for the multiplicity of discourses that enable and inform the text, Barker and Hulme are also concerned to

[8] Barker and Hulme, '"Nymphs and Reapers Heavily Vanish"', p. 204.

establish an 'ultimately hierarchical' relation and the 'domin-ance' of colonial discourse among them.

Their repeated term, 'dominant', itself has two dominant senses in post-structuralist discourse, one political and one structural, both of which seem to be in play. That colonial discourse is a discourse of domination, of 'hegemony' and 'oppression', and thus politically 'dominant' is clear enough; but that it is structurally 'dominant' in the sense of 'pre-eminent' or 'foregrounded' among the diverse discourses that reticulate the text, or that it is the 'articulatory *principle*' that underlies or generates them is certainly not self-evident. Nor is it clear how a return to its 'first inscription', while certainly putting the text back into touch with its forgotten or repressed discursive con-texts, can establish the priority of any one of them or the validity of interpretations based upon it. The argument for the structural dominance of colonial discourse as *primus inter pares* seems to turn on its power to elucidate certain traditional interpretive cruxes, notably that of Prospero's anxiety attack during the betrothal masque he stages for Ferdinand and Miranda in Act IV.

The breakdown of the masque, Barker and Hulme argue, registers the return of the repressed on Prospero's part, 'denial of dispossession' being the characteristic trope by which Euro-pean colonial regimes 'articulated their authority over land to which they could have no legitimate claim'. Nor is it possible at this point, so their argument runs, to preserve 'the text's unity by the familiar strategy of introducing ironic distance between author and protagonist'. No such recuperative reading of Prospero's anxiety in terms of dramatic irony is possible, because the play imposes *its own hierarchy of awareness and authority*:

The shakiness of Prospero's position is indeed staged, but in the end his version of history remains *authoritative*, the larger play acceding as it were to the containment of the conspirators in the safely comic mode, Caliban allowed only his poignant and ultimately vain protests against the venality of his co-conspirators . . . That this comic closure is necessary to enable the European 'reconciliation' . . . is . . . symptomatic of the text's own anxiety about the threat posed to its decorum by its New World materials . . . of a fundamental disquiet concerning its own functions within the projects of colonialist discourse.[9]

What finally establishes the structural dominance of colonial discourse is not merely Prospero's suppression of Caliban's claims and conspiracy at the level of dramatic action but the play's subordination of them at the level of dramatic genre. They form, after all, a mere comic subplot within a higher providential design.

Yet in order to arrive at so definitive and irreversible a conclusion, Barker and Hulme have had to perform certain 'repressions' of their own. Prospero's version of history 'remains *authoritative*' only in the sense that it is not explicitly contradicted, and not because it is incontrovertibly sanctioned. It is a notorious feature of the play that Antonio, whose version of the expulsion from Milan might have proved as challenging to Prospero's 'official history' of those events as Caliban's has to that of his usurpation of the island, withholds all commentary. Uniquely among Shakespeare's late romances, there is nothing like a theophany in *The Tempest*—unless it be the broken masque itself—Prospero himself having usurped not only the rule of the island but the role of 'god o'the island'. The quasi-divine validation provided in the previous romances through dream visions and oracular pronouncements is here reduced to a matter of communal consensus at most, precisely what Prospero *seeks* from the cast in the final act and from the audience through his singularly plaintive epilogue.

If the 'authoritative' status of Prospero's version of history thus remains open to question, so too does the explanatory power of colonial discourse to account for the anxious disruption of the masque. After all, other historical discourses—of 'magic', 'art', 'government'—have also been invoked within the tradition of criticism of *The Tempest* to account for a scene that remains a long-standing interpretive crux. This is not to suggest that the breakdown of the masque is inexplicable, but that it is in some sense *overly* explicable, susceptible of too many plausible explanations to permit any one of them an unquestionable authority or dominance. Rather than fixing the source of Prospero's anxiety and the dramatic problems it generates,

---

[9] Barker and Hulme, '"Nymphs and Reapers Heavily Vanish"', pp. 200, 203.

the return to first inscriptions and discursive con-texts provides further documentation of their fundamental overdetermination.

In so doing, the move from text to contexts serves as a timely and chastening reminder that sooner or later the textuality of history, and the indeterminacies it entails, come back into play at *every* level on which language is deployed. That includes the domain of 'discourses' and 'discursive formations' and 'con-texts' favoured by the new historicism every bit as unavoidably as the more exclusive preserve of canonical texts privileged— precisely for their self-consciousness in this knowledge—by deconstructive textualism. The unsettling force of the latter's insights into language and textuality cannot be eluded or elided by returning to first inscriptions, seeking out 'non-literary' texts, or furrowing among the archives of 'discursive forma-tions'. Where language is, there indeterminacy shall in-escapably be, even if—indeed, precisely because—it takes the form of an overdetermination of discursive formations and contexts.

It may also be clearer now why the claim that colonial discourse is structurally 'dominant', the 'articulatory *principle* of *The Tempest*'s diversity' should not go unchallenged. For the critical and political consequences of such a claim, pre-emptive as it is of the very resources of inscription available to the play, of the enabling structures of its signifying potential, are far-reaching indeed. Such a claim would mark the text from the beginning and for all time as decisively structured by an historical discourse beyond the power, because beyond the reach, of any contemporary re-inscription to recuperate. That structurally 'dominant' discourse, once disclosed, would effect-ively pre-determine the interpretive or performative destiny of the text. *The Tempest* would have to be seen as a text not merely informed but initially generated and for ever possessed by a discursive field dedicated to the legitimization of bondage and oppression. It would therefore be a text always already of the devil's party, whether or not earlier commentators recognized it as such.

So Barker and Hulme's reference to the '*still* crucial first inscription' of the text takes on a further, more ominous meaning, and the need to contest not the undoubted presence but the alleged priority of colonial discourse, a new importance.

To this end, their own argument that a partial surfacing of repressed and guilty knowledge explains the disruption of the masque can be turned against them. For just as Prospero may be said to know something that does not permit of complete repression, so too the play—perhaps even Shakespeare?—may be said to know something that prevents the decisive hier-archization of its new-world materials. *The Tempest*, I am arguing, knows something more than colonial discourse and its contemporary con-texts are supposed to know, and what it knows at once unsettles any attempt to impose the Euro-centricity of colonial discourse upon its materials and prevents the presumptive 'dominance' of the latter from ever being definitively established. There is, in sum, a knowledge at work in the play that differentiates *The Tempest* from its discursive con-texts as well as one that links it with them. Of course this distinguishing, even saving, knowledge must itself be mediated by a discourse.

What other discourses, then, are articulated with and within *The Tempest*, 'linked' perhaps to the discourse of colonialism, yet autonomous enough to resist the 'dominance' of the latter? Among the discourses 'linked' in this way, one candidate in particular is so obvious as to have become practically invisible. The discourse I have in mind is generated at the same moment as the colonial discourse, and arguably out of the same en-counter with and exploration of the new world. Not surpris-ingly, this cognate discourse is articulated through many of the same texts, including *The Tempest*, but it sounds the high end of their discursive register so that an ear attuned only to its low notes might well miss or mistake it. For this discourse is the dialectical 'other' of the discourse of colonialism, and as such bears a political and imaginative charge of equal intensity but opposite valency. It is familiar to every student of Renaissance literature and even owes its name to one of the best-known texts of the period, a canonical text itself the cynosure of an older Marxist commentary. I am referring, of course, to the 'discourse of utopia'.

THE DISCOURSE OF UTOPIA

In contesting the dominance of colonial discourse in *The Tempest*, I now find myself in the paradoxical position of nominating as its rival a discourse that by definition must be one of 'non-dominance'. What else could any properly 'utopian' discourse be? At the very least, I am committed to explaining how a discourse can perform at the level of formal structure the very thing it resists at the level of political reference. Moreover, these paradoxes will have to be resolved in historical terms if we are to meet Barker and Hulme on their own carefully delimited ground. We shall have to show, that is, that the 'dominance' of colonial discourse is held in check by a utopian discourse that not only knows no dominance now but knew no dominance then, at the moment of inscription of the play, and before the emergence of proto-revolutionary discourses of democracy and socialism a few decades later. How could such a discourse acquire the 'power' to counter the dominance of its dark *alter ego* without either replicating the power structures that define the latter or repudiating them in terms of a social order constituted on revolutionary principles?

Such paradoxes as these are already articulated within early colonial discourse, and nowhere more pointedly and self-consciously than in *The Tempest*. The first of a series of utopian moments in the play, Gonzalo's daydream of an island-commonwealth from which he has banished 'sovereignty' along with other social evils, is punctuated by Sebastian's sharp reminder that 'Yet he would be King on't' and deflated altogether by Antonio's conclusion that 'The latter end of his commonwealth forgets the beginning' (II.i.152–4). One critic has termed this problem of utopian discourse—the need to have power in order to abolish it—'Gonzalo's paradox', and sees it as one of poetics as well as politics. 'Since we are dealing with fiction,' he writes, 'we cannot submit [the Utopian] hypothesis to any empirical test. The author has it his way for the obvious reason that he is the author.'[10]

Authorial absolutism of this kind is clearly self-defeating, since it issues in utopian relativism. As in the case of the

[10] Harry Levin, 'Some Paradoxes of Utopia', in *The Myth of The Golden Age in the Renaissance* (London: Faber, 1970), 187–93.

politicized re-inscription we examined earlier and, with Barker and Hulme, found wanting, it makes everyone his own utopist by founding the will to utopia in individual subjectivity rather than in objective needs and collective desires. On Gonzalo's well-intentioned but self-contradictory lips, the full authoritarian potential of a discourse freed by the 'nowhere' of its setting from all material and historical accountability is released. Gonzalo's relation to his utopian construct, in both its poetic and political dimensions, is essentially despotic, albeit benevolently so.

Yet Gonzalo's paradoxically autocratic commonwealth is in certain respects more a parody than an exemplar of early utopian discourse. In contrast to Gonzalo, the eponymous 'Utopus', founder of More's Utopia, counters the authoritarianism of Utopia from within by building into it a communitarian dimension. Utopus commands his own conquering army to assist the conquered natives on equal terms in the digging of a channel that makes Utopia possible in the first place by making it an island (as well as an image of Britain). *Facile fertur quod omnibus commune est*, comments More in the margin: 'That which is common to all is borne lightly.'[11] Utopus' style of communitarian autocracy suggests a certain awareness of 'Gonzalo's paradox'—if not a resolution of it—on the part of More and alerts us to the analogous style of the *Utopia* itself.

For More's text can be seen as a rhetorical and political construct cunningly devised to avoid monologic assertion and autocratic domination alike. The indirections of its dialogue form and self-negations of its oxymoronic names enable More at once to distinguish himself from his spokesman for Utopia and to distance himself from the latter's—and indeed his own—utopian construct. At the same time, the social practices of Utopia, often as contradictory as its proper names—no lawyers in this stronghold of law, complete religious toleration but no atheism—jostle uneasily against one another and the rest of their author's *œuvre*, to unsettling and subversive effect. If 'the author has it his way for the obvious reason that he is the author', it has proved notoriously inobvious which way is the 'his way' this author presumably 'has it'.

[11] *The Complete Works of St. Thomas More*, iv, *Utopia*, ed. Edward Surtz and J. H. Hexter (New Haven: Yale University Press, 1965), 112.

If the discursive and political regime of More's Utopia—to which we shall return shortly—attempts to deny its own dominance, that of Montaigne's 'Of the Cannibals' manages, as we might say nowadays, to deconstruct itself altogether. Long recognized as the 'source' for Gonzalo's utopian monologue in *The Tempest*, the essay, like the play, is a case in point of the difficulty in deciding which discourse, colonial or utopian, is dominant. Montaigne's account of Amerindian life as a latter-day golden age is constructed out of, among other 'sources', the first-hand account of a household servant who spent 'ten or twelve' years in Brazil. Montaigne is at pains to represent his servant as a reliable witness, 'a simple and rough-hewen fellow: a condition fit to yield a true testimony', in contrast to 'subtle people [who] cannot choose but somewhat alter the story . . . and hyperbolise the matter'.[12]

Montaigne himself does not so much 'hyperbolise' the cannibals as ironize the Europeans. The most 'barbarous' customs of the former, including their cannibalism, are juxtaposed with analogous European practices culled from ancient or modern history. The effect is to familiarize the 'barbarous' and estrange the familiar. (Recall that More represents 'enclosure' as a form of 'cannibalism', in which sheep (or their owners) eat men, in Book I of *Utopia*.) The further effect is to relativize precisely that dominant Eurocentricity which structures colonial discourse. This process of systematic relativization, by which 'civilization' and 'barbarism' are shown to inhabit rather than oppose one another is certainly deconstructive; but it is also dialectical.

The historical encounter with—from the viewpoint of Europe—a blank new world apparently receptive or conformable to the mythic projections of power, wealth, and empire of the old, generates colonial discourse. But almost immediately, the sheer difference, indeed the recalcitrant otherness, of that new world begins to assert itself and impact back upon Europe. Europe is forced not only to look afresh at its own customs and institutions, to see them as less than the absolutes they were supposed to be, but to re-think the basis of the 'civilization' built upon them. That re-thinking constitutes one domain, in which brave

[12] Michael de Montaigne, 'Of the caniballes', *Essays*, trans. John Florio [1603], ed. J. I. M. Stewart (London: Nonesuch Press, 1931), i. 208.

new worlds serve as speculative inversions of tired old ones, of an emergent new-world discourse, the other side of the discourse of colonialism.

This broad and continuing historical process may be enacted, as we have begun to see, within a single text. Montaigne's idealization of life among the cannibals is also an inversion of life in contemporary France, whose household servants, boy-kings, and foppish *'haut de chausses'* all find their way, casually but uninnocently, into the text.[13] Similarly, the brave new world of Book II of *Utopia*—and *orbis novus* is More's punning term for it throughout—dialectically inverts the old world of poverty, homelessness, inflation, and crime arising from the enclosure discussed in Book I. The Utopian order is projected in both texts as a response to newly perceived historical contradictions that not only condition externally the discourse of Utopia but are inscribed within the very structure of its texts. The dialectical character of early utopian discourse obviously requires more extensive discussion than I can offer here. But at certain moments the texts at hand anticipate a later dialectical understanding in so striking a way as to require some comment.

Towards the end of 'Of the Cannibals', Montaigne recalls his own encounter with some native Caribbeans in 1562 at Rouen in the presence of Charles IX. On being asked 'what things of note and admirable they had observed amongst us', the cannibals replied how 'they found it very strange' that the tall, bearded Switzers of the king's guard should 'submit themselves to obey a beardless child'. They then turn the full clarity of their estranged perception from the specific absurdity of monarchy to a more general absurdity:

They had perceived there were men amongst us full gorged with all sorts of commodities, and others which, hunger-starved and bare with need and poverty, begged at their gates: and found it strange these moities so needy could endure such an injustice, and that they took not the others by the throat, or set fire on their houses.[14]

---

[13] These strands of social satire are tied together at the end of the essay, when Montaigne seems to laugh at the apparent expense of the cannibals, who 'wear no trousers' (*'ils ne portent point de haut de chausses'*). But as Harry Levin comments, 'the comparative nakedness of the Amerindians is juxtaposed to the ridiculous foppery of the breeches and hose then worn by French courtiers' (*The Myth of the Golden Age*, p. 78).

[14] Montaigne, *Essays*, i. 219. This striking passage, in which one central problematic of Marxism—why does the working class fail to see its real position, and then proceed

Montaigne does not go on to explain the strategies by which the poor are systematically deluded of that consciousness of their real position in a structure of inequality—so clear and painful to the cannibals—which is the precondition for any remedial action they might take.

If, however, these same cannibals, or their grandfathers, had talked with Raphael Hythloday in Brazil on his way to Utopia in 1503,[15] they might have gained from him some understanding not only of the class structure of European society, but of the containing strategies by which the rich defraud the poor not only of the full value of their labour but of the very consciousness that they have been defrauded:

When I consider and weigh in my mind all these commonwealths, which nowadays anywhere do flourish, so God help me, I can perceive nothing but a certain conspiracy of rich men procuring their own commodities under the name and title of the commonwealth. They invent and devise all means and crafts, first how to keep safely, without fear of losing, that they have unjustly gathered together, and next how to hire and abuse the work and labour of the poor for as little money as may be. These devices, when the rich men have decreed to be kept and observed under colour of the commonalty, that is to say, also of the poor people, then they be made laws.[16]

to do something about it?—is foreshadowed, has been strangely neglected by new-historicist commentary on *The Tempest*. Even Peter Hulme cites it only as a closing flourish to his *Colonial Encounters* (London: Routledge, 1986). The passage takes on even greater poignancy, across the cultural and historical differences it also highlights, in view of the communitarianism implied in the term used by the cannibals for the poor in relation to the rich. Montaigne refers to them as 'leurs moitiez' (Florio's 'these moyties'), explaining that the cannibals '*ont une façon de leur langage telle, qui'ils nomment les hommes moitié les uns des autres*', i.e. they have a way of speaking such that they call men one another's 'halves' (Montaigne, *Oeuvres Complètes*, ed. Albert Thibaudet and Maurice Rat [Paris: Gallimard, 1962], 212–13).

[15] Hythloday tells us he sailed with Amerigo Vespucci, whose account of his four voyages, entitled *El nuevo mundo* and published in 1507, was certainly one of the models for More's *Utopia*. Vespucci reports encountering, on his second voyage (1501), a nation where 'They have no private property but all things are in common . . . Of gold, pearls, jewels, and all such-like things which in Europe we regard as so valuable they think nought, and utterly despise.' (Recall that the chamber-pots of Utopia are made of gold.) It was on the fourth voyage, however, that Vespucci left behind twenty-four men in a garrison near Cape Frio, about a hundred kilometres from Villegagnon, where Montaigne's servant spent ten or twelve years. More represents Hythloday as one of these twenty-four, whose travels after the departure of Vespucci lead them to Utopia. See More's *Utopia*, trans. Ralph Robinson, ed. Harold Osborne (London: University Tutorial Press, 1936), 128.

[16] More, *Utopia*, ed. Osborne, p. 121. The passage has of course attracted much

More is of course free to express through the mouth of the malcontent Hythloday the proto-Marxist understanding of 'ideology' he might have been reluctant to express in his more public voices of lawyer, knight, and sheriff of London. Characteristically, he has it both ways by taking issue with Hythloday for his excess of zeal in things Utopian and by questioning the applicability of 'their common life and subsistence' to his own England. Such are the rhetorical indirections of the *Utopia* that not even the marginal directive *Haec annota lector* ('Reader, mark these words!') tells us quite where More stands.

There are of course historical constraints on the precocity of early utopian discourse, not least the real and embedded dominance of another political discourse in early modern European, namely that of monarchy. While More is at pains in both books of his *Utopia* to re-define the authority of governors well short of absolutism, his re-definitions themselves fall short of anything like a systematic redistribution of power. The 'prince' of Utopia (*principis magistratus*), though nominated by the people and elected by their representatives, is still essentially a monarch, if no longer an autocrat. He holds office constitutionally but permanently; unless of course he aims at 'tyranny', though the mechanism for identifying and removing a would-be tyrant, like so much else in Utopia, is not specified. Until discourses of government alternative to that of monarchy emerge in the seventeenth century, themselves enabled by the alternative beliefs and practices of nonconformist religion, the discourse of the new world was the only vehicle through which a radical re-thinking of the political structure could be conducted, albeit in a necessarily displaced form.[17]

In the sixteenth century, however, the redistribution of power had to be more difficult to imagine than the redistribution of wealth. This is not simply because of the intellectual dominance of monarchical discourse and the physical dangers of deviating from it, but because the redistribution of power, unlike that of wealth, is not reducible to the single symbolic gesture of communalizing property—the hallmark of all early

Marxist attention. Still forceful is Carl Kautsky, *Thomas More and His Utopia*, trans. H. J. Stenning (London: A. & C. Black, 1927).

[17] Cf. Christopher Hill, *The World Turned Upside Down* (Harmondsworth: Penguin, 1975) and Jonathan Dollimore, *Radical Tragedy* (Brighton: Harvester, 1983).

utopian discourse. Inseparable from materiality but not reducible to it, power is more like love or language than it is like
money or property. It is harder to measure, harder to locate,
harder to gain, lose, or exchange than money or wealth generally, harder indeed to systematize, because it has its existence
within a second-order sign system always already constituted
by more basic systems: power, that is, is not merely 'constructed' but embedded. This is what Montaigne's cannibals
failed to understand in the presence of the boy-king. Nor are the
cannibals alone; some new historicists also seem to think that a
redistribution of power will follow from its deconstruction as a
textual system.

But even a *systematic* understanding of power relations is
lacking to the entire sixteenth century, including More,
Montaigne, and arguably even Machiavelli. They understand
their own system of power relations from within; they know
enough, that is, to kneel before the king, boy or not, and know
what to expect if they do not kneel. But they believe the system
is divinely given and sanctioned; they do not understand it as
something culturally constructed, that is to say, as something
capable of being viewed from *outside*. Hence their decon-
structions of it may be satiric or ironic, but are always incomplete. Such an understanding, and the new discourses of
the social sciences in and into which it would develop, are
themselves made possible by the massive decentring and continuing relativization of European culture which began in its
encounter of a new world, and the new sense it enabled of an
'outside' to their system.

Limited on the 'right' by the dominant discourse of monarchy, and on the 'left' by an absent discourse of social and
political theory, early utopian discourse wanders between two
worlds, one whose days are numbered, the other whose life has
barely begun. The terms are simply not yet available to More
or Montaigne in which to contemplate what a later discourse
will describe, with the benefit of hindsight, as the transition
from 'traditional' and 'charismatic' to 'rational' and 'legal'
authority.[18] Unlike Max Weber, More and Montaigne know
only a world of kings—good and bad, strong and weak, but still

[18] See Max Weber, *The Theory of Social and Economic Organization*, trans. A. M.
Henderson and Talcott Parsons (New York: Oxford University Press, 1947).

kings. The best they can come up with under the circumstances are versions or inversions of the status quo, vaguely situated somewhere in the new world and held together by a happy combination of natural abundance, native wit, and authorial wishful thinking. These early utopias do not qualify as 'systematic' in any sense a modern social scientist might recognize. How could they, when they were invented before the very idea of system as something socially—as distinct from naturally or divinely—generated, was firmly in place?

What, then, is this early utopian discourse if it is not yet fully 'systematic'? Is it not rather what Lévi-Strauss terms '*bricolage*' —that 'primitive', mythopoetic cobbling together of the ready to hand, of ancient, contemporary, historical, fanciful, and philosophical bits and pieces into makeshift structures serving to mediate deep cultural contradictions? In their discursive incoherence and instability, these *ad hoc* ensembles are to the more systematic constructs of later political theory—Hobbes's *Leviathan*, for example, or the American Constitution—as Borges's 'Chinese Encyclopedia' is to the eleventh edition of the *Encyclopedia Britannica*.[19] No wonder the authoritarianism endemic to utopian discourse seems so muted or qualified in these early texts. After all, their very earliness has exempted them not only from the explicit authoritarianism of the monarchical discourse of their own cultures, but from the implicit authoritarianism of later, more 'enlightened' discourses, with their systematic capacity to bring every corner of the world—and all that it inherits—under a totalizing discursive regime.

Yet More's *Utopia* in particular does display an inkling of and instinct for system, a foreunderstanding that Utopia is actually unthinkable short of, or outside of, system. This prescience is not to be discovered in any particular aspect of the social

---

[19] In his fabulous encyclopedia, entitled the 'Celestial Emporium of Benevolent Knowledge', Borges classifies animals into: '(a) those that belong to the Emperor, (b) embalmed ones, (c) those that are trained, (d) suckling pigs, (e) mermaids, (f) fabulous ones, (g) stray dogs, (h) those that are included in this classification, (i) those that tremble as if they were mad, (j) innumerable ones, (k) those drawn with a very fine camel's hair brush, (l) others, (m) those that have broken a flower vase, (n) those that resemble flies from a distance' (Jorge Luis Borges, 'The Analytical Language of John Wilkins', in *Other Inquisitions, 1937–1952* (New York: Simon and Schuster, 1964), 103).

organization of Utopia, but in the rather more abstract form of a game played in Utopia:

They use two games not much unlike the chess . . . wherein vices fight with virtues, as it were in battle array, or a set field. In the which game is very properly shown both the strife and discord that vices have among themselves, and again their unity and concord against virtues. And also what vices be repugnant to what virtues; with what power and strength they assail them openly; by what wiles and subtlety they assault them secretly; with what help and aid the virtues resist and overcome the puissance of the vices; by what craft they frustrate their purposes; and finally by what sleight or means the one getteth the victory.[20]

More than a game *in*, this is the game *of*, utopia; and it is very much a system—a 'system of checks and balances' no less—in which the civic 'vices' are defeated by the civic 'virtues' as predictably as clockwork. Would not any utopia have to be a self-correcting system of this kind?

At this ludic and metamimetic moment, then, More's *Utopia* seems to disclose its own system, the deeper structure of relations that regulates its various parts. Yet what we glimpse here is not a system in the same sense that the Constitution of the United States outlines a 'system' of government or that political dissidents in that country twenty years ago used to anathematize 'the system' (though, curiously enough, the system to which they referred bore little resemblance to the one outlined in the Constitution). It is not simply that the underlying structure of *Utopia* is characteristically ludic, but that it is open to the point of emptiness. Just what are the extraordinary rules and uncanny moves in this game of moralized chess that enable the 'virtues' invariably to outmanœuvre and check the 'vices', do they their fiendish worst? To judge from the universal moral cast of the game, we seem to be closer to the theologically sanctioned model of the morality plays More is known to have enjoyed than to any specifically political system.

Though More inscribes into his *Utopia* intimations of tyranny, greed, and crime as more than individual vices, his

---

[20] More, *Utopia*, ed. Osborne, p. 57. On the ludic structure of Utopia, and its 'dialectical' relation to historical conditions, two essays are indispensable: Harry Berger, Jr, 'The Renaissance Imagination: Second World and Green World', *Centennial Review*, 9/1 (Winter 1965) and Michael Holquist, 'How to play Utopia: Some Brief Notes on the Distinctiveness of Utopian Fiction', *Yale French Studies*, 41 (1968).

discursive resources are not yet capable of representing them, or their reform, as functions of the social system as a whole. Nor are Shakespeare's in his utopia:

> It is not easy . . . to see how you can run a political state on the lines of a marriage bed, or precisely what purchase the brave new world of the young couple has. on, say, problems of economic inflation. At this point . . . *The Tempest* conveniently folds itself up by inviting the audience to applaud, thus breaking the magic spell by foregrounding the theatrical fictionality of its own devices. What it fails to draw attention to is the glaring contradiction on which its whole discourse effectively founders: the fact that this 'organic' restoration of a traditional social order founded upon Nature and the body rests not only on a flagrant mystification of Nature, gratuitous magical device and oppressive patriarchialism, but is actually set in the context of the very colonialism which signals the imminent victory of the exploit-ative, 'inorganic', mercantile bourgeoisie.[21]

'Shakespeare's utopian solution', Eagleton concludes, 'to the conflicts which beset him—an organic unity of body and language—is by definition unattainable.' Perhaps the framing of utopia is one of the 'many ways in which we have thankfully left this conservative patriarch behind' rather than one of the 'other ways in which we have yet to catch up with him'.[22]

But if the utopia projected by Prospero—or by Shakespeare—is 'unattainable', utopian discourse as such is represented, both within the play and in an important sense beyond it, as irrepressible. For the discourse of utopia may be contradicted but is not silenced by the discourses of either colonialism or *realpolitik* also inscribed in the play. The fatal gap between the body and language, between materiality and system, that vitiates Shakespeare's utopianism may also be seen as the space of desire within which it is generated in the first place and re-constituted over and over again. This internal split within new-world discourse between power and desire must proble-matize the realization of utopia but it must at the same time prevent the dominance of colonial imperialism from ever being decisive, or the reading of *The Tempest* as a document of that discourse from ever going unquestioned or unqualified.

In the texts and contexts of early new-world discourse this

---

[21] Terry Eagleton, *William Shakespeare* (Oxford: Basil Blackwell, 1986), 96.
[22] Ibid., pp. 97, x.

split is, as we have seen, already represented. In the case of *The Tempest*, it is repeatedly represented, foregrounded to the point of dominating not only the text but its subsequent interpretive history. In Gonzalo's interrupted monologue, as in Prospero's broken masque, as again in Miranda's fleeting impression of a brave new world, the utopian moment is contained, contradicted, but never quite cancelled in the imperialist moment. The discourses and structures of power frame and repress those of a desire they also constitute anew in that very moment of containment. The great literature generated by the historical encounter with the new world spectacularly instantiates this dialectical process. Such a dialectic of power and desire, of imperialism and idealism, structures not only the new-world discourse of the texts we have examined but the history of their reception and re-inscription.

Paul de Man's prescient remark that 'poetry is the foreknowledge of criticism' takes on an unexpected historical meaning in this connection.[23] In the case of a text like More's *Utopia*, or even more dramatically, that of *The Tempest*, whose critical history has fluctuated over the past two centuries between extremes of idealist and historicist re-inscription, its career was already implicit in its 'first inscription'. Both interpretive possibilities were encoded in the discursive structure of a text that only required the answering discursive structures of future contexts to become decipherable in alternative and antithetical terms. 'For the interpreter of a poetic text,' writes de Man, 'this foreknowledge is the text itself. Once he understands the text, the implicit knowledge become explicit and discloses what was already there in full light.' No text better illustrates the conclusion to which de Man's insight draws than *The Tempest*: 'The existence of a particularly rich aberrant tradition in the case of the writers who can legitimately be called the most enlightened, is therefore no accident, but a constitutive part of all literature, the basis, in fact, of literary history.'[24]

---

[23] Paul de Man, *Blindness and Insight* (New York: Oxford University Press, 1971), 31.
[24] Ibid., pp. 30, 141.

8

'Cultural Poetics' versus 'Cultural Materialism': The Two New Historicisms in Renaissance Studies

Historicism gives the 'eternal' image of the past; historical materialism supplies a unique experience with the past.
(Walter Benjamin, 'Theses on the Philosophy of History')

THE TEXTUALIZATION OF HISTORY

Of the diverse schools of criticism to emerge from the theoretical ferment of the 1970s, arguably the most influential in the 1980s—particularly in the field of Renaissance studies—has been the so-called 'new historicism'. Yet its high institutional profile has made it of late a target of critical and polemical attack from several quarters; so much so, that one might be excused for wondering how much longer it will remain alive as a critical movement, let alone influential. So swiftly do our paradigms now seem to shift, that the new historicism could conceivably pass from youthful vigour into obsolescence and decline without ever having attained intellectual and institutional maturity. Such a destiny would be regrettable, because its strengths would remain partly unrealized and its weaknesses imperfectly understood. It would have been denied, in sum, the full exposure, the moment in the sun—for better and worse— enjoyed by the schools it seeks to supplant: the old historicism on the one hand, and new and practical criticism on the other.

It is to some of those weaknesses that I now turn, albeit at the risk of hastening the demise of a critical movement from which I have learned a great deal and for which I have a corresponding respect. In mitigation, I can say only that unlike most recent attacks, the following strictures are *not* directed primarily at the politics of the new historicism, at a radical will which has occasioned the criticism that 'new historicists do not like "literature" '.[1] Nor are my remarks aimed at its style of radical will, which has led some to conclude that it is a 'male historicism and just not feminist enough'.[2] The following critique is directed not at the ideological soundness or unsoundness of the new historicism, which is of course far from ideologically monolithic, but at certain methodological and epistemological problems raised but not resolved by its practices. These problems arise, I shall argue, out of the difficulty or impossibility of producing a 'textualist' or 'post-structuralist' history, and are themselves contradictions of the new historicism's moment of emergence, indications of its underlying continuity with older habits of thought to which it is overtly opposed.[3]

To historicize the new historicism in this fashion, that is, to remind it of its own history, it will be necessary to ask at the outset whether the label, '*the* new historicism', is not something of a misnomer: are we really dealing with a single school of criticism? In saying this, I do not intend the sort of qualification that can, indeed should, apply when discussing any 'ism'. Since all 'isms' are umbrella-terms reared high above the diverse movements grouped under them, they are to that extent abstractions much less homogeneous or coherent than they tend to appear in discussion. But that is not the point I want to

[1] See Edward Pechter, 'The New Historicism and its Discontents: Politicising Renaissance Drama', *Proceedings of the Modern Language Association*, 102, 292–303.

[2] See Peter Erickson, 'Rewriting the Renaissance, Rewriting Ourselves', *Shakespeare Quarterly*, 38/3, 327–37; Lynda Boose, 'The Family in Shakespeare Studies', *Renaissance Quarterly*, 40, 707–41; Carol Thomas Neely, 'Constructing the Subject: Feminist Practice and the New Renaissance Discourses', *English Literary Renaissance*, 18, 5–18; and Judith Newton, 'History as Usual?': Feminism and the "New Historicism"', *Cultural Critique*, 9, 87–122.

[3] Since Jean E. Howard pointed it out in 'The New Historicism in Renaissance Studies', *English Literary Renaissance*, 16, 13–43, the reluctance of the movement to *theorize* its own practices has often been remarked. This reluctance was understandable and excusable, given the eclecticism and pragmatism of its project. The reluctance to *historicize* itself, though also understandable and excusable, given the demystifying thrust of that project, is now beginning to be overcome. See Don. E. Wayne, 'Power, Politics, and the Shakespearean Text: Recent Criticism in England and the United States', and Walter Cohen, 'Political Criticism of Shakespeare', both in Jean E. Howard and Marion F. O'Connor, eds., *Shakespeare Reproduced: The Text in History and Ideology* (London and New York: Methuen, 1987), 48–67 and 26–47 respectively. See also Louis A. Montrose, 'Renaissance Literary Studies and the Subject of History', *English Literary Renaissance*, 16/1, 1–12, and 'Professing the Renaissance: The Poetics and Politics of Culture', in H. Aram Veeser, ed., *New Historicism* (London and New York: Routledge, 1988).

make. 'The new historicism' is disunified within itself in a way that goes deeper than the disunified character of all 'isms'. It is disunified in ways that its opponents, preoccupied by its radical politics, have disregarded or discounted, and that it has itself been reluctant, given the institutional advantages of a united front, to acknowledge. The new historicism, even at the level of abstraction at which 'isms' operate, is at least two distinct historicisms.

To put the matter oversimply for purposes of exposition, there is an American and a British new historicism, and while they have much in common, they are in certain crucial respects not only 'different', as is now beginning to be perceived, but actually *opposed*.[4] What they have in common is a post-structuralist understanding of literature and history as *constructed textuality* or, to the extent that traditional oppositions between the 'literary' and the 'historical' have been shown by this school to be deconstructible, as *constructed intertextuality*. This way of proceeding is sometimes termed 'contextualism'; but more usefully for our purposes, it is also 'conventionalism'. This notion enables us to distinguish both 'new' historicisms from the 'old'; for their 'conventionalist' understanding of culture as an intertextual construction supersedes an older 'empiricist' or 'realist' identification of the meaning of an historical text with the biographical author's intention or his contemporary audience's understanding of it, as if such things were once monolithically present or linguistically transparent —even for the historical culture concerned—and retain an integrity untouched by the terms and methods of our enquiry into them.[5]

[4] See Cohen, 'Political Criticism of Shakespeare', p. 33 and Wayne, 'Power, Politics, and the Shakespearean Text', p. 51.

[5] For a lucid exposition of 'empiricism', 'realism', and 'conventionalism' as they have emerged in the history and philosophy of science, and a useful application of these concepts to cultural studies, see Terry Lovell, *Pictures of Reality: Aesthetics, Politics and Pleasure* (London: British Film Institute, 1980). See also Richard Rorty, *Consequences of Pragmatism* (Minneapolis: University of Minnesota Press, 1982). Whereas Lovell is concerned to avoid the relativist dangers of 'conventionalism' for Marxist aesthetics, Rorty is unworried by these consequences for the 'neo-pragmatism' he advocates. The uncertainty of new historicists themselves concerning the conventionalist status and implications of their enterprise is epitomized by Stephen Greenblatt in his introduction to *Renaissance Self-Fashioning: From More to Shakespeare* (Chicago: University of Chicago Press, 1980), 5–6: 'The significance [of sixteenth-century texts] for us is not that we may see *through* them to underlying and prior historical principles, but rather that we

Hence the centrality for both American and British new historicism of power and politics; for the interpretation of the text of history cannot be 'disinterested' or 'apolitical'. Just as there can be no 'motiveless creation', as Stephen Greenblatt puts it in the closest thing yet to a new-historicist 'manifesto',[6] so too there can be no motiveless interpretation. Both new historicisms are thus doubly political, not only in the sense that they are interested in the political motives of the texts they take up, but also in that the texts they produce are themselves politically interested and, generally speaking, make no secret of it—again in contradistinction to the older historicism. They seek, that is, to make a difference in the text of history by actively *rewriting* the Renaissance rather than passively reflecting on it.

Yet even before addressing the larger problems such a project entails, there are crucial differences between the American and British versions of 'the Renaissance'. Such differences reflect the particular political charge and commitment carried by each, and follow from the disparate positions occupied by 'English' within their respective cultures. Consider, for example, their common focus on Renaissance, particularly seventeenth-century, literature. As the moment of transition between medieval and modern England, the seventeenth century is the meeting-ground between historical alterity and contemporary identity, between cultural difference and presence, and as such holds special interest for any self-conscious historicism. Hence the oxymoronic term favoured by many new historicists: the 'early modern' period. The seventeenth century also holds, as the period of Shakespeare, Donne, and Milton, the strategic

may interpret the interplay of their symbolic structures with those perceivable in the careers of their authors and in the larger social world as constituting a single complex process of self-fashioning.' No less delicately balanced, and ultimately no less non-committal is Montrose in 'Professing the Renaissance': 'The post-structuralist orientation to history now emerging . . . may be characterised chiastically, as a reciprocal concern with the historicity of texts and the textuality of history. By *the historicity of texts*, I mean to suggest the cultural specificity, the social embedment, of all modes of writing—not only the texts that critics study but also the texts in which we study them. By *the textuality of history*, I mean to suggest . . . that we can have no access to a full and authentic past, a lived material existence, unmediated by the surviving textual traces of the society in question.'

[6] See his introduction to *Shakespearean Negotiations: The Circulation of Social Energy in Renaissance England* (Oxford: Oxford University Press, 1988).

high ground in a continuing institutional struggle for control of literary study on both sides of the Atlantic. For British new historicists in particular, 'English' is not just another subject, and involves more than the skills associated with 'literacy'. For them, 'English' is a matter of national identity, and the seventeenth century a revolutionary moment, a moment of social and constitutional crisis in the past with crucial implications for the political, indeed revolutionary, aspirations of the present. So the political valencies of these related critical movements, given their different institutional positions within the cultures that produced them, are not quite the same.[7]

And neither are their respective theoretical alignments, or the practical problems that arise in consequence in their dealings with Renaissance texts. For American and British new historicists have drawn on different intellectual traditions and pursued quite different methods in their respective critical practices. Let us consider the American position first. *Renaissance Self-Fashioning: From More to Shakespeare; James I and the Politics of Literature: Jonson, Shakespeare, Donne and Their Contemporaries; The Illusion of Power: Political Theater in the English Renaissance*—such titles, selected almost at random from the burgeoning shelf, have a lot in common. They announce their topic, and straightaway limit their scholarly focus to a specific set of authors, a king's reign, a historical period. Indeed, the form and style of these titles are distinctly academic; the conventions of the doctoral dissertation in which their authors were well trained are not far away, with watchful supervisors urging economical confinement within accepted historical divisions, and rigorous examiners ready to pounce on any extravagance unsupported by specialist expertise within the delimited field.[8]

---

[7] This basic difference is at last beginning to come home: 'In the British cultural context the field of literary criticism periodically takes on the appearance of a battleground on which a struggle is waged for control over the representational power of texts that are understood to be the nation's cultural patrimony—for better or worse' (Wayne, 'Power, Politics, and the Shakespearean Text', p. 52.)

[8] For an extensive bibliography of the new historicism, see Cohen, 'Political Criticism of Shakespeare', pp. 39–47. The studies named above are cited only for their formulaic titles, which may owe as much to the *imprimatur* of the university presses under which most works of American—as distinct from British—new-historicist studies first appeared, as to the conventions of the doctoral dissertation. Of course the two have been mutually sustaining in America for decades. The academic specialism of

More specifically, the academic convention at work in these titles is still that of an older historical empiricism. Its rationale necessitated the establishment of a clear demarcation of the historical subject matter under study and a carefully measured distance between that subject matter and its investigator. What such titles still signify, among other things, is 'research' with all its pseudo-scientific, empiricist connotations. 'Research' pre-supposes a cool, disinterested (indeed, invisible) interpreter bracketed off in the here and now, and an objective body of 'data' sharply visible in the there and then, each standing in a self-contained space and separated from the other by enough distance to enable independence and objectivity in the scrutiny. The historical data, in this case the authors and texts under study, are declared to be 'political'—that seems to be the working hypothesis at its most general—but the politics of the historical scholar—to judge from the titles of these studies—are still implicit or occluded.

Now you cannot judge a book by its cover, or by its title, and neither Stephen Greenblatt's *Renaissance Self-Fashioning: From More to Shakespeare* nor any of the other new-historicist studies cited above is quite the sort of book its title might lead you to expect. After all, these are not works of 'old' but of 'new' historicism, and that means they know better than to proceed upon the same 'empiricist' assumptions as the older historicism, or to pretend to the same 'objectivity'. Having delimited and

American new historicism is paradoxical, to say the least, in view of its wider political concerns. In America, where the academic system is so vast and complex as to constitute a social order unto itself, the political impulse tends to be confined and absorbed within the system, becoming 'institutional politics' or a politics of the subject, while any potential impact on the wider society is thus defused. If this proves to be the case with the new historicism, it will be a striking example of the success of that 'strategy of containment' which Greenblatt and others identify as a ubiquitous feature of Elizabethan culture, yet on which they remain strangely silent concerning its operation in their own. The new discourse of 'power' may well signify, within such a reading of the present, a displaced expression of institutional impotence on the part of left-wing humanists, and the thoroughgoing academicization in America of that discourse of power, a structural guarantee of their and its continuing marginalization. See Cohen, 'Political Criticism of Shakespeare', pp. 36–7: 'But if new historicist reductions of Shakespeare to an agent of royal power are hard to defend in the context of the Renaissance, they acquire a certain logic and justification in the context of the present . . . New historicism should accordingly be seen as a form of leftist disillusion-ment. From this perspective it is possible to account for . . . the abiding concern with state power; and for the strangely quietist feel of these radical critiques.' The British situation is, as we shall see, wholly different.

distanced the field of enquiry along older empirical lines, new historicists do not characteristically maintain the pretence of empirical objectivity toward its contents, least of all that of a 'naïve' empiricism. Quite the contrary: *nothing is now simply what it appears or as it presents itself to observation*, but something else, as anything and everything in the dramatic text reproduces, 'rehearses', and even 'reverses' the power relations of the cultural context.[9] Tamburlaine's extravagant career, for example, becomes 'an extraordinary meditation' on the destruction of a West African village by English merchant-sailors in 1586, while the rough magic with which Prospero controls his island is analogous to the martial law periodically imposed by the authorities upon the Virginia colony.[10]

This sudden, often surprising, interpenetration of text and context, theatre and culture—indeed, the dissolution of traditional boundaries between them—is of course characteristic of new-historicist practice. Partly because it began in the 1970s very much as a practice concerned to 'get on with' its work of politicization, and took theory on board only after the 'fact' and under pressure, the principles on which its subversive or transgressive readings proceed are not always explicit. One critic, not unsympathetic, goes so far as to describe its working assumption as one of 'arbitrary connectedness' between text and context.[11] This, as we shall see, is not quite the case. But if its persistent reading of Renaissance texts as dark conceits of official authority or ideological 'containment' is more than 'arbitrary', American new historicism is less than fully or clearly principled in its hermeneutic practices.

What is clear is that its political readings, such as those cited above, do not proceed under the straightforward regime of political allegorization familiar enough in empirical historicism, within which topical references encoded by the author are read off by contemporary audiences and historical critics 'in the know'. While this procedure was often at work in the early attention to the coterie—and conventionally allegorical—forms of masque and pastoral with which new historicism

---

[9] Greenblatt, *Shakespearean Negotiations*, pp. 7–9.
[10] Ibid., pp. 193–4; Greenblatt, *Renaissance Self-Fashioning*, pp. 148–63.
[11] Cohen, 'Political Criticism of Shakespeare', p. 34.

began,[12] later work rarely conforms to this residually empiricist model. Nor does American new historicism openly embrace—though it does flirt with—a more traditionally Marxist ideological critique, by which the interestedness of the text in promoting or legitimizing the political structure of its context of production is unmasked.[13]

The most explicit attempt to date to address such questions has been the 'retrospect' with which Greenblatt introduces his recent collection of essays on Shakespeare.[14] There, he recalls his increasing uneasiness 'with the monolithic entities that my work had posited', the 'sublime confrontation between a total artist and a totalizing society'. That Greenblatt should grow dissatisfied with his residually romantic and idealist conception of Shakespeare as a 'total artist' comes as no surprise. Less predictable, however, is his uneasiness with his other totalization, an Elizabethan society 'that posits an occult network linking all human, natural, and cosmic powers and that claims on behalf of its ruling élite a privileged place in this network'. He goes on to account for his growing discontent in terms of a heightened awareness, through the work of others, of the ways in which the 'discourse of power' in the period was itself contradictory and contested at virtually every point.

Far be it from me to dispute Greenblatt's account of his disillusionment with an historical hermeneutic that seems as questionable to me as it has come to seem to him. But I want to translate the terms of his disillusionment into those of my own argument, which attempts to identify a deeper source of unease than that which he acknowledges. For his 'totalizing society', whose power structure reinforces itself by appeal to a natural order conceived as rigidly and ubiquitously hierarchical, was not essentially different from that 'posited' by E. M. W. Tillyard and other older historicists forty years earlier.[15] Tillyard

[12] As, for example, in Stephen Orgel, *The Illusion of Power: Political Theater in the English Renaissance* (Berkeley: University of California Press, 1975), and Louis Montrose, ' "Eliza, Queene of Shepheards" and the Pastoral of Power', *English Literary Renaissance*, 16/1, 1–12.

[13] See Greenblatt, *Renaissance Self-Fashioning*, pp. 192–222, and 'Capitalist Culture and the Circulatory System', in Murray Krieger, ed., *The Aims of Representation: Subject/Text/History* (New York: Columbia University Press, 1987), 258.

[14] Greenblatt, *Shakespearean Negotiations*, pp. 1–20.

[15] See especially Tillyard's *The Elizabethan World-Picture* (London: Chatto, 1943), which has become a recurrent target of new-historicist attack.

documented a society and a Shakespeare for whom hierarchical order was nothing less than a 'world-picture'—and a good thing too. Of course the early Greenblatt, unlike Tillyard, repeatedly registers his astonishment and often his antipathy towards the 'totalizing' Tudor and Stuart culture that he chronicles first in *Sir Walter Ralegh* and more fully in *Renaissance Self-Fashioning*, in particular towards the absolutism with which its anxious and obsessive authoritarianism is enforced upon the wayward souls under its sway. One man's 'order' was certainly another's 'totalitarianism'.

My point, however, is that in moving from Tillyard to Greenblatt only the political valorization of such a society had been completely inverted; the terms of its cognition and construction deployed by Tillyard, the early Greenblatt, and many others were not essentially different. Those terms remain basically 'empiricist' or 'realist'. That is, they all 'posit' Elizabethan society as a historical reality not simply present—often oppressively so—and univocal to itself, but one whose historicity exists in its own right—and in a sense for all time—and remains independent of our efforts to reconstruct it—despite its survival only in the form of traces. 'Monolithic' indeed. And 'reconstruction'—as opposed to 'construction'—of the past is distinctly the objective within the logic of this historical 'realism': if no longer the fully positivist, documentary reconstruction pursued by the older historical scholarship of a Tillyard, then at least a plausible narrative representation. 'Representations', after all, names not only the journal Greenblatt has edited, with others, for nearly a decade, but the opening narrative gambit of virtually everything he has written.

The very term 'representation' at once recuperates and sublates this older historicist and naïvely realist objective of 'making present again' a past culture conceived not only as chronologically but *ontologically* prior to any construction of it. In so doing, it partly rehabilitates a residually referential aspiration, if not to 'commune', at least to correspond with the past. This is not the place to elaborate upon the problems raised (or, more often, repressed) by such a cognitive model. Against what, for example, could the claim to correspondence be tested, without independent access to historical 'reality'? How else could the accuracy, completeness, or vividness of that correspondence be judged? For such problems have already been confronted and effectively transcended by the post-structuralist move by which the 'traces' of history and the constructs of culture have been re-framed on the linguistic model of 'texts' and 'discourses' requiring an ever fresh and renewable 'construction' rather than the pseudo-empiricist model of 'documents' and 'facts' to be 'read off' in the effort of definitive reconstruction.

That major shift, in which Greenblatt's work has certainly participated, enables a rather different account of his change of attitude from the one he offers. For the transition he describes is a matter not merely of heightened awareness of complexity and conflict within the same conceptualization of the field but of a basic change in that conceptualization. In the course of the theoretical retrenchments of the 1970s and early 1980s, Green-blatt trades in his earlier 'realist' model of history, culture, and literature for a sleeker 'textualist' and inevitably 'conventional-ist' model. Or perhaps more accurately, he retains his older 'realist' model, but upgrades it by taking on board quite a lot of the new textualist technology arriving from several theoretical directions. The realist narrative structure that dominates his *Sir Walter Ralegh: The Renaissance Man and His Roles* is by no means relinquished. His essays still characteristically open with an historical 'event' narrated in quasi-documentary detail. But this tactic is now deployed with a new awareness of its status *as narrative*, as something more than a textual and rhetorical construct but less than a documentary 'given'.

The older 'realism'—marked in his latest work by such faintly pejorative terms as 'posit' and 'monolithic'—is now delicately and uneasily qualified by the newer 'textualism'. Thus his revised project is 'to inquire into the objective con-ditions of the enchantment [of the text], to discover how the traces of social circulation are effaced'.[16] With concepts like 'circulation'—let alone the 'traces' thereof—now in play, Greenblatt has repudiated (having always questioned) the historical empiricism of the likes of Tillyard, and its own traces in his earlier work. But to exchange the totalizing reifications of an older historical 'realism' for the differential relations of a

[16] Greenblatt, *Shakespearean Negotiations*, p. 5.

newer textualist 'conventionalism', while it might resolve some problems, is to encounter new ones. For the move from history as determinate 'fact' or 'event' to history as constructible 'text' renders this latest historicism open from within to the charge of 'relativism' as no previous historicism ever was, to being dismissed as merely one of many possible and no less plausible constructions of the historical text, and thus to conservative relativization and recuperation.

CULTURAL POETICS

At the same time, the anthropological emphasis and materialist inflection of the new history on which it depends, paradoxically expose it to a reductive 'universalism' and a new 'essentialism'. For beneath the specific Elizabethan historicity it seeks to identify is the concept of a 'deep structure' with which it cannot dispense, and towards which the surface structures of that culture consistently point. Does Greenblatt's latest terminology of 'circulation', 'negotiation', 'social energy' and 'exchange'— basically mercantile, even strangely monetarist, as it is—not effectively render Elizabethan England in terms of a generative grammar of economic exchange common to all societies? On this account, we might be excused for wondering whether we have blundered into a kind of universal bazaar teeming with rug dealers. What with so much exchange taking place in a culture that is, like all others, implicitly based on it, it is hardly surprising to find textual and contextual elements changing places handy-dandy with barely a trace, or the theatre 'rehearsing' or even 'reversing' some feature of the culture that might superficially appear remote and unconnected.

For these newly essentialist categories of 'energy', 'negotiation', and 'exchange' are so inclusive as to apply to virtually every activity conceivable within every historical culture under the sun. Hence the necessity, which Greenblatt himself recognizes, of further focusing the principles on which his 'poetics of culture' is to proceed if it is to identify and explore 'the objective conditions' of textual enchantment with any specificity, let alone the intertextual effacements on which it depends. Otherwise, a 'poetics' of culture with some claim to explanatory power would remain beyond reach, and the most we could expect would be another *ad hoc*, proliferating, and ultimately arbitrary hermeneutics. Have we not been here before? In Greenblatt's expressed interest in the 'objective conditions' of textual enchantment, is there not a certain sense of *déja vu*? Having exchanged an 'empiricist' for a 'textualist' model of history and culture, we should not be surprised to discover that a residual—if apparently antithetical—interest in identifying 'objective conditions' is still necessary for the construction of anything like a 'poetics'.

The typology Greenblatt goes on to outline in order to limit, specify, and systematize 'the whole spectrum of representational exchanges'[17] certainly creates a familiar illusion of object-ivity. Its primary category of 'symbolic acquisition', for ex-ample, through which social 'energy' and 'practice' are trans-lated on to the stage, is subdivided into 'metaphoric' and 'metonymic' or 'synecdochic' acquisition. If this sounds famil-iar, surely it is because Greenblatt's attempt to limit and objectify the potentially infinite variety of dynamic exchange is so openly modelled on the old, reliable opposition of metaphor to metonymy basic to structuralist analysis. For structuralist poetics and anthropology, despite their adoption of the conven-tionalist model of language, did not cease to think of themselves as 'realisms'. That was why 'deep structures' and 'underlying laws' were required and retained in the first place: to protect against 'relativism'.

The 'knowledge' promised by structuralism, be it of the operations of poetic language or of the cultural function of myth, was meant to be a 'knowledge' *of* something—of some-thing socially and conventionally constructed to be sure, and requiring theoretical work to be understood—but something that was not finally the projection of its own theories and methods. Be it the analysis of a sonnet, a myth, or a culture, structuralist method consisted in taking its object apart and reconstituting it in such a way as to reveal the laws of its functioning. There were a 'method', an 'object', and 'laws'. All three were important to the activity, and the 'laws' relating the various bits and pieces of the object under analysis were supposed to be independent of the method. After all, the

---

[17] Greenblatt, *Shakespearean Negotiations*, p. 8.

decoding at issue—as anyone recalling Lévi-Strauss' analysis of the Oedipus myth, or Jakobson's of poems by Baudelaire and Shakespeare, will attest—turned on the rigorous teasing-out of the *langue* of their *paroles*, the codes, rules, and grammars that regulated relations among the bits and pieces of the text at hand, the system of differences that made it congenial to analysis on the model of language in the first place. Structuralism was supposed to be a 'realism', whose object was language and its manifold textual and cultural instantiations.

It took a while for us to realize, however, that the system the text was thus forced to yield up was not as 'objective', or susceptible to objectification, as structuralist theory would have it. The text—whether sonnet, myth, or culture—was not structured *as* a language but *like* a language. And not even really like 'a language', but like language as structural linguistics constructs it. Shakespeare's sonnets beautifully illustrate the categories that structural linguistics (and its literary arm, structuralist poetics) consider to be constitutive, —and are so, but *constitutive of structural linguistics and structuralist poetics*. Similarly, the Oedipus myth responded obediently to the apparatus of structural anthropology; but how could it do otherwise, when it was re-constituted as a projection of it? A discipline that had conceived of itself as a 'realism' turned out to be a 'conventionalism' after all. One critic aptly invokes James Thurber's classic story of his fumbling efforts to master the use of the microscope, only to discover that the 'variegated constellation of flecks, specks, and dots' he kept seeing through it was the reflection in the lens of his own eye![18] Unfortunately, the analogy between 'cultural poetics' and structuralist poetics and anthropology goes deeper than its exponents might have wished.

For the new-historicist act of delimiting its subject matter along older empirical lines effectively cuts its 'Renaissance' out of the flow of history and turns it into a slice or cross-section of history. This can then be studied, like a slide, under the microscope, where it takes on the aspect of a synchronic system that is certainly culture-specific and conventional—and displays no shortage of 'energy' and 'circulation'—but one that

---

[18] See Frederic Jameson, *The Prison-House of Language* (Princeton: Princeton University Press, 1972), 206–7.

has been sealed off from any continuing historical process. For such questions as what 'writes' the cultural system under study, and to which culture—Renaissance or contemporary?—it belongs, remain unexplored and largely unasked. The microscope in use was not designed to investigate these matters. To be sure, it is no longer 'literature' or 'literary history' that is being isolated as a thing apart—Greenblatt is quite explicit and consistent on this point—but the cultural system within which 'literature' is inscribed.

The microscope in use, the method at work, however, is no longer that of historicism—'empiricist', 'realist', or any other—but of structuralism. And this puts into question the historical status of the enterprise, in so far as it is based on the principle that cultural, like linguistic, texts are to be analysed as synchronic systems operating in isolation from all prior and subsequent systems. Structuralist poetics and anthropology were never meant to be historical and can never be made historical. Unless Elizabethan literature and society are viewed, not simply as a textual *system* operating on its own terms—arbitrary, autonomous, as it were autochthonic—but as a cultural *moment*, laden with the traces of earlier and the latencies of subsequent moments, there can be any number of anthropological descriptions, 'thick' and 'thin', but no historical interpretation.

My point is not simply that American new historicism is not all that 'new'. I am arguing as well what may be both less clear and more important: that it is not genuinely *historical* or seriously political either, at least not from the highly politicized viewpoint of certain historical schools, including that emerging in Britain. In approaching Elizabethan culture as if it were a self-contained system of circulating energies cut off from his own cultural system, Greenblatt's cultural poetics relinquishes its potential for an historical understanding that might exert political influence upon the present. For such an understanding to arise, the past would have to be constructed not as a remote object—as in empiricism and structuralism alike—but as a vital issue; not in terms of discrete self-containment but of persisting relation. To qualify as a political—as distinct from an antiquarian, archaeological, or anthropological—discourse, the study of past cultures must have present import and consequence. There must be something in it for us beyond curiosity value. In sum, a genuinely *political* historicism inscribes the present as well as the past; it is not only diachronic, but at the very least *dialogic*, if not actually dialectical.

A striking illustration of the limitations of Greenblatt's cultural poetics occurs toward the end of his best known study.[19] There he discloses his considerable surprise when the 'self-fashioning' from More to Shakespeare he had set out to explore turned out not to be so fully or firmly 'there' as his modern assumptions had led him to expect. It attests to his honesty as a reader that he so openly acknowledges how the texts he reads— and which read him—have forced him to question his own falsely great, if never quite 'Californian', expectations concerning the scope for self-fashioning authorized or even thinkable within Renaissance culture. In these texts, the self-construction he expects keeps collapsing into the social construction he finds; Greenblatt can smell difference when he encounters it. But his surprise in the encounter also attests to an historical understanding insufficiently self-reflective to anticipate the encounter with alterity by inscribing in advance its own position relative to it. Greenblatt experiences history as a kind of 'shock of the old', for which his self-confident title has set him up. Without a philosophy of history that at once relates and differentiates past and present, the historical critic's encounter with the 'other' is bound to come as a shock.[20]

---

[19] Greenblatt, *Renaissance Self-Fashioning*, pp. 256 ff.

[20] Cf. Cohen, 'Political Criticism', p. 33: 'Unlike Marxism [new historicism] does not complement a lateral or horizontal approach with a vertical one: new historicism describes historical difference, but it does not explain historical change.' The antagonism between structuralist and historicist, synchronic and diachronic, approaches has long been recognized, particularly but not exclusively by Marxist critics. Montrose, for example, acknowledges the ahistoricity of structuralist analyses but still seems to think that more micrological historical and cultural studies modelled on Foucault can escape this structuralist limitation ('Renaissance Literary Studies', pp. 2–4). Yet Foucault's archaeologies of discourse have themselves been criticized—again, mainly by Marxist commentators—for the absence of any account of the transition from one discursive formation to the next: 'The emergence of such discourses is historically grounded in relatively perfunctory ways. Such discourses are concurrently in verbal, social, and material formations. But the whole question of process, of passage from one such problematic to the next, is left in abeyance' (Dennis Porter, '*Orientalism* and its Problems', in Francis Barker *et al.*, eds., *The Politics of Theory* (Colchester: University of Essex, 1983), 180.

CULTURAL MATERIALISM

These problems in the textual dealings of American 'cultural poetics' are largely absent from those of British 'cutural materi-alism'. This critical movement traces a path determined by different theoretical alignments and ideological allegiances, and carries in train a rather different set of problems. These are not simply a function of the less fully professionalized institu-tional structure and the more class-divided society within which the latter operates—more on this shortly—but of distinct intellectual traditions as well, the most obvious and important of these being, of course, Marxism. Whereas cultural poetics inhabits a discursive field in which Marxism has never really been present, its British counterpart inhabits one from which Marxism has never really been absent. This difference has, as we shall see, important consequences, one of which is to confer upon cultural materialism an enormous headstart in becoming a genuinely historical and political criticism. Its practitioners seem to have been born into this continuing discourse of history in something of the way the rest of us were born into our native language.

Once again, the titles of its recent productions, as distinct from those of its American counterpart, speak volumes. The auspicious title of *Re-Reading English*, the collection to which some of the critics with whom we are concerned contributed essays, foreshadowed an historical criticism oriented as much towards the present as the past, and one in which any safe distance between the two has effectively collapsed. Indeed, 're-making England'—to maintain their preferred present-parti-cipial mode—would have designated no less accurately its quite unhidden agenda. For these critics read and write to change the world, or at least the structure of British society, through the state ideological apparatus of higher education. And unacademic as it may seem to American scholars, they wear their political commitments on their dust-jackets: *Radical Tragedy, Political Shakespeare, Alternative Shakespeares, Re-Reading Shakespeare*, to cite just a few representative studies.[21]

---

[21] See Peter Widdowson, ed., *Re-Reading English* (London and New York: Methuen, 1982). British new-historicist studies, with their active, present-participial tendency, carry a similar message. Such titles might once have struck an American eye as not only

Ostensibly re-readings of the canonical texts of Elizabethan drama, these studies are hardly less obviously 'interventions' in a political drama closer to home. Such political explicitness contrasts sharply with the ambiguous, gestural, and mainly institutional leftwardness of American 'cultural poetics'. This contrast is not simply a function of differing institutional conventions, though it is that too, but of different philosophies —and experiences—of history. The work of Francis Barker and Catherine Belsey, for example, engages much the same historical problematic as that explored by Greenblatt of the emergence of a modern selfhood.[22] But they begin not with a determinate subject matter 'objectively' demarcated in the historical distance, but with the present subject-positions from which they construct and contemplate it. When Francis Barker subtitles his meditation on the fitful appearance of a tremulous, private, modern 'subject' in the literature of the seventeenth century, 'Essays on Subjection', he means it in every sense. The historical 'authority' of his work owes more to the self-reflective witness of his modern, liberal-bourgeois 'subjection' *malgré lui* than it does to professionalized, pseudo-objective scholarship.

In fact, Catherine Belsey's *The Subject of Tragedy* might be mistaken by its title for a politically innocent genre-study of an older kind, tragedy being the noblest 'subject' of them all within traditional, 'humanist' poetics and the form in which subjective 'self-fashioning' has been accorded the highest priority, at least since A. C. Bradley's reading of Shakespeare. (Is

unacademic but positively 'journalistic', though lately they have begun to be imitated. In Britain, as opposed to America, an intimate relation still obtains—even in the case of left-wing scholarship such as we are considering—between the academy and a wider public sphere of journalism, politics, and the media, the by-product perhaps of a smaller and more strongly class-articulated society. Concomitantly, the university presses have never achieved the virtual monopoly on scholarly publication that they have in America, perhaps because the doctoral dissertation is a relatively recent innovation as a professional requirement. All but one of the British studies mentioned above were issued by commercial or 'trade' publishers, most of them highly aggressive and profitable. Their titles may also suggest a marketing style aimed at an audience of student and 'general' readers broader than that of the libraries and scholars who purchase such books in America. Indeed, the role of Methuen (now Routledge) alone in mediating between the academy and the public sphere is a topic that deserves scholarly treatment in its own right.

[22] See Francis Barker, *The Tremulous Private Body: Essays on Subjection* (London: Methuen, 1984) and Catherine Belsey, *The Subject of Tragedy: Identity and Difference in Renaissance Drama* (London: Methuen, 1985).

this a cunning ploy on the part of Methuen, now Routledge, to sell books to the unsuspecting?) But her subtitle, 'Identity and Difference in Renaissance Drama', begins to re-frame the subject in question as not eternally given but of relatively recent cultural production and still more recent theoretical concern. In fact, our full-blown, modern preoccupation with 'character' in the plays of the period, however anachronistic and to that extent misplaced, is revealed to be a later stage of the same historical development. In both Barker's and Belsey's work, the inescapability of the historical interpreter's 'presentness' in appropriating the past is capitalized from the outset, in contrast to Greenblatt's attempts to minimize its importance and ignore its consequences.

In the very ease of acceptance and openness of admission of their own 'presentness', however, these cultural materialists exemplify a problem no less vitiating than the denial and back-projection of it by the cultural poeticians. It may actually be the other side of the same problem:

History is always in practice a reading of the past. We make a narrative out of the available 'documents', the written texts (and maps and buildings and suits of armour) we interpret in order to produce a knowledge of a world which is no longer present. And yet it is always from the present that we produce this knowledge: from the present in the sense that it is only from what is still extant, still available that we make it; and from the present in the sense that we make it out of an understanding formed by the present. We bring what we know now to bear on what remains from the past to produce an intelligible history.[23]

Here, in the opening paragraph of *The Subject of Tragedy*, 'history' is freely acknowledged to be a kind of storytelling towards the present, that is, a textual construct at once itself an interpretation and itself open to interpretation. Even the residual quest for 'objective conditions' seems to have been abandoned.

Perhaps the overt 'conventionalism' of this history of social construction, the self-confessed 'subjectivity' of its 'story of the subject', are only fitting. But before returning to the epistemological status of such a 'history', let me risk crudifying it by attempting to sum it up. For the terms, the discourse, in which

[23] Belsey, *The Subject of Tragedy*, p. 1.

this story is told are more than usually inseparable from its subject matter, story and discourse being in this case one and the same. The story, in outline, begins in what Barker has termed the 'radical alterity' of the Middle Ages, when subjectivity as we know it did not exist as such. The plot thickens only in the latter sixteenth and seventeenth centuries when something like an 'early modern' subject begins to precipitate out of the consolidation of Protestant nonconformism, private enterprise and property, parliamentary democracy, and scientific empiricism. Only then does what Belsey terms the 'discursive knowledge' of the late Middle Ages give way to the 'empirical knowledge' of the modern world.

With it comes a wholly different understanding of the subject, the self, and of course dramatic character. The individual subject, source and site of consciousness and arbiter of the phenomenal world, becomes sovereign, or gathers to itself the illusion of sovereignty. The self, formerly the playground of good and evil, God and the devil, that is, of discursively produced and maintained forces external to it, now becomes an autonomous agency in its own right, no longer constituted as a position in and product of a larger discourse, but constituting its own meaning and truth through observation and ratiocination. The power of defining the human subject hitherto vested in the mutually reinforcing structures of church and monarchy, a power visible, embodied, and enforced in signifying practices of perfect and universal intelligibility, increasingly devolves on to the 'free' individual, a newly autonomous agent capable of self-determination through the exercise of ethical and political choice. Power that was monolithically manifest is now everywhere yet nowhere, inalienable yet invisible in its new inwardness.

In respect of dramatic representation, the sovereign subject's new powers of self-determination have tremendous consequences. They enable and support the rise of illusionism in the theatre, and the separation of actors and audience by the transparent fourth wall of the proscenium arch. The spectator takes on new interpretive and evaluative prestige as the point of origin of his own 'realistic' perspective, and the actor, no longer the emblematic embodiment of moral roles and social types within a universal discursive system, becomes the imitator of newly individual and psychological beings for whom character is destiny—a notion utterly unthinkable within the culture that produced the *theatrum mundi* of the moralities, but one that would come to be taken for granted in theatrical production and interpretation of the nineteenth and early twentieth centuries.

The story is fresh enough, yet deeply familiar. Where have we heard its like before? Certainly in Michel Foucault's archeologies of discourse, influential upon all new historicism, cited early in Belsey's book and crucial to Barker's study of progressive 'disembodiment'. After all, the shift at issue here may be viewed as a local variation on the much larger transition described by Foucault between the medieval and classical epistemes. Foucault's terminology is certainly echoed in these studies, as are the larger conceptual structure and specific institutional focus that go with it. But the nostalgic tone of these British cultural materialists is not really Foucauldian in decisive respects we shall soon examine. Moreover, the concentration on native dramatic texts at the crux of their thesis seems to me to have a more local, though much less obvious and—to the critics in question—less welcome precedent, and I am not referring to the formative influence of Raymond Williams in particular or of British Marxism in general.[24]

In fact, the thesis that the Elizabethan drama is at best discontinuously 'realistic', that it is an unhomogeneous patchwork of medieval and modern representational modes, and that attempts from the late eighteenth century onwards to discuss it as if it were consistently psychological, are a distinctly modern distortion of it, is not of course new. In revealing the discursive discontinuities and instabilities of these plays, as Barker does in his striking discussion of 'presence' versus 'interiority' in *Hamlet*, and as Belsey does in her analyses of conflicting female subject-positions in a number of plays, we are not all that far from the work of Bernard Spivack, Anne Righter, and other 'older' literary historians, who argued the transitional status of

---

[24] The term 'cultural materialism', and its basic theory and practice, derive from the later work of Raymond Williams. See particularly his *Marxism and Literature* (Oxford: Oxford University Press, 1977). Its application to Renaissance literature is discussed in the introduction by Jonathan Dollimore and Alan Sinfield, eds., to *Political Shakespeare: New Essays in Cultural Materialism* (Manchester: Manchester University Press, 1985).

Elizabethan dramatic technique against earlier, anachronistic presumptions of a thoroughgoing, if imperfect, naturalism.[25] The focus has shifted, to be sure, from theatrical form as an end in itself to the wider configuration of signifying practices within which it operates and interacts. But the contour of the argument, this new contextualist inflection having been registered, is already in place.

NOSTALGIA FOR THE FUTURE

The major native precursor of the cultural materialist position, however, remains to be named. Before naming him—indeed, to prepare for the utterance of so dreadful a name—I want to examine the frequent, perhaps inevitable, connection between historicism and nostalgia. In the work of Barker, Belsey, and British new historicists generally, we encounter not the nostalgia for presence that suffuses Greenblatt's work, not a longing to enter into the past across the time and distance so painstakingly established, and once there, 'to speak with the dead'.[26] We encounter something rather more subtle, but no less wishful: a kind of nostalgia for the future. I employ this peculiar term to distinguish their practice from the simple back-projection of present political belief upon the text not uncommon among older Marxist critics, and at the same time, from a straightforward, prospective utopianism also endemic to Marxism. Their utopianism expresses itself not in projection, forward or backward, but in nostalgia, literally understood as a communitarian longing for home, for an England that in certain respects once was and might be again.

This new-historicist nostalgia should also be distinguished from that of the old. For Renaissance scholarship, particularly that devoted to unearthing the medieval roots of the Elizabethan drama, has often been the medium of historicist nostalgia. 'There was once a theatre in these islands', writes Glynne Wickham in the preface to his *Early English Stages, 1300–1600*, 'whose stage was the world instead of a drawing-room and

---

[25] See, for example, Bernard Spivack, *Shakespeare and the Allegory of Evil* (New York: Columbia University Press, 1958) and Ann Righter, *Shakespeare and the Idea of the Play* (Harmondsworth: Penguin, 1961).

[26] Greenblatt, *Shakespearean Negotiations*, p. 1.

whose players were men and women, body and soul, of every walk of life instead of two or three gathered together for luncheon, high tea or even for a cocktail party.'[27] Wickham's privileging of the native and medieval above the cosmopolitan and modern (hence the snide allusion to Eliot) suggests the nostalgic, nationalist—and not infrequently jingoistic—motives of so much of the older historicism, so different from those of the new. From the textualist viewpoint of the latter, Wickham's account of English theatrical history is a myth of presence akin to that of the 'Merrie England' of which Professor Welch's lecture in *Lucky Jim* is the comic *locus classicus*.

The consequences for cultural materialism of its open textualization of history and culture now become clear—by contrast with an older empiricist and a newer structuralist version of them—and come home to roost. Wholly undeluded that the story they tell can be anything other or more than a 'text', cultural materialists—unlike their empiricist and Marxist precursors and even their structuralist counterparts—have abandoned all hope of re-entering the past or reconstructing it in its 'reality'. The abandonment of that nostalgia for 'historicity' is important, for once 'history' is framed as a textual and discursive construct never again to be confused or equated with the past 'itself' but separated from it for ever by the 'difference' of textuality, the only story that *can* be told becomes 'only a story'. There can be no more accounts of or appeals to an 'authentic' past on which a present political standpoint or future political programme with special claim to validity or necessity can be based.

For such a 'textualist historicism' there can be only 'readings'; if 'discursive knowledge' is all that it claims, then the only validity it can hope or long for will consist not in an objective or transhistorical 'truth' but in its communal acceptance: the truth of 'conventionalism', not of 'empiricism' or 'realism'. Hence the peculiar nature of cultural-materialist nostalgia, with its longing not for the historical *presence* of the past, but for the social coherence it reads out of it, and hopes to find again in the future. In Barker's reading of *Hamlet*, for example, the play stages through its action the conflict of two discourses: an older

[27] Glynne Wickham, *Early English Stages, 1300–1600*, vol. I (London: Nonesuch Press, 1966), p. ix.

discourse of embodied, externalized presence, of 'spectacular corporeality', informing the opening court scene in the royal 'presence-chamber', and a newer discourse of modern, interiorized subjectivity foreshadowed in Hamlet's comments to his mother—'I have that within which passes show'—and further explored in his soliloquies. It is entirely consistent with the cultural-materialist position, I am arguing, that Barker's interpretive energies and sympathies are clearly on the side of the older public discourse of embodiment and presence—itself a discourse of 'conventionalism'.

His antipathy to the newer discourse of subjective interiority struggling in and through Hamlet to emerge—and shifting uncertainly between distinct modes of expression—is registered as much in the imagery of traumatic violence—itself recalling the Jacobean drama—that characterizes his prose as in its explicit statement:

That the body we see is so frequently presented in fragments, or in the process of its effective dismemberment, no doubt indicates that contradiction is already growing up within this system of presence, and that the deadly subjectivity of the modern is already beginning to emerge and to round vindictively on the most prevalent emblem of the discursive order it supersedes.[28]

In the case of Hamlet, his ironic image of himself as a 'pipe' to be manipulated and sounded marks the metaphysical hollowing of a fully signified, because public and embodied, selfhood and the emergence of a modern and disembodied self-consciousness: 'this interiority remains in *Hamlet*, gestural . . . at the centre of Hamlet, in the interior of his mystery, there is, in short, nothing.'[29] Yet there is still hope; for 'despite the violence unleashed against the body, it has not yet been quenched. However much it has been subsequently ignored, it remains in the texts [of Jacobean drama] themselves as a vital, full materiality.'[30]

If this newer discourse of interiority has been denied the status of 'transcendental'—or 'central'—signified ascribed to it by so much modern criticism, that status has been effectively re-assigned to the older discourse of presence, an inversion of privilege made possible only by reading strenuously against the

[28] Barker, *The Tremulous Private Body*, pp. 24–5.
[29] Ibid., pp. 36–7.   [30] Ibid., p. 25.

grain of the text. That is, the privileging of an older cultural semiotics of extroverted fullness and presence above a more precocious semiotics of inward subsidence and subjective slippage is itself peculiarly modern, and is already represented within the play, but represented *ironically*. For Claudius' enactment of the panoply of signified monarchy, his full-dress instantiation of the king's two bodies, *is perceptibly an enactment*, a rhetorical and theatrical mimicry of a discourse and a ritual existing in the play not 'authentically' but only in the mode of recollection, that is, at a distance and in the past, if not in the 'mind's eye' or memory of Hamlet alone. And in re-enacting them, Claudius hollows them out further, whether or not they were always already hollow.

At the same time, Hamlet's descent into the new selfhood of interiority is represented as a quest for a basis for action more 'authentic' than that of the familial, social, or dramatic—i.e. public but *in*authentic—roles available to him and insouciantly (and disastrously) played out by the Polonius family. Through his indictment of the disembodied subjection of our bourgeois contemporaneity, Barker seems to express—a bit like Hamlet himself at times—a kind of nostalgia for feudalism: if not for its punitive regime of split noses and mutilated ears as such, at least for the clarity and publicity of the thoroughgoing and fully social subjection they signify. Do we really want to return to corporal punishment, let alone to the older social order figured, with grim irony, in the 'old commandant' and his 'infallible' judicial machinery in Kafka's *The Penal Colony*— even if we could?

In Belsey's work, too, the thoroughgoing 'conventionalism' of the older social and institutional order is also privileged, but it is the regime of scholasticism rather than feudalism. From her opening analysis of the discursively regulated instabilities of the hero in *The Castle of Perseverance*, a later, empirical construction of the subject is implicitly under attack, not merely for its anachronistic distortion, through its own self-projection, of the older drama under scrutiny, but for the selfhood that it projects: 'In the problematic of discursive knowledge understanding is a preparation for the dissolution of the self. It is empirical knowledge which promises dominion. In empiricism as Locke would define it,' she concludes, 'the subject of humanism takes, in effect, the place of God.'[31] Whereas in Foucault's work all epistemes are created morally equal, even if that means equally oppressive and objectionable, in Belsey's they are clearly not.

The 'discursive knowledge' institutionalized in medieval scholasticism and bearing the *imprimatur* of church and state is *good*, i.e. ideologically sound, because within it the subject is socially constructed and defined. It is the 'empirical knowledge' newly available to the ambiguously sovereign subject that is *bad*, i.e. ideologically unsound, because, no longer regulated by a monologic social authority, it is potentially unbounded and anarchic and, in its untrammelled individualism, plumes up the will to God-like power. Between the lines of Belsey's consistent privileging of 'discursive' over and against 'empirical' knowledge lurks a nostalgia for a universal and absolute social authority long since unavailable, presumably for the reasons she explicitly traces. In a study that ostensibly, even ostentatiously, celebrates 'difference' on its title-page, the undeclared object of desire is 'identity', defined no longer individualistically, to be sure, but *socially*—as if that made all the difference. Do we really want to bring back censorship, the Index, the Inquisition—let alone 'God'?

For such an ideological apparatus is surely what it would take to regain for 'discursive knowledge'—however re-defined —its lost status, and to maintain it, once regained, in place. It is thus no accident that a pre-modern 'discursive knowledge' tends to be privileged within cultural-materialist criticism; for once the move into textualism has been made, that is the only kind that is available to it, even potentially: a knowledge that consists in the consensus of an 'interpretive community' rather than in correspondence to a reality outside discourse. If empirical science represents—or once represented—the paradigm-case of the latter kind of knowledge, then that of the former must be (and for some still is) religion. The thought is not quite as discouraging as it sounds, since an independently verifiable knowledge has never been necessary for political change, provided communal assent could be achieved. As Fulvia Morgana, the Marxist semiotician in *Small World*, astutely replies when

---

[31] Belsey, *The Subject of Tragedy*, p. 74.

asked 'What follows if everybody agrees with you?': 'What follows is the Revolution.'[32]

Strange as it may sound, we are not very far from the poetics and politics of—at last he can be named—F. R. Leavis. What links so apparently ill-sorted a trio as Leavis, Barker, and Belsey is not only their common desire for a restored univocality of the sign, poetic and social, but their nostalgia for a time when it is supposed to have actually existed. For Leavis, that univocality, which went under such names (some of them borrowed from Eliot) as 'realization', 'unified sensibility', and 'tradition', was grounded in the vision of the 'organic community' that was supposed to have existed before the 'dissociation of sensibility' set in during—when else?—the seventeenth century. In Belsey's nostalgia for England's future, in contrast to Leavis's, the key term is 'discourse' rather than 'sensibility', and the communitarian vision is systemic rather than organic, a matter of active cultural production rather than serene natural growth. These displacements having been registered, the similarities between her cultural materialism and Leavis's essentialist humanism are as striking as their differences.

It is surely significant in this connection that the opening essay in the founding number of *Scrutiny* was entitled 'A Note on Nostalgia'. Though not by Leavis but D. W. Harding, it argued that social nostalgia—as distinct from psychological regression—could legitimately combine with 'realism' in preferring the past while resolving to act in the present. Leavis too held this view, that 'the memory of the old order [of the "organic community"] must be the chief incitement towards a new, if ever we are to have one.'[33] Formed in the depths of an economic depression that made the incitement of a 'new order' seem an urgent necessity to many others as well, Leavis's social vision was so near and yet so far from that of the Marxists with whom he could never quite come to terms. While insisting that his project was one of social reform, the role of 'high culture' in general and 'literature' in particular as the means to that end grew to such proportions as to become an end in itself and an

---

[32] David Lodge, *Small World* (New York: Secker and Warburg, 1984), 319.

[33] F. R. Leavis and D. Thompson, *Culture and Environment* (London: Chatto, 1933), 97. Quoted and usefully situated by Francis Mulhern, *The Moment of* Scrutiny (London: Verso, 1979), 59.

insuperable stumbling block to any possible merger with the Marxists. For them, the key to a 'new order' was to be found not in the cultural superstructure but in the economic base of society; and not in the past but in the future.

That moment of high Marxism, at once 'humanist' and 'scientific', has passed; yet for a current generation of Marxist academics, post-imperial and post-industrial Britain is no less in crisis now than it was in 1933, and the need for a 'new order' no less peremptory. If an older vision of proletarian revolution arising from the imminent collapse of capitalism—once thought an historical inevitability predictable by 'objective', 'scientific' analysis—has come to appear an all but forlorn hope, the Marxist project has not been abandoned but re-conceived. Having withdrawn its faith in the 'realism' of economic necessit-arianism, post-structuralist Marxism has re-invested it in the 'conventionalism' of ideological criticism, through which a progressive community of the future can be educated in a certain reading of the textuality of the past. While this meta-morphosis of Marxism from an 'historical' into a 'cultural' materialism has raised problems of historical validation and political agency, it has certainly not spelled the end of Marxism. Perhaps an older claim to scientific 'truth' could be confidently maintained only as long as science itself could make the same epistemological claim, and that moment might also have passed.

Yet the new problems arising from a 'textualist' or 'con-textualist'—and inescapably 'conventionalist'—reading of history and literature cannot be ignored or dismissed either. While the perpetuation of the class structure—and struggle—virtually guarantees cultural materialism a significant 'market share' in the teaching of literature, this should not exempt its practitioners from concern over the weakened philosophical basis for the historical claims they still want to make—unless they are content to preach only to the converted, i.e. their own 'interpretive community'.[34] To accept the relativism of their

---

[34] This concern is sometimes registered by the cultural materialists themselves, as for example by Francis Barker and Peter Hulme: 'While a genuine difficulty in theorizing "the text" does exist, this should not lead inescapably to the point where the only option becomes the voluntaristic ascription to the text of meanings and articula-tions derived simply from one's own ideological preferences. This is a procedure only too vulnerable to pluralistic incorporation, a recipe for peaceful co-existence with the

position—'pluralism' is its cultural and institutional extension —would not only be to abandon the 'struggle', but to invite extinction at the hands of a dominant culture only too ready to dismiss all historical and literary studies as a luxury society can no longer afford. How much easier for it to do so when the 'knowledge' delivered by the latter is only a 'reading', a matter of opinion or interpretation. Whether one is interested primarily in the political or the philosophical dimensions of historical texts—or sees them as inextricable—the problem of 'conventionalism', with its inescapable relativism, looms large at a moment when the value of studying those texts within an increasingly reactionary culture is an open question.

dominant readings, not for a contestation of those readings themselves.' See ' "Nymphs and Reapers Heavily Vanish": The Discursive Con-Texts of *The Tempest*' in John Drakakis, ed., *Alternative Shakespeares* (London and New York: Methuen, 1985), 193 ff.

9

The Tempest in our Time

Then it occurred to Robyn that this was a suspiciously humanist train of thought and that the very word *classic* was an instrument of bourgeois hegemony. 'Of course', she added, 'they're often read simply as wish-fulfillment romances . . . You have to deconstruct the texts to bring out the political and psychological contradictions inscribed in them.'

'Eh?' said Wilcox.

(David Lodge, *Nice Work*)

FROM 'SACRAMENTAL ALLEGORY' TO SOCIAL REALISM

Fourteen years ago, at the meeting of The International Shakespeare Association in Washington, Bruce Erlich offered a Marxist interpretation of *The Tempest*. He argued that there are times—the then present being one of them—when we have a duty to look beyond the 'purely aesthetic or "beautiful" dimensions' of the play in order to recognize 'how a work of profound social realism can be written in the mode of romance and "sacramental allegory"'.[1] It is difficult to say whether Erlich's paper helped precipitate the sea-change soon to overtake *Tempest* criticism on both sides of the Atlantic, or merely participated in it. In any case, I cite these remarks of 1976 in order to suggest that there are times when certain ideas are 'in the air', ready, as it were, to be thought and, just as importantly, credited. Or as we say nowadays, when certain 'discursive positions' are emerging to be occupied, even to become dominant—at least for a time.

---

[1] Bruce Erlich, 'Shakespeare's Colonial Metaphor: On the Social Functions of Theater in *The Tempest*', *Science and Society: A Marxian Quarterly*, 41 (1977), 43–65. An important forerunner of Erlich's paper, and of new-historicist criticism at large, is Leslie Fiedler's *The Stranger in Shakespeare* (London: Croom Helm, 1973).

The mid-1970s were just such a time. One did not have to be a Marxist to know that anti-authoritarian, anti-elitist, and anti-aesthetic doctrines were in the wind in a recently politicized academia. How would Shakespeare, of all authors, fare within such a changed climate? One did not have to be a magus to divine that he would be, was already being, de-idealized and demystified. And in the case of his most idealized and mystified play, it was only a matter of time before a social-realist *Tempest* of some sort would displace the allegorical—or was it 'archetypal'?—romance from the strategic position within Shakespeare studies that it, along with the other late romances, had only just regained.

A 'social-realist' *Tempest*? How oxymoronic, how literally unthinkable and incredible, would such a notion once have been! Between 1947, the year of Wilson Knight's *The Crown of Life*, and the early 1970s, studies of *The Tempest* and the other late romances appeared with increasing frequency: not one, to my recollection, had much to say about its social realism, profound or superficial. Hence the auspiciousness of Erlich's remarks in 1976; the time was right for a new fit, a new mesh between text and context that would make what was formerly unthinkable and incredible seem plausible and even inevitable. A social-realist *Tempest*—we would soon wonder how this aspect of the play could ever have gone unnoticed!

Indeed, barely fourteen years since the play was thus described, the positions have practically reversed themselves. What Shakespearean now would be oblivious or audacious enough to discuss *The Tempest* as anything *other* than 'a work of profound social realism'—which is to say, discuss it from any critical standpoint other than a historicist or feminist or, more specifically, a post-colonial position? Would anyone be so foolhardy as to concentrate on the so-called 'aesthetic dimension' of the play? To dote thus on such luggage would be to risk being demonized as 'idealist' or 'aestheticist' or 'essentialist' by a critical community increasingly determined to regard itself as 'materialist' and 'historicist'. No less a student of *The Tempest* than Frank Kermode has succumbed, in more than one recent article, to such a fate.[2]

---

[2] See Kermode's influential introduction to *The Tempest*, New Arden Shakespeare (London: Methuen, 1954), xi–lxxxviii. Kermode's view of the play is contested,

Having recognized itself over the past decade—somewhat belatedly, it might be said, in relation to criticism at large—to be at one of those moments in its history when a 'return to history' is on the agenda, Shakespeare criticism is not about to linger before such aesthetic luggage as 'pastoral tragicomedy', 'art and nature', 'masque elements'—I am merely transcribing the subheadings of Kermode's introduction to the play—without historicizing them anew. Nor has it much time for such old and unreconstructed chestnuts as Shakespeare's spiritual autobiography and 'farewell to the stage'. This despite the fact that such-like issues were thought to arise 'naturally' enough from the text for much of its interpretive history. But that was in another, less ideologically sound and theoretically enlightened, era. Since the 'death of the author' and the 'end of man', it is no longer Shakespeare's personal history, let alone his 'spiritual autobiography' that matters, but the larger history and discourse of colonial imperialism that are inscribed in *The Tempest*, and that can now, at the moment of breakdown of the power that held us in thrall to them, be read out of the play.[3]

among other places, in Francis Barker and Peter Hulme, '"Nymphs and Reapers Heavily Vanish": The Discursive Con-texts of *The Tempest*' in John Drakakis, ed., *Alternative Shakespeares* (London and New York: Methuen, 1985), 191–205.

[3] In addition to the two articles cited above, the critical literature performing this re-reading is already substantial. See, in chronological order, Stephen Greenblatt, 'Learning to Curse: Aspects of Linguistic Colonialism, in the Sixteenth Century', in Fredi Chiappeli, ed., *First Images of America: The Impact of the New World on the Old* (Berkeley: University of California Press, 1976), ii.568–76; Charles Frey, 'The Tempest and the New World', *Shakespeare Quarterly*, 30/1 (Winter 1979), 29–41; Trevor R. Griffiths, '"This Island's Mine": Caliban and Colonialism', *Yearbook of English Studies* 13 (1983), 159–80; Paul Brown, '"This Thing of Darkness I Acknowledge Mine": *The Tempest* and the Discourse of Colonialism', in Jonathan Dollimore and Alan Sinfield, eds., *Political Shakespeare: New Essays in Cultural Materialism* (Manchester: Manchester University Press, 1985), 48–71; Peter Hulme, *Colonial Encounters: Europe and the Native Caribbean, 1492–1797* (London and New York: Methuen, 1986), 89–136; Malcolm Evans, *Signifying Nothing: Truth's True Contents Revealed in Shakespeare's Text* (Brighton: Harvester, 1986); Thomas Cartelli, 'Prospero in Africa: *The Tempest* as Colonialist Text and Pretext', in Jean E. Howard and Marion F. O'Connor, eds., *Shakespeare Reproduced: The Text in History and Ideology* (London and New York: Methuen, 1987), 99–155; Stephen Greenblatt, 'Martial Law in the Land of Cockaigne', in *Shakespearean Negotiations* (Oxford: Oxford University Press, 1988), 129–63; Alden T. Vaughan, 'Caliban in the "Third World": Shakespeare's Savage as Sociopolitical Symbol', *Massachusetts Review*, 29/2 (1988), 289–313; Meredith A. Skura, 'Discourse and the Individual: The Case of Colonialism in *The Tempest*', *Shakespeare Quarterly*, 40/1 (Spring 1989), 42–69; Deborah Willis, 'Shakespeare's *Tempest* and the Discourse of Colonialism', *Studies in English Literature*, 29/2 (Spring 1989), 277–89.

Yet the post-colonial *Tempest* produced in our time is still very much an allegorical romance. I am suggesting, that is, that the recent politicization of *The Tempest*—and no Shakespearean text has been subjected to greater political pressures than this one to tell us what we want to hear—has been only superficially successful, in so far as the allegorical romance continues to work its spell on us even as we think we are demystifying it. *The Tempest* goes on leading, in Kermode's aptly biblical phrasing, 'even scholars into the wilderness of undisciplined allegory'.[4] The latest archaeological scholarship, which has delved into the play's participation in the early discourse of the 'new world' and discovered the colonial skeletons in Europe's imperialist closet, is actually no less allegorical than that to which Kermode refers. Only the particular allegories have changed, and changed surprisingly less—as we shall soon see—than might have been expected.

Yet it is important to recognize, as Kermode did not, that none of the allegories of the play, old or new, is really 'free' or 'undisciplined' at all. They are in fact doubly disciplined: on the one side by the discursive structure of the text, its system of relations and oppositions ('art–nature', 'white versus black magic', 'old world–new world', etc.); and on the other, by the discursive forestructure of understanding already in place in its various contexts of reception and re-inscription (civilization–cannibalism, Christianity–paganism, whiteness–negritude, imperialism–nationalism, etc.). For an allegory can come into being only if a mesh, a fitment can be found between the two; if not, the 'other' that allegory is supposed to express could never be read out of it. The 'farewell-to-the-stage' allegory had to focus on, and thereby foreground and privilege, different discursive features of the text from the 'welcome-to-colonialism'

---

[4] Kermode, introduction to *The Tempest*, pp. lxxxii–lxxxiii. Northrop Frye, whose readings of *The Tempest* in terms of archetype and myth have been no less influential than Kermode's, is more tolerant of allegorical interpretation generally and more penetrating into its processes: 'It is not often realised that all commentary is allegorical interpretation, an attaching of ideas to the structure of poetic imagery. The instant that any critic permits himself to make a genuine comment about a poem (e.g., "In *Hamlet* Shakespeare appears to be portraying the tragedy of irresolution") he has begun to allegorise. Commentary thus looks at literature as, in its formal phase, a potential allegory of events and ideas' (*Anatomy of Criticism* [Princeton: Princeton University Press, 1957], 89). Frye, however, has little to say concerning contextual determinations and constraints upon *particular* allegories of the text.

allegory. The former fixed on Prospero as *magician*, on the power of *art*, on his collaboration with his *spirits*, and of course on his repudiation of magic and departure from the island; the latter on Prospero as *usurper*, on the art of *power*, on events *prior* to the play, particularly the attempted rape of Miranda and its unfortunate aftermath.

In the case of the post-colonial reading—of all the play's political allegorizations, and there have been several—the crucial moment or movement in the text is Prospero's imposition of hierarchy upon difference. His dispossession and domination of Caliban, justified in the name of cultural, moral, and even biological superiority, make the play potentially allegorical of *all* hegemonic structures, that of colonial imperialism being only one of them. The discursive homology that conditions and enables this particular allegory is formulated by one critic as follows: 'If Prospero might dispossess Caliban, England might dispossess the aborigines of the colonies.' This analogy lies at the core of all the recent post-colonial readings of the play, different as they apparently are.

In fact, the comment so neatly encapsulates the play's potential for post-colonial allegorization that it will serve to illustrate the kind of depersonalized discursive positioning with which we began. That is, it expresses not the unique viewpoint of a personal author but the underlying structure of all post-colonial re-writings and re-readings of the play. It could have been written by Francis Barker and Peter Hulme in the course of teasing out the play's complicity in early colonial discourse. Perhaps it is by Paul Brown, who has at once broadened and sharpened that colonial context to include the very real Irish question of the time. Or is it to be found in Trevor R. Griffiths's illuminating study of stage performances of Caliban over the past century and a half, instinct as he has shown them to be with the social and political issues of the day? Does the phrase 'aborigines of the colonies' identify our author as an Australian cultural nationalist, for whom the play signifies the ending of the dream-time with Captain Cook's arrival at Botany Bay two centuries ago? For even this re-writing of the play has actually occurred.[5]

---

[5] Perhaps I stretch the point, but certainly no further than Malcolm Evans in *Signifying Nothing*. See Randolph Stow, *A Haunted Land* (London: Macdonald, 1956).

But such concreteness, though not fanciful, is surely mis-placed; the formulation is pregnant in precisely the degree it remains abstract and open-ended. In fact, Caliban has been played more than once as an Australian aboriginal, as well as identified in theatrical and critical interpretation with an American Indian, a West Indian, an Indian, an African, a Boer, a 'red republican', a 'missing link', a 'Hun', and, as just mentioned, an Irishman.[6] Such an array of allegorizations, it is worth emphasizing, is not simply the product of critical or directorial whimsy; each is conditioned, indeed disciplined, by two things: by the ideological configuration of the moment; and by the structure of relations of the text. The oppressed group to whom Caliban has not yet been assimilated is that of women— an idea whose time might have come, and (let us hope) gone.

The 're-writing' of *The Tempest* in this century from a colonial or ex-colonial viewpoint at once anticipates and continues the 're-interpretation' of the play in criticism and performance. See Cartelli, 'Prospero in Africa', as well as Diana Brydon, 'On Rewriting *The Tempest*', *World Literature Written in English*, 23 (1984), and Chantal Zabus, 'A Calibanic *Tempest* in Anglophone/Francophone New World Writing', *Canadian Literature*, 104 (Spring 1985). For a more extensive bibliography on relevant post-colonial developments, see Hulme, *Colonial Encounters* and Bill Ashcroft, Gareth Griffiths, and Helen Tiffin, *The Empire Writes Back: Theory and Practice in Post-Colonial Literature* (London and New York: Routledge, 1989).

[6] Most of these identifications are to be found in Trevor R. Griffiths's account of theatrical productions since the turn of the twentieth century, but some go back into the nineteenth. Horace Howard Furness, ed. *The Tempest*, New Variorum edition (Philadelphia and London, 1892), 383 ff., alludes to Caliban's 'mutterings of red-republican-ism, or perhaps, socialism' in his summary of Ernest Renan's political rewriting of the play, *Caliban* [1878]. In *Caliban: The Missing Link* (Oxford, 1873), Sir Daniel Wilson, Professor of English Literature at University College, Toronto, crudifies Browning's 'Caliban upon Setebos' into a 'pre-Darwinian realisation of the intermediate link between brute and man'. (Although the phylogenetic scale is a hegemonic structure if ever there was one, no 'animal-liberationist' readings have yet, to my knowledge, emerged. But give them time.) In this connection, the most whimsical nineteenth-century identification of Caliban was made by Bernard Shaw at a meeting of the Browning Society on 25 April, 1884, after a paper on 'Caliban upon Setebos' by the positivist James Cotter Morison. Shaw is reported by Katharine Tynan (*Twenty-Five Years: Reminiscences* [London: Smith, Elder, 1913], 313) to have commented: 'that if Caliban was now alive he would belong to the Philharmonic Society'. Sir Walter Raleigh re-situates Caliban in Germany and renames him 'Fritz' or 'the Boche' in the 1917–18 *Proceedings of the British Academy*, 407–8. See Terence Hawkes, 'Swisser-Swatter: Making a Man of English letters' in Drakakis, ed., *Alternative Shakespeares*, pp. 26–46. The image of an African Caliban goes back at least as far as Hogarth, who painted a scene from *The Tempest* around 1735 in which he depicts Caliban as a savage fantasizing rape of Miranda. See David Dabydeen, *Hogarth's Blacks: Images of Blacks in Eighteenth Century English Art* (Coventry: Dangaroo Press, 1985), 80–1.

Sometimes the text throws up more resistance than even the most wilful interpreters can overcome.

COLONIALISM AND THE CANON

But who did make explicit the analogy on which all these political allegories depend? In fact, it was none of the new historicists cited above, nor any other, for there is nothing 'new' about it. The idea was expressed exactly a century before Bruce Erlich's comments to the Marxist seminar, with which we began. And its author, far from being a Marxist, was none other than James Surtees Phillpotts, editor of the Rugby edition of the play published in 1876, the year Victoria was proclaimed 'Empress of India'. What *Tempest* criticism is now experiencing is actually a *second* flowering of colonial allegorization. The first corresponded to a series of divisions within British imperialist policy in the late nineteenth century, the second to its total collapse in the two decades after the Second World War. For it is mainly at moments of breakdown, or at least trepidation, that such massive historical structures as colonial imperialism cease to be taken for granted by those occupying positions within them, and become available in consequence for theatrical representation and critical interrogation.[7]

So Phillpotts, writing very much from a *pro*-imperial position, overhears something in the play that chimes with something in his own time:

The character [of Caliban] may have had a special bearing on the great question of a time when we were discovering fresh colonies . . . Even if there were special dangers to savage races when first brought into contact with civilization, yet we might justify the usurpation of power by those who were mentally and morally the stronger, as long

---

[7] A 'new' British imperialism, anxious and belligerent, emerged in the decades following 1870, owing to, among other things, Bismarck's imperial designs after the Franco-Prussian War and Disraeli's support of the imperial idea in his Crystal Palace speech of 1872. What had been a pragmatic, loosely administered, somewhat rag-tag 'empire' now underwent formalization. For an excellent account of these developments, see C. C. Eldridge, *Victorian Imperialism* (London: Hodder and Stoughton, 1978); Richard Shannon, *The Crisis of Imperialism, 1865–1915* (London: Paladin, 1976); and V. G. Kiernan, *The Lords of Human Kind: European Attitudes Towards the Outside World in the Imperial Age* (London: Weidenfeld & Nicolson, 1969).

as that usurpation was only used to educate and humanise the savage.[8]

Whether or not colonial expansion was the great question of Shakespeare's time—was it really a 'question'?—it had certainly become one by Phillpotts's time; but the official answer to it, allowing for a few terminological changes in the discourse of colonialism, echoes faithfully Prospero's protestations of 'pains, | Humanely taken' (IV.i.189–90), and it is as Eurocentric as ever.

For us there are other echoes as well: 'the Rugby edition'. The very name of the inexpensive series of octavo volumes, edited by Phillpotts for 'Rivingtons' School Classics', is like a bell to toll us back to that time, with its resonant connotations of Englishness, of public-school privilege, of the chapels and playing fields where young upper lips were stiffened for the rigours of colonial administration and the *longueurs* of countless pink gins at the Raffles Hotel. Of course it was not only the consolidation of an already precarious British empire that was at issue in 1876 but the formation of the emerging canon of English literature, and in this connection the name 'Rugby' conjures up the son of its best-known headmaster. From the moment Matthew Arnold quoted a line from *The Tempest*, a line resonant of the classics in its syntax and diction, as a touchstone

---

[8] Introduction to *The Tempest*, ed. J. S. Phillpotts (London: Rivingtons, 1876), xviii–xix. This inexpensive octavo edition, clearly aimed at a school market, is one in a series entitled 'Select Plays of Shakespeare: The Rugby Edition', itself a subseries of 'Rivingtons' "English School Classics"'. These opportunistic ventures were doubtless occasioned by the recent Education Acts of 1870 and 1876, extending compulsory schooling to the age of thirteen. Phillpotts himself was Headmaster, not of Rugby, but of Bedford Grammar School. He also produced a German grammar, several beginners' texts in ancient Greek, and an edition of Scott's Lay of the Last Minstrel in 'Storrs' English School-Classics'. Phillpotts is not, incidentally, the first to read *The Tempest* as a colonial allegory. That honour should be attributed, thanks to Jonathan Bate, to William Hazlitt, responding to Coleridge's view of Caliban 'as an original and caricature of Jacobinism': 'Caliban is so far from being a prototype of modern Jacobinism, that he is strictly the legitimate sovereign of the isle, and Prospero and the rest are usurpers, who have ousted him from his hereditary jurisdiction by superiority of talent and knowledge . . . He is the Louis XVIII of the enchanted island . . . Even his affront to the daughter of that upstart philosopher Prospero, could not be brought to bar his succession to the natural sovereignty of his dominions . . . Why does Mr. Coleridge provoke us to write as great nonsense as he talks?' *The Complete Works of William Hazlitt*, ed. P. P. Howe, xix (London and Toronto, 1933), 207. See Jonathan Bate, 'Shakespeare and the Literary Police', *London Review of Books*, xxix (September 1988), 26.

of the highest seriousness, Shakespeare's plays were destined to form, in effect, the canon within the canon.[9]

This is not the place to rehearse the story of the foundation of English, with Shakespeare at its cornerstone, as a university discipline; though the relevance, to a discipline committed to historicism, of historicizing its own discourse can hardly be questioned. This is the place, however, to point out that a crucial episode in that larger story is the establishment, on 'scientific' grounds such as the nineteenth century would credit, of the authenticity and chronology of Shakespeare's plays. In this essential task of canon-formation, concurrent as it was with the work of empire-building, *The Tempest* plays a crucial role. For it was not until the last quarter of the century that the case for *The Tempest* as the jewel in Shakespeare's crown, the fitting culmination of an exemplary career, was convincingly made. Until then, *The Tempest* was still sometimes viewed as a revision of an earlier play, and sometimes of an earlier play not even by Shakespeare. Its promotion to sublime, even quasi-religious, standing within a newly allegorized professional career— Shakespeare was now 'on the heights' when he wrote the play—was as much the work of F. J. Furnivall as it was of Edward Dowden, to whom it is usually attributed.[10]

---

[9] Arguably the most Miltonic line in Shakespeare: 'In the dark backward and abysm of time' (*The Tempest*, I.ii.50). It is quoted by Arnold in his enormously influential introduction to the popular collection, Ward's *English Poets* (London, 1880). Many links between canonization and colonialism had of course already been forged by this time. See particularly Gauri Viswanathan, 'The Beginnings of English Literary Study in British India', *The Oxford Literary Review*, 9/1–2 (1987), 2–25. Margreta de Grazia has called attention to the literal and emblematic imperialism of the 'Globe edition', published in 1864, whose sun began to set not much before a century later ('Introduction' to Plenary Session, 'Shakespeare and Colonialism' at the Shakespeare Association of America Meeting, 1 April 1988).

[10] It was on the pseudo-scientific basis provided by Furnivall for Shakespeare's chronology that Edward Dowden erected his vastly influential 'spiritual biography'. Through his *Shakspere: His Mind and Art* (1875), Dowden constructed the vision of a late Shakespeare serenely 'on the heights' that would dominate criticism of the romances for the next generation. Dowden warmly alludes to his links with Furnivall through the New Shakspere Society, and these are confirmed by his spelling of 'Shakspere', a hobby-horse of Furnivall's. Professor of Oratory and English at Dublin University, Dowden was an Irishman, more specifically an Anglo-Irishman. It does not seem overly strained to see in Dowden's career an emblem of the internal colonization of the British Isles, begun under the Tudors and nearing cultural completion in the work of this Anglo-Irish Matthew Arnold. Dowden was Irish Commissioner of Education from 1896 to 1900, and towards the end of his life became Trustee of the National Library of Ireland.

The original for Rat in *The Wind in the Willows*, Furnivall is an intriguing figure in whom a number of the currents we have dipped into converge.[11] Active in his youth in the Christian Socialist movement, Furnivall turned his missionary zeal to the cause of literary and cultural nationalism by founding the Chaucer Society, the Early English Text Society, and in 1873 the New Shakspere Society. He launched the last with the publication of a pamphlet entitled *The Succession of Shakspere's Works*, in which he sets out the 'scientific' principles of verse-testing, by which earlier disintegrationist speculations were to be discredited, and the integrity and order of Shakespeare's work established once and for all.

'Carefully and faithfully', he writes, 'is every Englishman *bound* to follow the course of the most splendid imagination of his bard, and to note its purpose in every mark it leaves of its march. Shakespeare *must*', Furnivall characteristically asserts, 'be studied chronologically and as a whole.'[12] The pursuit of that purposeful march through the plays, which leads to Prospero/Shakespeare's hard-earned retirement to the quint-essential Englishness of 'quiet Avon's side', is urged by Furnivall upon his countrymen as a patriotic duty, even com-pulsion, akin to national service, which in a way is just what it is. With Furnivall and Dowden, the recently established Shake-speare industry turns its ideological apparatus to the production of an English subject fitted to the needs of empire.

In moving from the pro- to the post-colonial moment of *Tempest* criticism, from the old chauvinism to the new historicism, we seem to have illustrated Walter Benjamin's dictum that 'there is no document of civilization which is not at the same time a document of barbarism',[13] if only because it was made possible through violence and exploitation. A text regarded at the end of the last century as a document of the highest civilization, in which the noble vocations of English imperialism and English literature coincide, has become at

---

[11] Furnivall actually persuaded its author, Kenneth Grahame, to join his New Shakspere Society. See William Amos, *The Originals: Who's Really Who in Fiction* (London: Cape, 1985), 432.

[12] F. J. Furnivall, *The Succession of Shakspere's Works* (London: Smith, Elder, 1874), xx (italics in original).

[13] Walter Benjamin, 'Theses on the Philosophy of History', vii in *Illuminations*, trans. H. Zohn (New York: Schocken, 1969), 258.

the end of our own century, at a counter-moment of decolonization, a document of barbarism. For the barbarous history of colonialism, so long eclipsed by the magic, music, and spectacle of the play, has now emerged, making it difficult any longer to maintain its ideality or innocence in view of that history. Worse yet, through the canonization of the play over the past century, its systematic idealization through such institutional practices as theatrical productions, scholarly editions, and school examinations, *The Tempest* takes on a kind of complicity in the making and legitimizing of that colonial history, if only by masking the actual barbarism it entailed.

So runs the new-historicist argument, and one does not have to be politically radical or paranoid to see how Phillpotts's edition of the play in Rivingtons' 'English School Classics', for example, might well have served such interests. For it is very much a conspiracy of cultural interests, rather than personal intentions, with which we are concerned. At a moment when colonialism and canonicity are seen to be in close cahoots, when the latter is widely suspected of being little more than an ideological reflex or tool of the former, and when the function of criticism is held by many to be that of unmasking such interests and complicities—at such a moment, *The Tempest* stands as a test case for the viability of the canon itself. Is there, then, no other direction open to a politically progressive criticism, and no other destiny possible for canonical texts? Have they outlived their century, as Horace required of a classic, only to be unceremoniously consigned to the dustbin of history?

THE COLONIALISM OF THE CANON

Before facing up to these hard questions, we should take note of certain unforeseen side-effects of the new-historicist attack on the institutional hegemony of the canon. In the attempt to combat this other colonialism, the colonialism *of* the canon, by dissolving 'literature' back into the more egalitarian ground of history, culture, and textuality whence it so recently emerged, the new historicists may actually have enhanced its power and prestige. For if the disclosure and deconstruction of colonial discourse has changed our reading of *The Tempest*, it has certainly not *stopped* our reading of *The*

Tempest, or theatrical production of it, or the teaching of it at every level of the curriculum, or any of the interconnected institutional and cultural practices that constitute and perpetuate canonicity. Since the new-historicist re-inscription of *The Tempest* got under way a decade ago, the canonical standing of the play is at least as high, arguably higher than ever. If *The Tempest* is any indication, the canon may turn out to lead a kind of 'charmed life', invulnerable to the ideological critique levelled against it by new historicists, no matter how demystifying or decanonizing its intent.[14]

This 'boomerang effect', whereby the very acknowledgement of power, albeit negative, turns into an affirmation of power, requires closer inspection. For there seems to be a sense in which even the most negative critique works to reinforce its canonical object in direct proportion to the strength of its negation, as if both were caught up in a system that defies entropy by re-containing the subversive energies it generates, thereby reconstituting itself. No Shakespearean play has more thoroughly absorbed the political interest and energy of the new historicism than *The Tempest*; yet as a consequence of this attention, no critical movement, not even the bardolatry of the nineteenth or the myth-criticism of the twentieth century, has done more to sustain the canonicity of the play. Canonical text and anti-canonical critique have actually been mutually reinforcing. If the new historicism requires *The Tempest* to demonstrate its case for an oppositional politics, *The Tempest* also relies on the new historicism to read it afresh and thereby renew its

---

[14] The new-historicist attack on the privileged status accorded to 'literature' and 'the canon' has been undertaken from various standpoints and with varying intensity, ranging from the modest disciplinary reforms urged by Stephen Greenblatt in the introduction to *Renaissance Self-Fashioning: From More to Shakespeare* (Chicago: University of Chicago Press, 1980) to John Drakakis's eschewal of 'coverage of all those texts which are generally thought to occupy pride of place in the Shakespearean canon, since what is being challenged here, on a very broad front, is the concept of a distinct "canon" itself' (*Alternative Shakespeares*, p. 24) to a still more extreme abolitionism: 'The raw material of a canon which is rigorously defended for any number of reasons . . . in the end best produces a knowledge of the timeless values and truths which can be recognised in the texts . . . This is not so much a conspiracy as an effect of the sublime status which criticism has achieved in relation to other branches of the humanities' (Simon Barker, 'Images of the Sixteenth and Seventeenth Centuries as a History of the Present', in Francis Barker, *et al.* eds., *Literature, Politics, and Theory* [London: Methuen, 1983], 182).

claim to cultural centrality—even if the two interests seem to be diametrically opposed.

If any of this sounds familiar, it is because these ironies of negative affirmation and negative determination have not gone unnoticed by the new historicists themselves, albeit in a way that renders them hard to recognize as contemporary issues. For in new-historicist criticism, particularly in its American manifestation, this institutional and ideological process goes by the name of 'containment' and its 'strategies', and tends to be located in the relations between Elizabethan literature and official Elizabethan power. Such back-projection of a cultural process that would, if recognized as present and pressing, threaten the viability of a political criticism more concerned than most to 'get on with it' is certainly understandable. The question of the oppositional reinforcement of established authority is thus displaced in their work to the relative safety of historical distance: did the Elizabethan theatre serve as a vehicle for the expression of subversive, even radical, energies, and if so, did it also serve as a vehicle for their strategic containment by the very authority against which those energies were directed?[15]

The new-historicist containment of the question of containment within an historical period, however, might also be symptomatic of the continuing operation of this same cultural process upon the new historicists themselves, as the equivocal and inconsistent answers they offer to their own question suggest. For new-historicist critics stand in a no less ambiguous relation to an official authority at once sponsoring and censoring than the Elizabethan playwrights they write about: namely, the state ideological apparatus of the modern university and its interrelated research and funding agencies. This too exemplifies an extraordinary capacity to absorb the most shocking and

---

[15]   The concept of 'containment' within Marxist criticism is discussed by Frederic Jameson, *The Political Unconscious: Narrative as a Socially Symbolic Act* (London: Methuen, 1981), 52–3. New historicists are divided on the question of whether Elizabethan drama was politically conservative or subversive. Their division is epitomized in the final paragraph of Stephen Greenblatt's influential essay, 'Invisible Bullets: Renaissance Authority and its Subversion, *Henry IV* and *Henry V*' in Dollimore and Sinfield, eds., *Political Shakespeare*, p. 45. Though revised for reprinting in his *Shakespearean Negotiations*, pp. 21–65, its position *vis-à-vis* Elizabethan containment remains unchanged in its fundamental ambivalence: 'There is subversion,' Greenblatt writes, significantly paraphrasing Kafka, 'no end of subversion, only not for us.'

ferocious challenges to its institutional survival by giving its challengers from the margins—blacks, women, gays, Marxists —a place on the programme and sometimes a place in the sun. The opposition is thereby *institutionalized*, that is to say, at once 'contained' and 'neutralized'. In the case of American new historicism, the speed of whose rise to respectability, indeed centrality, must have set a new world record, the process of containment within the bland and indiscriminate rotarianism that characterizes institutions of the humanities in that country seems to have worked with remarkable efficiency.

Yet significantly, that efficiency has not been total. While no new historicist, to my knowledge, has so far refused the obvious benefits of institutional containment, some remain sufficiently alert to its 'strategies' to thematize—and even up to a point to theorize—its operations, albeit in the reluctant mode of dis-placement and ambivalence. But ideological containment, as a form of collective repression, can be completely effective only if its workings are unavailable to consciousness altogether; only then can the very possibility of critique be eliminated from within the psychic space meant to be contained. The fact that 'containment' and its 'strategies' remain sufficiently available to consciousness even for displaced historical thematization— could *Elizabethan* power be countered from within the theatrical space it controlled?—suggests that the repressive embrace of contemporary containment has been incomplete, even in Amer-ica. The institutional structure within which such discussions arise has clearly not succeeded in neutralizing *totally* the poten-tial opposition. Its strategies of pluralist containment must therefore operate with less than the insidiously perfect efficiency that the same new historicists who raise these issues are inclined to claim for its Elizabethan counterpart. A position from which such issues can be raised at all cannot have been fully contained in advance.

New historicists know all this already, but in the perverse way of denying in theory what they assume in practice. For if the canon and its institutional support system were the strategically contained space some of them claim or imply, there would be no point in contesting it in the name of a politicized critical pedagogy or anything else. Not only would the very idea of contestation be unthinkable from within such a space but, if it came from outside, it would be foredoomed to quixotic defeat. Yet the recent history of *The Tempest*, in which post-colonial re-writings and new-historicist re-readings have joined forces, suggests a rather different cultural function for canonical texts. The long dominant 'aesthetic' inscription of the play having been all but displaced by a political reading now institutionally dominant (though not yet culturally so), the recent history of *The Tempest* seems to exemplify the capacity of the canon to resist containment by official ideology, and to serve as a space of struggle among ideologies, official and unofficial, always already in progress.

For it was only at the 'moment of canonization' of *The Tempest* in the later nineteenth century that the discursive field of its reading could be fairly described as 'contained' by official ideology, and even that is arguable. At a time when the subject of 'English' had begun to trickle upwards from the schools, the Working Men's Institutes, and indeed the colonies to challenge the hegemony of Classics in the education of the ruling and middle classes,[16] *The Tempest* came to hold, as we have already seen, a central position within the newly institutionalized discipline whose very name was redolent of official, indeed imperial, ideology, and whose emergent professional practices were permeated by it: 'English'. If the systematic representation of its own local and historical interests as universal and eternal truths is, as we have come to see, the inevitable reflex of every ideology, then it was doubly inevitable that an *imperialist* ideology should construct the literary canon as a repository of values not merely British but universal, and not of an age but for all time. If 'Shakespeare' did not exist, he would have had to be invented. And so 'He' was. An era of eternizing, universalizing readings—autobiographical, allegorical, aesthetic, and archetypal—had begun.

Yet the construction of the liteary canon, like the enunciation of Victoria's own imperial status at just this time, might also signify not the robustness of imperial ideology but the beginning of its breakdown. For just as the effort to deny the canon may be the measure of its strength, so the effort to affirm it may be the

---

[16] See Terence Hawkes, *That Shakespeherian Rag: Essays on a Critical Process* (London and New York: Methuen, 1986), 55–6; and especially Viswanathan, 'The Beginnings of English Literary Study in British India'.

measure of its need for reinforcement, that is, of its weakness. It could be argued, for example, that the various discourses of authority within which *The Tempest*, with Prospero/Shake-speare at its centre, has until recently been re-inscribed, though not without their own cultural power and prestige, represent so many displacements from the strong form of Phillpotts's explicitly colonial and canonical inscription. It seems more than accidental that the loftiest claims for the 'classic' since Matthew Arnold were made by an expatriate American amid the ruins of the blitz in 1944, and more than a little ironic, under the circumstances, that those claims are fully instantiated for him only in the great Virgilian epic of *translatio imperii*.[17] For at that very moment, the *imperium* was set to translate from an old world to a new once again, the social composition of universities on both sides of the Atlantic to be transformed, and the basis of 'English' in class and nationalism—if not quite yet in ethnicity and gender—to change for ever.[18]

SAVING THE BATTLEFIELD

It therefore seems unhistorical to project the canon, as the new historicism is inclined to do, as the continuing stronghold of ruling-class ideology, particularly in view of its more recent function as a battlefield of ideological contestation. Is it still possible for us to think in terms of national literatures comprised of a stable set of texts clearly distinguishable from other texts by an inbuilt moral and/or aesthetic superiority and an immanent 'richness of meaning'? Such an ensemble of assumptions might have enabled the founding of 'English', and been shared during the rising phase of its institutional history even by such overtly opposed and occasionally antagonistic schools as the 'old' historicism' and 'new' and 'practical' criticism, albeit in varying configurations of emphasis. But the theoretical ferment of the 1970s journalistically known as the 'crisis in English' effectively put an end to all that, and appears in retrospect to have been a

---

[17] T. S. Eliot, 'What is a Classic?', in *On Poetry and Poets* (New York: Farrar, Strauss and Cudahy, 1957), 52–74.

[18] I refer to the Butler Education Act and the GI Bill, passed in Britain and America respectively at the end of the Second World War. The effect of both was to open universities to a much wider social cross-section, including returning servicemen.

crisis *of* English, as not even the boundaries of the subject have emerged consensually intact. Like the 'text in itself' of which it is an extension, the 'canon in itself' looks increasingly like the nineteenth-century idea, residually religious and royalist, that it is. The canon can no longer be defined in terms of some essential 'literariness' that lifts it above the fray of historical circumstances, cultural differences, and political struggle.

Quite the contrary: it is by just such mundane processes as these that the canonical text is now held to be determined.[19] As we have seen in the case of *The Tempest*, even—especially—a secular scripture serves an ideological function within the cultural system, and the more exalted the function, the more elaborate the support system required in turn to maintain it in place. Within late capitalist societies now struggling to maintain the material standards and expectations to which they have grown accustomed, the canon, literature, and the humanities generally have lost much of their quondam prestige. Their future within an institutional system increasingly technocratic and utilitarian is an open question. At the same time, the ideological function of naturalizing these new priorities has shifted to other texts, media, and institutions. Such cultural and institutional re-positionings, of which the 'crisis of English' was a symptom, are admittedly more complex than I can take account of here; but to ignore them altogether would be even more derelict than to acknowledge them inadequately.

Whether experienced as death by a thousand cuts at the hands of free-market governments or as threatening murmurs by newspaper editors and federal bureaucrats, the marginalization of literary studies cannot help but evoke a response from its institutions. This seems to have taken two principal forms, though any particular response is likely to combine elements of both. One has been the further *professionalization* of the subject,

---

[19]   The argument against the 'intrinsic' value of canonical texts is well made by Jane Tompkins, 'Masterpiece Theatre: The Politics of Literary Reputation', in *Sensational Designs: The Cultural Work of American Fiction 1790–1860* (New York: Oxford University Press, 1985), 3–39. In arguing that canonization is a political process, Tompkins is only half right in her voluntarist emphasis. What worked for Hawthorne does not necessarily work for other writers, such as the sentimental female novelists she wishes to promote. No effort at canonization can succeed unless the text in question meets, and continues to meet, the contextual demands of successive cultures. So Horace and Dr Johnson are not completely wrong after all.

the replication at the cultural margins of the technical, routinized, utilitarian operations that characterize those other learned professions—law, medicine, engineering—more securely and respectably esconced astride the social and economic mainstream. I say *further* professionalized, because as a nineteenth-century discipline institutionalized literary study has had a 'professional' dimension virtually from the beginning.[20] The extension as far as possible of 'professional' norms of objectivity and scientificity in literary studies, or the appearance of them, is a predictably self-protective response to the threat of anachronism posed by accelerating technological change.

The other principal response has been a *politicization* of the subject. While literary studies, as is often remarked of late and as we have seen for ourselves, has always been implicitly political, it is becoming more explicitly so, and not only from the 'left'. From the 'right', the marginalization of the humanities has been perceived as a crisis of 'literacy', and has been met by a 'back-to-basics' strategy designed to reinstate history, philosophy, and literature within the core curriculum, and thereby restore that sense of cultural continuity and coherence which seems to be slipping away along with literacy.[21] This politicization from the right thus carries with it a conviction and purpose that the empty technicism of professionalization does not, and in that respect a stronger resistance to the marginalization of the humanities in the face of advancing technology. At the same time, the promise of a curricular fix capable of arresting the galloping illiteracy conditioned by technology, *without the need for fundamental social change*, has brought its exponents a cultural prominence and material success rarely achieved by academics. Whatever the plight and destiny of the

---

[20] It was already in evidence in the pseudo-scientific procedures for establishing authorship and chronology that F. J. Furnivall imposed upon his New Shakspere Society, procedures that anticipate the more refined positivism of bibliographical, textual, and historical scholarship of this century. There have been a number of recent studies of professionalism that bear directly on the issues under discussion. See, for example, Burton J. Bledstein, *The Culture of Professionalism* (New York: Norton, 1976); Magali Sarfati Larson, *The Rise of Professionalism: A Sociological Analysis* (Berkeley: University of California Press, 1977); and Gerald Graff, *Professing Literature: An Institutional History* (Chicago: University of Chicago Press, 1981).

[21] See Allan Bloom, *The Closing of the American Mind* (New York: Simon and Schuster, 1987); and E. D. Hirsch, *Cultural Literacy* (Boston: Houghton, 1987).

humanities, these humanists have certainly solved the problem of their own marginalization.

But the anterior question remains of whose version of history, literature, and culture they are reinstating. Only the politicization from the left raises the question in broad and fundamental terms, and implies the necessity of radical social change in its answer to it. For, in its attempt to reinvigorate the historical study of literature once central to humanistic culture, the new historicism has brought to bear a radical tradition of ideological critique and unmasking of the role, unacknowledged by the old historicism, played by literature in serving dominant interests and preserving official power. In Britain especially, where this critique is articulated through a continuing discourse of Marxism, there can be no mistaking its present political orientation. For it is directed against a radically conservative regime bent on reversing long-standing social-democratic reforms in the name of a 'resolute approach' supposedly authenticated by Elizabethan precedent.[22] So not only *its own* institutional survival but the national destiny is at stake. In reinterpreting Renaissance literature, 'cultural materialism' is engaged in present struggle against a very different and dominant 'cultural materialism'. Indeed, it is not only an overtly oppositional, but a fully dialectical response to it in every sense.

Though ostensibly oppositional to a dominant culture hardly less exploitative, militaristic, and self-righteous than that of Britain, American 'cultural poetics' is more deeply complicit with the forces and structures it overtly opposes. We have already noted the displaced and ambivalent way its critique tends to stop with the Elizabethan cultural forms at which it is directed. What present political concerns it seems to have are partly obscured by a residual historical empiricism that contains its enquiry within an historical period demarcated and distanced in advance, thereby limiting its potential for present cultural commentary. The history it constructs foregrounds alterity at the expense of continuity. Yet it may be precisely this sublation of older historicist procedures that has facilitated the accommodation of the new historicism within the academic establishment. At the same time its ready acceptance of the

---

[22] Simon Barker, 'Images of the Sixteenth and Seventeenth Centuries', p. 173.

elaborate machinery of professionalism would not have hurt its institutional chances either. But the very compatibility that has enabled so rapid a rise to institutional power and prominence has also blunted the trenchancy of its cultural critique and limited its capacity for political opposition.

In so far as it thinks of itself as a political criticism, I am arguing, the new historicism has generally mistaken its real adversary by directing its energies against older constructions of the canon rather than the enveloping structures of professionalism. Even the reconstructed canon of professionalism would be a worthwhile object for political concern. For professionalism still requires a canon on which to practise its skills and demonstrate its specialist expertise, though only in the depoliticized form of an arbitrary or consensual body of texts without positive or political value in their own right. In fact, the avoidance of potentially contentious valorizations of this kind is precisely what is professionally required. Here post-structuralism helped by coming up with just what the doctor ordered in the 'productivity' of writing and the 'open' text.

Unlike the various older versions of essential 'loftiness', essential 'openness' makes possible a pluralist canon purged of political or cultural prejudice. Such a canon works by inviting rather than excluding not only an expanded and ever negotiable range of texts but the proliferating array of new approaches to them resulting from the explosion of theory. Even older classics can now be renewed through the back-projection on to them of a precocious and anachronistic post-modernity, thereby demonstrating yet another resource of a pluralist and technicist professionalism. Let a thousand doctoral dissertations bloom! Having been rendered *scriptible*, plural, open, the canon can thus be updated and re-tuned in response to all the potential 'interpretive communities', in the name of whose supposed 'difference' these elaborate professional services have been laid on. As always with professionalism, however, the only 'community' whose interests are actually—rather than hypothetically—served is its own.

Within the ideology of professionalism the canon is preserved not as a real but as an illusory battlefield, where actual battles with winners, losers, and social repercussions have ceased to take place. Though no longer a blatant stronghold of nationalist or imperialist ideology, this newly 'open' canon would still have to be seen by new-historicist lights as a strategy of containment, a limiting condition on political thought, albeit a more subtle one than previously required. For whatever exchanges over the canon might now take place are bound, as exchanges among a specialist clerisy operating at the margins of society, to be literally inconsequential. Only the 'embedded professional', as Stanley Fish unironically characterizes her or him, could be content to remain so institutionally celebrated and culturally insulated.[23] Certainly no new historicist, already labouring under 'a nagging sense of professional, institutional and political powerlessness or irrelevance' would knowingly collaborate in such a strategy of containment and marginalization.[24]

Yet that is what new historicists unwittingly do when, like Homeric heroes gone berserk, they turn their frustrated fury against the battlefield itself and level their own space of cultural struggle. In so doing, they deprive themselves of strategic advantage in the wars of literacy. Their point, after all, was that reading should make a difference beyond the institution, not end up filling 'casebooks' to illustrate the variety of current 'approaches'. If a canonical text is a text with a history, that history is more than the sum of its critical approaches set out in chronological order on a contents page. It is the history of struggle represented by their successive attempts to displace one another and occupy, but not annihilate, the space of the text. The history of re-inscription that marks out the canon is also the only inscription of history that is specifically available to literary studies. This is why the historicization of literary studies need pose no threat to the canon, and why the canon need offer no obstacle to the historicization of literary studies. Without a canon and its record of re-inscription, there would be no ground on which literary studies could oppose the state and its strategies of containment by teaching the curriculum against the grain. Nor would there be any basis without it on which to construct the newer historicism some of us might envision.

[23] Stanley Fish, 'Guest Column: No Bias, No Merit: The Case Against Blind Submission', *Proceedings of the Modern Language Association*, 10/5 (October 1988), 747.

[24] See Louis A. Montrose, 'Professing the Renaissance, The Poetics and Politics of Culture' in H. Aram Veeser, ed., *New Historicism* (New York and London: Routledge, 1988).

Index